# SECURITY POLICY DYNAMICS

*To My Parents, Wife, Son and Daughter*

# Security Policy Dynamics

Effects of contextual determinants to South Korea

BYUNG-OK KIL
*Center for Asia-Pacific Studies, Seoul, Korea*

Routledge
Taylor & Francis Group

LONDON AND NEW YORK

First published 2001 by Ashgate Publishing

Reissued 2018 by Routledge
2 Park Square, Milton Park, Abingdon, Oxon OX14 4RN
711 Third Avenue, New York, NY 10017, USA

*Routledge is an imprint of the Taylor & Francis Group, an informa business*

Notice:
Product or corporate names may be trademarks or registered trademarks, and are used only for identification and explanation without intent to infringe.

Publisher's Note
The publisher has gone to great lengths to ensure the quality of this reprint but points out that some imperfections in the original copies may be apparent.

Disclaimer
The publisher has made every effort to trace copyright holders and welcomes correspondence from those they have been unable to contact.

A Library of Congress record exists under LC control number: 2001093298

ISBN 13: 978-1-138-70114-4 (hbk)
ISBN 13: 978-0-415-79290-5 (pbk)
ISBN 13: 978-1-315-21010-0 (ebk)

# Contents

# List of Figures

# List of Tables

# Preface

There have not, as of yet, been sufficient theoretical and analytical explanations that integrate institutional determinants of domestic politics into security policies or examine security policy dynamics. Causal relations between external and internal systemic fluctuations and a state's security policy behavior have been an intriguing puzzle. A fundamental question is: Under what conditions do domestic politics matter more than international politics, or vice versa?

*Security Policy Dynamics* attempts to clarify the extent to which shifts in the international systemic and domestic institutional factors have contributed to South Korea's security policy change. Among the most important changes are the areas of international security structure, economic interdependence and institutional arrangements of South Korea's domestic politics. The book develops a historical-comparative analysis, which attempts to understand the changing nature and the process of South Korea's security policies in the Northeast Asian region.

The book aims to examine the relative explanatory power of internal and external determinants of South Korea's security policy change during the Cold War, transitional phase and post-Cold War era. It also aims to discover the importance of domestic political institutions and institutional arrangements in explaining changes in South Korea's security policies. This inquiry contends that a policy change also occurs as the result of alterations in domestic institutional arrangements, although international systemic factors determine the general route of security policies.

The significance of the book is largely fourfold: to explore security policy determinants that generate the state's distinctive security policies and policy changes; to broaden theoretical and analytical perspectives by including the impact of institutional dynamics on domestic policies in security studies; to enrich policy formulation and implementation for policy-makers by illustrating how states respond to external and internal crises and events; and to explain why states act as they do in international politics.

# Acknowledgements

First and foremost, my appreciation goes to the Center for Asia-Pacific Studies and the Department of Political Science of Kent State University that provided invaluable support to finish this project from beginning to end.

I have benefited greatly from the advice and assistance of a number of individuals. No words can express my debt to them. First of all, I would like to express my deepest appreciation to Dr. John J. Gargan and Dr. Steven W. Hook, without whose guidance this book would be impossible. Special thanks are due to Dr. Steven R. Brown and Dr. Dennis M. Hart of the Department of Political Science, Kwang-Sae Lee of the Department of Philosophy, and Dr. Frederick W. Schroath of the Graduate School of Management for their extremely valuable comments and suggestions.

My appreciation is extended to staff members who provided assistance in collecting and analyzing data at the Asian Studies Centers and Korean Studies Centers at the University of California, Harvard University, and Columbia University. I owe a great debt to Dr. Chang-Nam Kim of Kyung Hee University and Jin-Chul Jung of the Hyundai Research Institute for their encouragement and support throughout the research. I also appreciate my mentors and friends, Dr. Richard Robyn and Mr. Um Soo-Hyun, who reviewed the book and gave so generous support. Most importantly, In-Sun Kil, Tong-Neun Kim, Im-Sun Kim, Yong-Sik Kang, Sun-Sub Shin, Kyung-Sook Kang, Kyung-Whan (Jeremy) Kil, and Ji-Hyun Kil have furnished spiritual sustenance from the preparation to the completion of this project. Finally, I would like to thank the editors and staff of Ashgate Publishing Company whose editorial attentiveness and processing skills improved the manuscript from its early drafts into its final form.

It is my hope that this case-study will offer the reader a better understanding of how a state's security policies are taken in the Northeast Asian context. It is also hoped that this manuscript can contribute to a better explanation of South Korea's security policy behaviors vis-à-vis regional major powers and serve as a resource for security policy makers.

# 1. Introduction

Since the birth of the Republic of Korea in 1948, a number of significant changes in international and domestic politics have influenced that country's security policy. Among the most important shifts are those of regional security structure, regional economic interdependence, and institutional arrangements of domestic politics. The Northeast Asian security structure has been transformed from a bipolar or bi-triangular system to a pluralistic or multiple bilateral system.[1] Bipolarity, structured by ideological antagonism between the United States allied, with South Korea, and the Soviet Union, allied with North Korea, was the result of the World War II settlement and Korea's independence in 1945. Despite global détente during the 1970s, the Soviet Union and China included North Korea as their strategic ally while the U.S. extended its deterrence strategy to South Korea and Japan. This structure resembled two antagonistic triangular geopolitical systems.

The demise of the bi-triangular system was accompanied by economic normalization among South Korea, China, and the Soviet Union during the late 1980s and their diplomatic normalization during the early 1990s. Regionally, economic interdependence was also intensified and diversified with the advent of the Asia Pacific Economic Cooperation (APEC).[2] The remaining security structure entails a multiple bilateral system among the U.S., Japan, China, Russia, and South Korea, while China maintains its friendly relationship with North Korea.[3] Recently, there have been numerous forums and dialogues for the establishment of multilateral security alliance mechanisms in Northeast Asia.[4]

Internally, South Korean democratization in 1987 led to a new security initiative of *nordpolitik* (northern policy) and had a great impact on its international relations in the region. The new democratic government found that rigid anti-communism was no longer suitable or credible for the relaxation of military tensions with North Korea as well as the former communist countries. Ideological tolerance was necessary to normalize economic and diplomatic relations. At the same time, primary policy-making institutions were expanded and have included agencies, departments, and think tanks that were excluded from the security policy-making process during the Cold War. The subsequent reformation of the national security machinery has led to a greater flexibility in formulating security policy goals and objectives. In addition, military and especially economic superiority over the North has mandated that the South recalculate its perceived threats, re-examine the effectiveness of military postures and alliance formations, and revise its future security policies.

Reflective of these international and domestic changes, South Korea's post-Cold War policy-making behavior displays both convergent and discontinuous characteristics in its formulation and implementation of security policies. The most salient example is the "stick and carrot," or "quid pro quo" approach, as evident in the recent preventive efforts of the North's nuclear ambition and missile program. This approach is to provide incentives such as economic aid, diplomatic recognition, and provisions of alternative energy sources in exchange for the dismantling of the North's nuclear and missile programs. South Korea endeavored to persuade Pyongyang that going nuclear was against its interests in security and opening its system to the outside world. South Korea perceived that intensifying geo-economic interdependence and creating a stable regional security structure via diplomatic channels were more feasible for peaceful unification. An important analytic framework for understanding the shifts of the Northeast Asian security structure was prescribed by geo-political and geo-strategic factors.

South Korea's security policy dynamics offer possibilities for developing and testing several theoretical insights. Theories that look at the causal mechanisms have pinpointed international factors as the critical determinants of the state's security policy behaviors. The international sources include the anarchic structure of the international system, balance-of-power system, relative distribution of power, international economic interdependence, and international organizations. The causal arrow flows from international politics toward domestic politics. However, an intriguing question left unanswered is why states in certain situations take active stances in dealing with international issues while taking passive roles on other occasions. An example is South Korea's international behavior toward China. It took a passive stance in normalizing relations with China during the early 1970s while actively pursuing diplomatic rapprochement during the late 1980s. Another question is why states with similar international systemic situations often act differently, and vice versa. These questions underscore that states do not always implement policies determined by changes in international systemic factors.[5] Instead, states often implement security policies due to variations in domestic politics factors.

As a result, an overemphasis on structural determinants in international politics generates a lack of attention paid to domestic politics, particularly security policy-making institutions' responses to internal and external changes. Those who reverse the arrow from domestic politics toward international politics point out a uniqueness of states in the international system, regime types, domestic institutional arrangements, bureaucratic politics, decision-making processes, and defense expenditures. However, theoretical causal claims that over-emphasize international politics are significantly flawed, just as are international systemic explanations that stress domestic politics. An intriguing puzzle in this study is the causal relationship between South Korea's internal and external systemic determinants and its security policy changes.

There has not, as of yet, been a sufficient theoretical explanation that integrates institutional determinants of domestic politics into security policies or examines security policy dynamics. As Kenneth N. Waltz points out, the third image describes the framework of world politics, but without,

> the first and second images there can be no knowledge of the forces that determine policy; the first and second images describe the forces in world politics, but without the third image it is impossible to assess their importance or predict their results. (1959: 238)

This means that an understanding of the third image (or the anarchic international system with no world government) alone does not make it possible to understand the state's security policy behavior without also comprehending the first (or rational actors) and the second (or domestic politics) images. Theoretical limitations are evident on the one hand in attempts to explain systemic dynamics in international politics, and on the other in explanations of policy change affected by political realignments in domestic politics. Thus, the primary research questions of this study are: Under what conditions do domestic politics take precedence over international politics, or vice versa? How do variations in international and domestic politics lead to changes in the state's security policy? What is the relationship between the "restructuring" of the state's institutional arrangements and security policy changes? How have security policy-making institutions responded to systemic transformations in both domestic and international politics? Are security policy-making institutions capable of adapting to internal and external changes?

These questions demand that the nature and the process of changes in the state's security policy behaviors be re-evaluated. Due to endogenous and exogenous sources, security policies change in a predictable fashion, but in international relations theories, the finger has been predominantly pointed toward exogenous systemic factors as the determinants of the state's security policies. There is a need to clarify the "linkage" between domestic and international determinants of the state's security policy behaviors. Linkage is defined as "any recurrent sequence of behavior that originates in one system and is reacted to in another" (Rosenau, 1969: 44). More fundamental questions are when and how, and under what conditions, "linkage politics" occur. In other words, under what conditions do domestic institutional factors influence the state's security policy changes more than international structural factors, and vice versa?

In order to examine the causal relations, both critical determinants in domestic and international contexts are analyzed and compared to South Korea's security policy behaviors. The dependent variable to be explained is South Korea's security policy change. The concept of change is defined as the restructuring of the state's behavioral manifestations resulting from transformations of domestic institutional and international systemic factors.[6] South Korea's security policies are the government's official security policies as declared and stated in the Republic of Korea (ROK), the Ministry of National Defense, *Defense White Paper* and the Ministry of Foreign Affairs, *Diplomacy White Paper*. For the most part, South Korea's security policies have changed from anti-communism to mutual antagonism (1961/1980), to *nordpolitik* (1987-1988), and then to globalization/sunshine (1993/1998). Its security policy shifted from a defensive deterrence policy of the Cold War era to a governed interdependence policy of the post-Cold War era.[7] South Korea's broad trends of security policy change are laid out later in this chapter.

The independent variables that explain South Korea's security policy change include international and domestic determinants. They are used to test causal claims or hypotheses of the existing theories. Causal links between domestic institutional and international systemic factors and South Korea's security policy changes are examined to determine which factors have had more influence in the Cold War era, transitional phase, and post-Cold War era. International factors include geo-structural factors of regional security and economic structures, geo-strategic factors of alliance formations, geo-economic factors of economic interdependence and financial alignment mechanisms, and geo-political factors of diplomacy and international institutions. Domestic factors include types of government, legal-institutional setting, policy-making machinery, and national capabilities.

In analyzing South Korea's security policy dynamics, this study will use a historical-comparative approach, multilevel or interactive analysis, theory-testing, and descriptive statistics. A historical-comparative approach explores historically continuous and discontinuous patterns of South Korea's security policy influenced by international systemic and domestic institutional factors.[8] It is designed to explore why, when, and how the state's security policies fluctuate. In order to assess the changing nature of security policies, I will compare critical determinants of South Korea's security policies during the Cold War era (1954-1987), transitional phase (1988-1992), and post-Cold War era (1993-1998).[9] Each chapter of this study will contain a brief historical overview or description of security policy, review of empirical evidence or data-based analysis informed by theoretical hypotheses, and theoretical interpretation.

For the design and implementation of a historical-comparative approach, I will utilize an integrated level of analysis, combining system-level and state-level analyses.[10] Variables relevant to system-level and state-level analyses will be used to test the causal claims and hypotheses drawn from different theoretical insights.[11] The specific relationships between the international and domestic variables and South Korea's security policy changes will be examined to identify causal mechanisms. In this vein, this study will test the theoretical explanatory power of security policy change, rather than creating logical causal mechanisms. Theory-testing is used to verify, falsify, and refine the existing theories by examining their causal claims and specifying how variations in one variable are related to variations in another variable. Thus, theory-testing should help to examine the relative power of theoretical causal claims to explain South Korea's security policy dynamics. Evaluative criteria in examining the relative explanatory power of international systemic and domestic institutional factors include variations in the relative distribution of power, the US-ROK alliance system, formal diplomatic and trade relations, types of government, power sharing in the government and the National Assembly, and national military and economic capabilities.[12] Descriptive statistics are used to summarize the association between variables and bring out the salient features or patterns of the data. Accurate estimation of figures is extremely difficult because of secrecy, ambiguity, and under- or over-estimation of data. However, the goal is to analyze overall patterns and trends of relations among variables.

As discussed earlier, the primary purpose of this study is to examine the linkage politics between domestic and international determinants of South Korea's security policy change. It also examines how security policy-making institutions react to their contextual factors, while adapting and updating the policies and rules that govern their behaviors. The objectives of this study are largely five-fold: (1) to understand the changing nature and character of security environments that generate the state's distinctive security policies and policy changes, (2) to clarify the linkages between international systemic/domestic institutional factors and the state's security policy change, (3) to broaden theoretical and analytical perspectives by including the impact of institutional dynamics on domestic politics in security studies, (4) to enrich policy formulation and implementation for policy-makers by illustrating how states perceive external threats and define their security goals, why they choose alternative policies and reject others, and how they respond to external and internal crises or events, and (5) to explain, and more importantly to test, why states act as they do in international politics.

This inquiry contends that security policy changes occur as the result of international systemic transformations as well as alterations in a state's institutional arrangements. The configuration of the external determinants such as the regional security/economic structures, geo-strategic factors, economic interactions, and diplomatic alignments, no doubt shapes the kinds of stimuli to which South Korea is constrained to respond. So, too, do the domestic institutional factors of political types, legal-institutional setting, policy-making machinery, and economic/military capabilities structure South Korea's security policy behavior. As a result, both bi-triangular system/authoritarian regimes during the Cold War era and multiple bilateral system/market democracy provided important systemic constraints on and opportunities for South Korea's security policy change. Fluctuations in international and domestic determinants generate different security policies in different situations.

Comparative analysis of evaluative criteria illustrates the relative importance of critical determinants. To a large extent, the principal sources of South Korea's security policy change were international systemic factors. Except for the late 1980s, variations in the international system determined its policy shifts toward mutual antagonism, *nordpolitik*, globalization and sunshine policies. Specifically, during the Cold War era (1954-1987), domestic institutional determinants were closely related to authoritarian governments' regime security, while external systemic factors led South Korea to retain a strategic deterrence policy. Interestingly, South Korea's new international orientation resulted from alterations in domestic institutional factors in the years of 1987-1988, but domestic factors were not solely responsible for the change. Its *nordpolitik* was derived from the realistic calculation of strategic interests, reflective of fluctuations in the international security structure during the early 1990s. Globalization and sunshine policies in the post-Cold War era (1993-1998) were instituted to meet international trends of economic interdependence. Geo-economic factors have had a profound impact upon post-Cold War Northeast Asia, even in situations in which geo-strategic factors are salient. South Korea's economic engagement policy was instituted to resolve the new security problem of the North's nuclear ambition and to induce the North to open its society to the outside world. In short, shifts in South Korea's systemic postures have had a greater impact upon its security policy change than have those in domestic institutional arrangements.

As pointed out, the time-frame ranges from 1954 (or the end of the Korean War) to 1998. In analyzing the shifting patterns of South Korea's security policy, this study is concerned with the levels, scope, and timing of security policy change. In this chapter, South Korea's security policy dynamics are compared in terms of its international orientation, security goals/problems, security programs, and security adjustment changes. This comparison is made to acknowledge South Korea's strategic response to the transition in both international and domestic politics. Before the comparative analysis, I will briefly discuss the historical legacy of South Korea and its general trends of security policy change. A primary focus is given to South Korea's international relations and its strategic response to external systemic constraints and incentives. Finally, I will summarize the overall trends and framework for comparative analysis employed to explain South Korea's security policy change.

## Historical Legacy Prior to the Cold War

Korea's place in the Northeast Asian international system should be viewed within the context of the regional balance among the U.S., the Soviet Union/Russia, China, and Japan. Historically, its roles in the region and its security policy, for the most part, have been largely reactive to these major powers. Until the formal opening of "the Hermit Kingdom" during the late nineteenth century, Korea's security policy "vacillated between a policy of absolute isolationism and one of occasional informal contact with the outside world" (Koo and Han, 1985: 3).[13] But since then, Korea's foreign relations have had much to do with the big powers' strategic calculations in the context of their power competition that determined the routes of its own destiny. A traditional "elder brother/younger brother" relationship with China and its successive attempts to view Korea as a tribute state explain best Korea's foreign policy until the second half of the nineteenth century in East Asia.[14]

A significant change occurred in this center and semi-periphery relationship during the Opium Wars (1840-42 and 1856-60). There was a power vacuum when China could not deal with the Western powers, and Japan, newly armed with Westernized armor, then attempted to fill the power vacuum. Following the Sino-Japanese War (1894-95), China recognized Korea's independence from the traditional "brotherhood" relationship, signing the Treaty of Shimonoseki in April 1895.[15] But Russia attempted to have a strategic influence on the Korean peninsula. The result was the first instance of bipolarity in Northeast Asia as Japan and Russia competed to maintain their spheres of influence. Japan claimed superiority over Northeast Asia when it defeated Russian forces in the Russia-Japanese War (1904-5). When the Peace of Portsmouth was signed in 1905, Russia acknowledged Japan's paramount geo-strategic interests on the Korean peninsula.[16] From 1910 to 1945, Korea was annexed and Japan was in absolute control of Korea's foreign relations.

Japanese imperialism ended when Japan declared "unconditional surrender" in August 1945. But the harbinger of the Cold War on the Korean peninsula began to emerge during the settlement phase of Korea by the Allied Powers. At the Cairo meeting of November 1943, President Roosevelt promised Korean independence "at the earliest possible moment," but later changed this to "at the proper moment," while Prime Minister Churchill favored the term "in due process."[17] At the Teheran Conference of November 1943, President Roosevelt told Soviet Premier Stalin that Korea needed a period of apprenticeship before full independence might be attained, perhaps a period of 40 years.[18] Stalin agreed. Later, Roosevelt proposed a 20- or 40-year tutelage. Stalin's view was that the shorter the period the better. Both agreed that no foreign troops should be stationed in Korea. At the Yalta Conference of February 1945, the United States suggested "a short-term, four power trusteeship," although the independence of Korea was guaranteed.[19] There was no detailed discussion on how to manage this trusteeship. But finally at the Potsdam Conference, on July 26, 1945, the Potsdam Declaration was issued to Japan in the name of Truman, Churchill, and Chiang Kai-shek: "unconditional surrender."[20]

However, early Japanese surrender would preclude Soviet entry into the Pacific War that might lead to Russia's occupation of Korea and Manchuria. As Japan collapsed, the Soviets and the Americans came in. The Soviet Union declared war against Japan on August 8, 1945 and moved into northern Korea.[21] On August 15, 1945, President Truman sent the draft of the 38th parallel division to the British, Soviet, and Chinese governments as a means of facilitating the Japanese surrender in Korea. No objections were made. Thus, General MacArthur sent Lt. General John R. Hodge as Commander of the United States Army Forces in Korea. On August 24, Col. General I. M. Chistiakov's 25th Army entered Pyongyang.[22] On September 4, 1945 the U.S. Army arrived in Seoul. MacArthur, on September 7, 1945, issued a proclamation to the Koreans, promising Korean independence "in due process" and that south of the 38th parallel "all powers of government" would be exercised under his authority.[23] Thus, formally the U.S. ruled southern Korea from September 12, 1945 until August 15, 1948, and a divided Korea was a reality. The settlement of World War II resulted in the division of the two Koreas, and the Cold War emerged thereafter and remains until today.

**The Cold War Order and South Korea's Security Policy**

Korea was liberated but the consequence of this liberation was not independence. Nowhere was the Cold War confrontation between the U.S. and the Soviet Union more obvious than in the divided Korea, ultimately creating two disparate governments for an otherwise homogenous nation (Cumings, 1981, 1997). Subsequently, the division eventually caused the U.S. to become engaged in the Korean War (1950-53) to prevent perceived communist encroachment from the North supported by China and the Soviet Union.[24] Since then, the two Koreas have played geo-strategic roles as useful buffer states among the United States, Japan, the Soviet Union, and China. Much of the structure of Northeast Asian international politics has been shaped by how these four powers defined their interests and identified their strategic allies and adversaries. The Truman Doctrine was the basis of the dominant paradigm for South Korea, which aimed to contain the perceived spread of communism and Soviet expansionism. South Korea's security agenda was dependent upon the U.S. global strategy of ideological competition with the Soviet Union. Its primary security goal was to deter North Korea's military aggression and maintain the Northeast Asian balance of power system. National defense from external threats was the highest priority in domestic policy and budget allocations.[25] As a result, South Korea adopted a military deterrence policy and a mutually opposing strategy against the North and the communist countries.

During the Cold War, South Korea's security policies were characterized by absolute anti-communism, non-alignment, mutual antagonism, competitive diplomacy, extended deterrence, and economic/military modernization.[26] By advocating a "total defense" against communism, the first President of ROK, Syngman Rhee, did not align with any countries friendly to communism. As antagonistic stances continued, both North and South Korea sought to maintain mutual hostility or reconciliation to justify their political regimes and sustain political unity. In certain situations these policies were mixed, and in the aggregate these policies seemed to be implemented in contradictory directions, with one policy quite often favored over the others. In this section, these policies are explored to account for South Korea's defensive deterrence policy. Defensive deterrence means that South Korea's security policy is by nature defensive or reactive and aims to deter North Korea's military aggression with the aid of the US-ROK Combined Forces and the U.S. security guarantee.

The Rhee administration's (1948-1960) security policy was characterized by the following: (1) absolute anti-communism, (2) maintenance of friendly relations with anti-communist countries, and (3) absolute rejection of the doctrine of "two Koreas."[27] Experiencing catastrophic bloodshed all over the Korean peninsula during the Korean War, the Rhee regime would not make any distinction between communist regimes and non-aligned nations.[28] President Rhee's anti-communist stance was most vividly portrayed in the letter sent to his close friend Dr. Robert Oliver on February 25, 1954: "We are going to invite all anti-communist groups…to hold a Conference with a view to starting up an anti-communist crusade…within Europe and Asia" (Oliver, 1978: 444). For Rhee, the choice to be made was between right and wrong and between freedom and communist tyranny. The Rhee regime maintained friendly relations with free nations, with particular reliance on the United States, but the Rhee government was as anti-Japanese as anti-communist in word and deed.[29] Indeed, Japan and its people were described as "the savage and unfeeling Japanese," "the punished little criminal," and "the unscrupulous *nouveau riche*" gained from the Korean War (Koo, 1975: 220-221).

From the Rhee administration's view, "restoration of the status quo" or "two governments within one nation" was unacceptable. Thus, the Panmunjom

Peace Negotiations or the Armistice Agreements of the Korean War were unacceptable since the collective security objective of the UN was "the establishment of a united, independent, and democratic Korea and the punishment of the aggressor [North Korea]."[30] President Rhee clearly stated that the Korean question could not be settled unless the punitive action against the aggressor (or North Korea) was implemented. Nevertheless, the two Koreas were restored and the US-ROK Mutual Defense Treaty was signed on October 1, 1953. Overall, no policy adjustment was made while President Rhee was in office, although many policymakers pointed out the need for UN admission, normalization of Korean-Japanese relations, and expansion of diplomatic relations toward non-aligned nations.[31]

The first major change in South Korea's security policy was made by the military government led by Park Chung Hee, who came to power in the May 1961 military *coup d'etat*. The Park administration (1961-1979) changed South Korea's primary security programs in the following areas: (1) strengthening security alliance with the U.S., (2) exploring avenues for mutual antagonistic existence with the North, (3) normalizing economic relations with Japan, (4) promoting diplomatic relations with the non-aligned nations in the Third World, and (5) establishing communication channels with the Soviet Union and China. Modified somewhat by the Chun Do Whan administration (1980-1987), which extended the levels and scope of the Park administration's security policy, both regimes' underlying purposes were to achieve deterrence against the North's military aggression and communist expansionism.[32]

South Korea relied on U.S. military support, and the presence of the U.S. forces in South Korea provided a security guarantee and extended deterrence. This alliance has been maintained by arms transfers and formally declared alliance, such as the 1953 US-ROK Mutual Defense Treaty. Extended deterrence is "a confrontation in which the policymakers of one state [the U.S.] threaten the use of force against another state, that is, a potential attacker [North Korea], in an attempt to prevent that state from using military force against an ally [South Korea] of the defender"(Huth, 1988: 424). The South's decision to go to Vietnam was an extension of this alliance formation.[33] However, South Korea often assumed militarily aggressive postures that independently employed limited offensive action and counter-attacks to deny a contested area or positions to the North.[34] In 1979, President Park attempted to "go nuclear" as a response to President Carter's proposal to withdraw U.S. forces. A military strike against the North's strategic military bases was proposed, but not initiated, when the North attempted to assassinate President Chun Do Whan and killed his aides in Burma in 1983.

For both North and South Korea, it was useful to promote domestic solidarity by maintaining a relationship of "hostile reliance" toward each side's adversaries.[35] An opposing antagonistic security policy was put into action and the two Koreas "sought partial tension and strife as a means of justifying their own regimes and solidifying internal conflicts in the midst of economic difficulties, systemic uncertainty, and political unrest" (Lee J.G., 1995: 73). Both the Park and Chun regimes used this strategy, switching people's interests from social demands to security concerns, for the maintenance of authoritarian governments and societal control. But in the event of détente, South Korea maintained mutual conditions of partial cooperative actions aimed to explore a means for dealing with the problem of national division and reunification. North-South dialogues and Red Cross talks, although not successful, were the notable examples. Thus, in a complete departure from its old policy of non-recognition of the North or absolute objection of the two Koreas, South Korea "began to soften its tone toward *de facto*, if not *de jure*, recognition" (Kang, 1985: 65).[36] Subsequently, both regimes fostered, at least partially, positive reaction to a meeting between President Chun Do Whan of the South and Premier Kim Il Sung of the North. However, North Korea continued its forward deployment of troops near the demilitarized zone (DMZ), even during the time various peace negotiations were taking place.

Another major security program change accompanied the ROK-Japan Economic Normalization Treaty, signed in June 1965.[37] It was purely an economic, rather than political, factor that made the treaty possible. Instead of being dictated by anti-Japanese sentiments, the Park regime was strongly influenced by commercial and financial needs to propel the economic miracle on the Han River.[38] President Park was concerned about the future withdrawal of US troops and reduction of US foreign aid, and the need to manufacture more military hardware to compete against the North's military build-up. Thus, the goal of "security-first," or deterrence policy, was to be achieved through the means of economic catch-up and the modernization of the military derived from linkage effects of a heavy industrialization drive. From Japan's perspective, promoting economy in less-developed countries was necessary to transplant declining industries in Japan, utilize cheap labor, and implement its visions of the product cycle theory.[39] Specifically, the year 1966 was the turning point, and South Korea's growth rates reached double digits with capital/technology provided from Japan and the West, and with the labor/land of South Korea. The separation of political factors in relations with Japan continued into the Chun regime.

In the early 1970s, South Korea declared its readiness to open its doors to other Communist countries that were not hostile to the Republic of Korea. There had been a détente between Moscow and Washington and a move toward normalization of relations between Peking and Washington, accompanied by a substantive change in relations between the Soviet Union and Japan and between China and Japan. Eventually, Moscow regarded Beijing as its major adversary in Northeast Asia. However, South Korea did not make any formal diplomatic normalization as Japan had done. Rather, to Presidents Park and Chun, establishing communication channels with Moscow and Beijing was of major importance to facilitate simultaneous entry of North and South Korea into the UN as member states and to effect a cross-recognition of the two by the four major powers, namely, the United States, the Soviet Union, China, and Japan. This system of cross-recognition is called "a bi-triangular geopolitical system."[40] Another major objective was to expand its relations with a wide range of states by relaxing the earlier stance toward countries with which North Korea already maintained formal relations. Although South Korea's gestures were intended to ease tensions, at least partially, in the international relations, the underlying logic was based on the goals of deterrence, economic development, competitive diplomacy, and reunification on its own terms.

**Security Policy during the Transition and the Post-Cold War Era**

South Korea's security policy has been dualistic since its democratization in 1987. On the one hand, it demands that the U.S. continue its positive security guarantee against the North's military posture. On the other hand, it attempts to build its own new regional security alignment mechanism. With increased military capability, the South plans to reduce military tensions by providing economic assistance to and diplomatic channels with other regional powers. Ideological tolerance toward rigid anti-communism is also necessary, and the new democratic government of 1987 found that an antagonistic deterrence strategy was no longer credible for the relaxation of military tensions. To achieve this new international orientation, *nordpolitik*, globalization, and sunshine policy have been implemented.[41] As mentioned earlier, these policies are also integrated, with one policy quite often favored over the others. In this section, South Korea's security policy in the transitional period and the post-Cold War era is transformed into a governed interdependence policy. The governed interdependence policy aims to control the process of international interdependence or globalization in military, political, and economic domains of security.

*Nordpolitik* was implemented not only to reduce military tensions but also to establish a regional security mechanism for a peaceful process of unification. South Korea used economic incentives to promote the North's economic opening and delay the timing of unification through economic aid, rather than an ideologically antagonistic strategy to compel the North. Militarily, South Korea pursued a cooperative security strategy, using extended deterrence through its alliance with the U.S. so that it could eliminate the security threat from the North. At the same time, the South, by improving its naval and air capabilities, made plans to take over some of the responsibilities that the U.S. had covered over the years.[42] This is planned, not only to provide for a manageable unification, but also to prevent an abrupt collapse of the North.[43] Although South Korea acknowledges the fact that the North cannot be prevented from collapsing, it prefers a gradual integration as blueprinted under the globalization policy. However, those who foresee the North's collapse also believe that a "soft-landing" is not possible.[44] To them, offering unilateral assistance via the sunshine policy is useless; if the current regime in the North remains, it would be the people who would suffer, not the regime. All in all, the post-Cold War security policy stresses mutual and contingent interdependent interactions with regional powers, including North Korea, to maintain stability and order.

Under the new policy initiative of *nordpolitik* in South Korea's international orientation, the Noh Tae Woo administration (1988-1992) successfully negotiated formal diplomatic relations with all the Communist countries except Castro's Cuba and North Korea. In addition, both North and South Korea joined the United Nations and signed the Basic Agreement on Reconciliation, Non-aggression, and Exchanges and Cooperation in 1991. The primary goal of *nordpolitik* was the following: (1) the promotion of mutually beneficial relations with the Soviet Union/Russia and China, (2) facilitation of the North's entry into the world economy and *de facto* recognition of the North, (3) increasing regionalization of trade and the link to wider security concerns, and (4) relaxation of military tensions towards the North and promotion of an exchange of correspondence, visits, and contacts between the nations' representatives.[45]

The initial statement of *nordpolitik* was presented in the inauguration address of President Noh in February 1988. The foremost goal "was to realize cross-recognition of South Korea by the Communist allies of North Korea, in exchange for cross-recognition of North Korea by the South's allies" (Kihl, 1995: 127). The South attempted to improve military and security postures in relation to the North via the latter's allies, the Soviet Union/Russia and China. President Noh met Premier Gorbachev in San Francisco in June 1990 and President Yeltsin visited the Cheju island of South Korea in 1992. South Korea offered economic assistance to Russia and the latter wanted to initiate trade and investment. China also was moving toward a market economy, and economic normalization between Seoul and Beijing was established after the 1986 Asian Games in Seoul; diplomatic relations followed in 1992.[46] Eventually, South Korea's new international orientation had transformed economic power into diplomatic influence and strategic advantage over the North.[47]

Seoul's northern plan was instituted to provide a feasible alternative to Pyongyang and to facilitate the North's entry into the world economy.[48] Its aim was to relax military tensions and promote contacts among representatives and relatives dispersed in both parts of Korea. Internally, *nordpolitik* was also intended to gain political support. However, these plans were idealistic rather than realistic, since the success of the northern policy was dependent upon how the North responded to the South's gestures. As witnessed during the early 1990s, the North chose to go nuclear as opposed to opening its closed society to the outside world. Actually, the northern policy left the North in both strategic and diplomatic isolation, since the North's nuclear ambition was to offset the military and geostrategic balance of power after it lost strategic allies Russia and China.

Permanent nuclear freezing or dismantling of the North's nuclear reactors was a primary objective of the Kim Young Sam administration (1993-1997). The possible reason for Pyongyang's nuclear and missile programs was its desire to reverse the military imbalance, diplomatic isolation, and autarchic economic situation.[49]  From Pyongyang's perspective, possessing nuclear weapons might generate a countervailing deterrence against the US-ROK conventional military superiority. Nuclear weapons also can function as a strategic equalizer to compensate for the loss of allies, using these weapons as bargaining chips for diplomatic recognition and economic aid from the West. Whatever the North's motivation might have been, the result was the 1994 Korean Peninsula Energy Development Organization (KEDO).[50] The KEDO is an ad hoc consortium that provides economic aid, two light-water reactors and diplomatic recognition for dismantling nuclear programs during the next 10 years. The KEDO is operated by the consensus of South Korea, Japan and the U.S.

Factors such as North Korea's missile and nuclear programs, the possibility of its political and economic breakdown, the question of security for economic interactions, trade frictions among regional states, and territorial disputes all contributed to possible conflicts in the post-Cold War Northeast Asian security structure. The collapse of the Berlin Wall in November 1989 and the subsequent unification of Germany as well as the collapse of the Soviet Union all generated new policy agendas and concerns. The rise of Japan as an economic power and the growth of China's military and economic power affected shifting patterns of power politics in Northeast Asia. Diplomatic and economic normalization among South Korea, Russia, China, and the former communist countries illuminated extended international alignment mechanisms. All of these led to the demise of the Cold War. This systemic transformation ended with the formal alignment between South Korea and China in 1992, and the post-Cold War era emerged. However, the relatively pluralistic power structure in the post-Cold War era has produced uncertainty due to the potential for competition in establishing political and economic preponderance and complexity in terms of the type and source of threats.

Currently, the post-Cold War structure includes multiple bilateral security alliances and broadened economic and diplomatic alignments among regional states. The U.S., Japan, China, Russia, and South Korea have maintained bilateral alliance and alignment relations, and only China maintains friendly relations with North Korea.

Adjusting to the changed international security structure, the Kim Young Sam government proclaimed "open and global diplomacy" or globalization that included the following: (1) creation of an international environment conducive to peace on the Korean peninsula and gradual unification of the two Koreas, (2) implementation of economic diplomacy, and (3) expansion of international cooperation and extension of its spheres of activity throughout the world. Globalization means not only the liberalization of the market but also includes efforts to create an economic community in which the North can be included. For the phased reunification, the Kim government provided economic rewards to sustain the Kim Jong-Il regime.[51] The South's unification scenarios were planned as a gradual process: economic integration by the year 2000, political integration by 2010, and a unified Korea by 2020.[52]

At the same time, South Korea attempted to extend its economic and diplomatic influence in order to compel the North to open its isolated system and to lead to eventual reunification in South Korean terms. Efforts also had been made for the establishment of a pluralistic security community which includes the attempt to procure the Conference on Security and Cooperation in Northeast Asia, North Pacific Cooperative Security Dialogue, and the Hexagon ("two plus four") security alliance system.[53] The most recent attempt is the proposal for a "two plus two" dialogue, including the two Koreas, China, and the U.S., put forth in April 1996 by President Clinton and South Korean President Kim Young Sam for North-South Korean dialogue. This proposal does not set any preconditions, and North Korea is encouraged to bring up any issue it wants to discuss at the proposed talks. The Kim government proclaimed that the Cold War competitive diplomacy was over and that the implementation of economic diplomacy in the pursuit of practical interests was a better alternative for the post-Cold War era.

Economic diplomacy aimed to widen the South's international spheres of activities from politico-military and regional issues to trade, environment, development and other areas. The South expressed its willingness to expand cooperation with Asia-Pacific countries at the summit meetings of the Asia Pacific Economic Cooperation (APEC), and announced that it would substantially increase aid to developing countries at the United Nations World Summit for Social Development in 1995.[54] In addition, an active role would be played in the United Nations, including peacekeeping activities in Somalia and Morocco. Membership in the World Trade Organization (WTO) in 1995 and admission to advanced economies' Organization for Economic Cooperation and Development (OECD) in 1996 also enabled the South to use its new international position to gain support and to widen international contacts. South Korea's economy was gradually liberalized in the areas of trade, finance, and investment, following the scheduled liberalization set by APEC, the WTO, and the OECD. However, reversed capital flows, ineffective financial regulations, symbiotic relationships between the government and business, and relatively high costs of land, labor, and capital caused South Korea's financial and economic crisis of 1997.[55] Fortunately, with $57 billion of the International Monetary Fund (IMF) bailout, the crisis did not cause any significant changes in its economic diplomacy toward North Korea.

All in all, the Kim Young Sam administration's globalization policy supported the view that economic diplomacy and active participation in world politics might "lure" North Korea to a more acceptable path, and that economic aid would, in the long run, lead to a penetration of the closed market for a phased unification.[56] However, the policy of gradualism lacked any concrete details. It seemed more speculation than a "blueprint" by which economic and political union could be gradually achieved through negotiations between the North and the South. Moreover, the North-South dialogue, regarded as the essential precondition of multistage integration, was suspended by Pyongyang. The Kim administration drew a fairly optimistic picture of national reunification in its own terms without specifying any detailed means to reach its goal.

The Kim Dae Jung administration (1998-present) called for a "sunshine" policy that aimed to improve inter-Korean relations in line with peaceful coexistence, reconciliation and cooperation. The sunshine, as opposed to strong wind, policy included the former administrations' mutual reconciliation and democratic unification policies, but adjusted its program to direct economic engagement with the North.[57] The policy toward the North is based on economic appeasement or separation of economics from politics rather than economic absorption by the South. It is "intended to enable North Korea to voluntarily remove its coat of isolation and hostility and give up its vision of liberating the South, while institutionalizing peaceful coexistence with South Korea, thereby fostering the establishment of regional structure ripe for peace for unification" (Yang, 1998: 51). The goal of the sunshine policy is to maintain reciprocal North-South mutual cooperation.

**Overall Trends and Framework for Comparative Analysis**

The characteristics of South Korean security policies have been evolutionary, shifting from strengthening military and economic capabilities to advocating the creation of regional economic interdependence. A dramatic restructuring of South Korea's security policy also occurred in its international orientation toward the communist countries including North Korea. Largely, there have been three major changes in South Korea's security policy: (1) from absolute anti-communism to mutual antagonism during the Cold War era, (2) from defensive deterrence to governed interdependence during the transitional phase, and (3) from *nordpolitik* to globalization and sunshine policy during the post-Cold War era.

The Syngman Rhee administration's (1948-1960) policy of absolute anti-communism and no-two-Koreas changed to the Park Chung Hee (1961-1979) and Chun Do Whan (1980-1987) administrations' mutual antagonism. The latter two regimes' goal was to achieve economic development, political legitimacy, and deterrence against the North's military aggression and communist expansionism. The deterrence policy shifted to a governed interdependence policy during the Noh Tae Woo administration (1988-1992). That administration initiated *nordpolitik* and attempted to promote mutually beneficial relations with the communist countries. Along with democratic reforms and economic liberalization, the Kim Young Sam administration (1993-1997) and the Kim Dae Jung administration (1998-present) called for open economic trade and investment with regional powers as well as with North Korea. Their globalization and sunshine policies were meant to induce the North to open its society to the outside world. Since the transitional phase, South Korea has prioritized the issues of economic liberalization, political reforms and democratic consolidation, and economic interdependence with North Korea. As shown in Figure 1.1, these three major changes in South Korea's security policy will be analyzed in chapters 4, 5 and 6. Each chapter will examine the relative explanatory power of international systemic and domestic institutional factors critical to South Korea's security policy change.

**Figure 1.1.    Framework for Comparative Analysis of Security Policy Change**

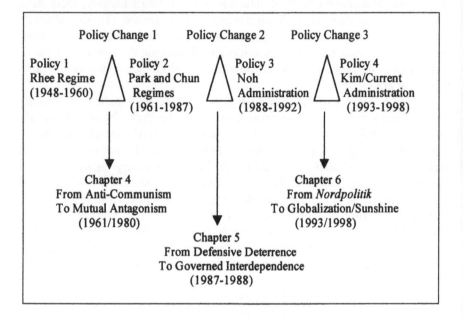

## Notes

[1] In the 1970s, the United States, China, and Japan formed a "trilateral diplomacy" or "geopolitical triangular." The bi-triangular system consisted of the United States, Japan, and South Korea on the capitalist side and the Soviet Union, China, and North Korea on the communist side.

[2] APEC was established in 1989 as a way to manage and facilitate economic interdependence and began as an informal grouping of 12 Asia-Pacific economies: Australia, Brunei, Canada, Indonesia, Japan, South Korea, Malaysia, New Zealand, the Philippines, Singapore, Thailand, and the United States. In 1991, the so-called "three Chinas"—China, Hong Kong, and Taiwan— joined the forum. At the 1993 Seattle meeting, Mexico, Chile, and Papua New Guinea were invited to join, bringing APEC membership to 18. At the 1997 meeting, the APEC invited Vietnam, Peru, and Russia to join in 1998, after which there is now a 10-year moratorium on new members. See Deng (1997) and Dutta (1999).

[3] The Russia-DPRK (The Democratic Peoples' Republic of Korea) Defense Treaty was formally abrogated in 1996. China also officially announced that it would not support any North Korean military aggression against South Korea. See Ministry of National Defense, *Defense White Paper* (Seoul: MND, 1998).

[4] Patrick Cronin defines an alliance as a "latent war community" designed to permit states to collaborate on military or security affairs. Examples include military exercises of the Team

Spirit and the Rim of Pacific Asian Countries (RIMPAC). In contrast, alignment takes the form of economic and diplomatic relationships instead of security commitment; thus, alignment can be "asymmetrical or coincidental rather than reciprocal or explicit" (Cronin, 1992: 209). Therefore, many of the recent proposals for multilateral security fora in Northeast Asia are regarded as proposals for alignment rather than for a security alliance. Examples of alignment systems are the APEC and security fora of the Council for Security Cooperation.

[5] For detailed treatment of these questions, see Lynn-Jones and Miller (1993), Gerner (1995), Neack, Hey, and Haney (1995), and Rothgeb (1995).

[6] For the study of security policy change, see Buzan and Jones (1981), Katzenstein (1989), Rosenau (1992), and Rosati, Sampson, and Hagan (1994).

[7] Deterrence by definition refers to the relationship in which nation A, through its behavior (verbal and non-verbal), convinces nation B not to take any action against nation A. Defense means reducing one's own costs and risks and attempting to nullify the effectiveness of the enemy's attack. If deterrence is successful, then defense never has to take place. Thus, defensive deterrence means that South Korea's security policy is by nature defensive or reactive and at the same time the South attempts to deter any military adventure from the North through deterrence by the US-ROK Combined Forces and extended deterrence. Governed interdependence refers to the government-controlled mutual and uneven international interaction in military, political, and economic domains of security. The concept represents a fusion of neoliberal and neorealist visions of the international system. Specifically, states are related to each other on both economic and political-security terms in an interdependent neo-mercantile global system, as Gilpin argues. See Snyder (1961), Gilpin (1987), Keohane and Nye (1989), and Huth (1993).

[8] For the review of a comparative-historical approach, see Przeworski and Teune (1970), Ragin and Zaret (1983), George and McKeown (1985), Skocpol (1985), McMichael (1990), and Thelen and Steinmo (1992).

[9] The Korean War of 1950-1953 saw intervention by major powers whose interests both intersect and clash in the Korean peninsula. An understanding of the relationships among the United States, the Soviet Union, China, Japan, and the two Koreas takes on practical significance. This inquiry looks at the overall trends among them from 1954 to 1998.

[10] Rosenau (1971) emphasizes the scientific study of five levels of analysis: system-level, state-level, societal/political culture-level, group-level, and individual-level approaches. In this study, an integrated model of system-level and state-level approaches is applied. See Rosati, Sampson, and Hagan (1994), pp. 18-20; Gerner (1995), pp. 17-32; and Hughes (1997).

[11] Theoretical causal claims are discussed in Chapter 2.

[12] The analytical rationale for choosing these criteria is in Chapter 3.

[13] Formal relationships with other nations were concluded in the latter part of the nineteenth century: Japan (1876), the U.S. (1882), Germany and Great Britain (1883), Italy and Russia (1884), France (1886), and Austria (1892). See Kim and Kim (1967) and Reese (1988).

[14] See Walker (1975) for traditional Sino-Korean relations. Historical legacies and foreign relations in Northeast Asia are well explained by Koo and Han (1985), Reese (1988), and Eckert et al. (1990).

[15] See Koo and Han (1985), p. 4; Jung (1984), p. 65; and Cumings (1997), pp. 86-138.

[16] *Ibid.*

[17] See Jung (1984), pp. 73-75; Reese (1988), pp. 74-76; and Cumings (1997), pp. 139-184.

[18] *Ibid.*

[19] *Ibid.*

[20] *Ibid.*

[21] See Kihl (1984), pp. 27-42; Eckert et al. (1990), pp. 327-346; and Cumings (1997), pp. 185-236.

[22] *Ibid.*

[23] *Ibid* and Matray (1995), pp. 17-38.

[24] For recent accounts on the role of China and the Soviet Union during the Korean War, see Cumings (1981), Ha (1990), Chen (1994), Park M. (1996), Spanier and Hook (1998), and Seo (1999).

[25] During the Cold War, South Korea consistently spent about 5% or above of its GNP for military expenditures. Seventy percent of the expenditure was used for military maintenance and operations and thirty percent for improvement and purchasing. See Ministry of National Defense, *Defense White Paper* (Seoul: MND).

[26] The sources of this categorization are Ministry of National Defense, *Defense White Paper* (Seoul: MND) and Ministry of Foreign Affairs, *Diplomacy White Paper* (Seoul: MFA).

[27] The doctrine of "two Koreas" was later known as the Hallstein Doctrine, which described "the rupturing of diplomatic relations with nations establishing formal diplomatic ties with North Korea" (Koo, 1975: 212). The fundamental basis of 'no-two-Koreas' was the UN General Assembly Resolution 195 (III), December 1948, which recognized South Korea as 'the only lawful government' on the Korean peninsula.

[28] About 3.5 million people were either wounded or killed during the Korean War. This figure includes the North and South Korean military personnel and civilians, Chinese volunteers, and UN military personnel. See Kihl (1984), p. 42.

[29] For President Rhee's autobiography and remarks on communism, see Koo (1975), Oliver (1978), Kihl (1984), and Cumings (1997).

[30] See U.S. Senate, Committee on Foreign Relations, *Hearings on the Mutual Defense Treaty with Korea*, 83rd Congress, 2nd Session, 1954, p. 53.

[31] See Institute of International Affairs, *Korean Defense Yearbook* (Seoul: IIA, 1990).

[32] See Ministry of National Defense, *Defense White Paper* (Seoul: MND, 1985).

[33] Premier Nguyen Gao Ky and President Johnson made official requests and President Park dispatched troops in 1965 until early 1973. About 312,000 South Korean military personnel were dispatched and about 13,000 were either killed or wounded, including missing in action. See Lee and Jung (1996), p. 232.

[34] See Institute of International Affairs, *Korean Defense Yearbook* (Seoul: IIA).

[35] A mutually hostile opposing policy was initiated by President Park's *Yushin* reform of 1972, stressing "total defense" as a guiding ideology of defensive deterrence, military modernization, and an economic catch-up mentality (Min, 1978; Sohn, 1989).

[36] When the North Korean representative for the North-South Korean Dialogues Kim Yong-Ju met the Director of the Korean Central Intelligence Agency Lee Hu Rak on July 4, 1972, they agreed, although interpreted differently, to refrain from slandering or defaming each other as well as from committing armed provocation, to send mails among separated families during the Korean War, and to install a hot line between Seoul and Pyongyang. See *Dong-A Daily News*, July 4, 1972 and Scalapino (1976), pp. 65-66.

[37] Despite the normalization, there are still a number of unresolved problems: (1) the status of Korean residents in Japan, (2) Japan's claim to Dokdo island, (3) problems concerning the sea line, (4) compensation for "comfort women," and (5) Japanese possession of Korean art treasures. See Koo (1975), pp. 220-222 and Institute of International Affairs, *Korean Defense Yearbook* (Seoul: IIA).

[38] Detailed explanations of the process of South Korea's industrialization during the take-off period (1962-1972), the heavy industry drive period (1973-1980), and high-tech knowledge intensive period (1981-present) are found in Amsden (1989), Kwon (1990), Wade (1991), Todaro (1992), and Blomqvist (1997).

[39] For more explanations on the product cycle theory or "flying geese model," see Cumings (1984), Blomqvist (1997), Castley (1997), and Islam and Chowdhury (1997).

[40] For the analysis on the bi-triangular system in Northeast Asia, see Barnds (1976), Kihl (1984), Gong and Leng (1995), and Kwak and Olsen (1996).

[41] See Ministry of National Defense, *Defense White Paper* (Seoul: MND) and Ministry of Foreign Affairs, *Diplomacy White Paper* (Seoul: MFA).

[42] The South Korean military has attempted to restructure the composition of its armed forces to create both a defensive-oriented and an offensive competence to strike at an adversary's strategic locations. The military now has peacetime operational control of its forces implemented in December 1994, and operational control at war has been in the US-ROK Combined Forces Corps since 1978. As a part of "burden-sharing," the South contributed $330 million in 1997 and $175 million in 1998 for the costs of the US Forces in South Korea. See Ministry of National Defense, *Defense White Paper* (Seoul: MND, 2000).

[43] The condition of a collapsed system in the North is not clearly defined yet. Generally, the circumstance of the North's collapse is speculated as being in a situation of structural dysfunction in which the system cannot recover from social revolts, economic decline and breakdown of the command and control system in the military. Military coup d'etat in the North is one of the possible outcomes in that situation, but the question is how the South will respond to the military-dominated North. Economic absorption and military takeover are proposed as other alternatives, but the timing and method of such alternatives are not yet clear.

[44] In particular, collapsists point out that economic stagnation and food shortages in the 1990s may be signals of the North's systemic collapse. According to South Korean authorities, a large number of North Koreans might die of starvation or flee their country into neighboring states. Considering systemic breakdown, officials also commented that a crisis of either collapse or aggressive action is only a matter of time.

[45] See Ministry of Foreign Affairs, *Diplomacy White Paper* (Seoul: MFA).

[46] In 1987, "trade offices were established in Seoul and Beijing, but the cost was the breaking of the long established formal relationship with Taiwan" (Middleton, 1997: 165).

[47] Although the North opposed the separated entry of two Koreas into the UN, China and Russia did not veto to block the entry. Given the wide support for the joint entry, the North had little choice but to follow suit. See Olsen (1993), Sanford (1993), and Kihl (1995).

[48] The Economic Planning Board made public announcements that opened trade with North Korea in 1988. Trade between the two Koreas totaled $1 million in 1988 and reached about $230 million in 1994. These figures also include indirect trades. See Institute of International Affairs, *Korean Defense Yearbook* (Seoul: IIA, 1995).

[49] Pyongyang's interest in nuclear deterrence includes shifting the military balance incorporating ideas such as countervailing deterrent, changing alliance, international status, bargaining chip, *juche*, and shield for terrorism (Bracken, 1993; Kim B., 1993; Mack, 1994).

[50] This agreement was negotiated by the former Assistant Secretary of State Robert Gallucci and Vice Foreign Minister of North Korea Kang Sok-Ju in Geneva, 1994. It includes reaffirmation of the North's membership in the Nuclear Non-proliferation Treaty, provision of 500,000 tons of heavy oil annually and return to the North-South dialogue. For further details, see Lehman (1994) and Ministry of National Defense, *Defense White Paper* (Seoul: MND, 1995).

[51] Although South Korea provided 150,000 tons of rice to help with food shortages in the North as a way of reassuring the North and prolonging its existence, South Koreans were not convinced that people in the North benefited from such provisions. About 70% of the South Korean people opposed the food aid to the North. Thus, the South eliminated the direct food aid program except for international humanitarian aid through non-government agencies such as the Red Cross. See Ministry of National Defense, *Defense White Paper* (Seoul: MND, 1995).

[52] See Koo and Kim (1993) and Ministry of Public Information, *Globalization Blueprint: 1995-2000* (Seoul: MPI, 1995).

[53] The best example of a pluralistic security community is the Conference on Security and Cooperation in Europe (ESCE). For more discussions, see Cronin (1992), Tow (1993a), and Lee J. G. (1995).

[54] South Korean aid amounted in 1994 to only 0.04% of GDP compared with the average of 0.38% for OECD countries. See Ministry of Foreign Affairs, *Diplomacy White Paper* (Seoul: MFA, 1998).

[55] Detailed treatments on the causes of South Korea's financial and economic crisis are in Chapter 6.

[56] For the role of economic aid to North Korea, see Park M. (1995) and Middleton (1997).

[57] See Ministry of National Defense, *Defense White Paper* (Seoul: MND).

# 2. Security Policy Analysis: A Theoretical Guide

After the demise of the Cold War, critics argued that mainstream theories in the area of international relations failed to predict substantial changes in international politics.[1] Systemic transformations include the collapse of the former Soviet Union, the rise of a "new world order," and the recent economic crisis in East Asia. Dominant international theories, primarily neorealism and neoliberalism, can be faulted on the grounds that they lack adequate explanations of the dynamics of international structural determinants and domestic institutional forces. Theory development at this level of security policy change has received comparatively little attention. International relations theories "tend to bias historical and theoretical analyses too much toward continuity...[and] rarely find a way to introduce discontinuities into theory" (Gaddis, 1992/3: 52). In short, the primary theoretical pitfall is that established theoretical approaches in the field of international relations have over-emphasized continuity at the expense of change.

If the theoretical objective is the explanation or anticipation of what happens, rather than "problem-solving" (Waltz, 1986), then a precise description of international phenomena is essential. Explanatory and causal claims, at both empirical and theoretical levels, reflect an ability to explain what happened and to offer adequate descriptions or forecasts of what will happen. The theoretical failure to anticipate the dynamics of international politics encourages one to speculate on the explanatory power of existing theories and their methodological tools. The consideration of security policy changes also raises the issue of how states behave to internal and external changes. Under what conditions do states react to international changes? When and why do states' security policies change? This chapter addresses various aspects of theoretical debates in light of security policy change, and is divided into three subsections: historical overview of security policy analysis, theoretical causal claims, and theoretical deficiencies and further research.

**Historical Overview of Security Policy Analysis**

The study of security policy is "a diverse set of activities, dedicated to understanding and explaining...behaviors of actors in world politics" (Neack,

Hey, and Haney, 1995: 1). The evolution of this field and theoretical causal claims about state behaviors have been marked by both continuity and change over traditional approaches between the first, second, and third generations of security policy analysis (SPA).[2] These studies frequently overlap temporally; hence, the generational change is neither complete nor specific to a particular year. The study of security policy as a sub-field of international relations has become conceptually rigorous, methodologically diverse and sophisticated, and theoretically inclined. SPA as a field of study may lack the theoretical integrity of a discipline, but it has served as a bridge between the studies of world politics and comparative politics.

The generational change of security studies embraces a broad scope of analysis and has always been diverse and dynamic. The main theoretical foci are domestic politics and international affairs, ranging from individual to state to systemic levels of analysis. What has been recognized as the sources of the state's security policy change include the state's size and status associated with national capabilities in the international system, levels of socioeconomic developments, the types of political and ideological order, organizational or bureaucratic attributes of domestic politics, and psychological traits of decision-makers. Theoretical importance has been given to establishing some *a priori* judgments about what kinds of factors have most influenced the state's security policy behaviors. As Joseph Nye and Sean M. Lynn-Jones argue, the field includes:

> Basic theoretical work on the causes of conflict and war in the international system, the dynamics and outcomes of conflict, the nature and perception of threats, and efforts to ameliorate or resolve conflicts caused by such threats. Analysis of the problems of nuclear strategy, arms control, and deterrence,... the determinants of the defense policies of states,... and military history are familiar parts of the field. Economic, sociological and psychological dimensions of threats and institutional responses to security dilemmas are equally important. (1988: 6-7)

The study of interstate relations is "as old as the existence of nation-states themselves; however, foreign [or security] policy analysis as a distinct theoretical enterprise didn't exist before World War II" (Hudson and Vore, 1995: 212). The roots of SPA are generally found in the studies of international relations, comparative politics, and the international society. In the field of international relations, critical determinants of security policy resided in the nature of the international political system. The structural condition of anarchy had been the general starting point for the study of SPA. In *Politics Among Nations: The Struggle for Power and Peace*, Hans Morgenthau, as a founding father of realism, argued that international anarchy, as the ordering principle, led states to maximize their strength and ability to survive in power politics. Largely, studies in comparative politics, refining Weberian and Marxian analyses of the state, have attempted to explain why states do what they do, treating states as members of a class of phenomena, generalizing the sources of states' behaviors, and focusing on bureaucratic politics and decision-making processes. Idealist thinkers following Woodrow Wilson have searched for regional and international mechanisms or communities that would prevent war and build peace. Studies of the international society or world community also maintain that the world can secure its stability and order through international law as Hugo Grotius proposed. Consequently, most traditional approaches focused on the ways of sustaining international order at the systemic level.

The first generation of SPA emerged from the revolutionary impact of nuclear weapons and within the positivist era of comparative and international politics in the 1950s-60s. Assuming security studies to be those dealing with conflicts between states under anarchy, scholars devoted extensive efforts to explain the causes of peace and war (Wright, 1942; Waltz, 1959; Wohlstetter, 1959; Hoag, 1961; Claude, 1962), nuclear deterrence strategies (Kaufmann, 1956; Schelling, 1960; Snyder, 1961), and arms control and limited war (Brennan, 1961; Bull, 1961; Schelling and Halperin, 1961; Osgood, 1966).[3] Studies of conflict resolution, peace and world order, and defense and military affairs were utilized to model the state's security strategies and facilitate quantitative methods, event data, and case studies. In this vein, the first generation of scholarship can be labeled as politico-military strategy analysis (POMSA). These first-generation scholars paid explicit attention to the specification of anarchic situations under which change or disorder took place. The security dynamics of the state are only implicitly discussed as adjuncts in analyses of war and power; i.e., war "is deemed to be a symptom of disorder [and] the balance of power is a means to create order" (Dunn, 1981: 72).

Theoretically, POMSA scholars hoped to establish a normal science of security study in the Kuhnian (1970) sense and concentrated on rational actor assumptions and stressed ideas, national types, social characteristics, cognitive-psychological modes, and systematic decision-making models.[4] However, there were inherent deficiencies. The common accusation centered on the claim that rationality has objectively dual forms; i.e., one is rational and the other irrational. The two hegemonic blocs were caught in a building up of conventional weapons and massive destructive capabilities against the adversary, attempting to increase "spheres of influence" in world politics.[5] A theoretical deficiency was that rational actor assumptions over-shadowed various aspects of domestic political factors, which also determined state behaviors. By treating the state as the unitary-rational actor, internal political factors such as party politics, bureaucratic procedures, and institutional realignments are overshadowed. Another deficiency was a lack of cumulative case studies and systematic evidence to support hypotheses and policy recommendations drawn from POMSA. Still another deficiency was that the theoretical treatment of change was limited in describing politico-military conditions or power politics in the international security structure. As a result, POMSA was seen as being largely atheoretical and descriptive.

Due to this theoretical impasse, studies of peace and war started to decline. In addition, causes for the field's decline in the mid-1960s included "unresolved controversial issues of rational deterrence paradigm, the failure to produce Ph. D. students, and the Vietnam War" (Walt, 1991: 216). U.S.-Soviet détente also discouraged scholars' interests in security studies. The disillusionment over Vietnam made SPA in the U.S. "less fashionable and illogical." However, a renaissance of security studies began in the mid-1970s with the end of the Vietnam War and the oil crises of 1973 and 1979. This encouraged scholars to study not only military and strategic issues, but also issues of economic development and dependency. The study of economic development also made Western scholars look at relations with non-Western states. Issues of state- and nation-building created a need for more diverse theoretical and conceptual tools in the study of security policy. Explicitly, study was extended to the explorations of socioeconomic and cultural factors at various levels of analysis. Labeled as international security analysis (ISA), the scope of security study utilized by second-generation scholars has been interdisciplinary and has covered a wide range of issues in international politics.

The theoretical foci of ISA were the historical analysis of deterrence (George and Smoke, 1974; Steinbruner, 1976; Jervis, 1979; Sagan, 1985; Achen and Snidal, 1989), conventional warfare (Fischer, 1976; Mako, 1983; Cohen, 1988; Posen, 1989), the security and insecurity dilemma (Jervis, 1978; Ayoob, 1984, 1995; Buzan, 1991; Job, 1992), regional security studies (Jackson and Rosberg, 1982; Grabendorff, 1984; Kim, 1988; Moon, 1988), and policy-relevant security policies (George and Smoke, 1974; Leffler, 1984; Posen, 1984; Posen and Van Evera, 1987). These second generation scholars incorporated diverse theoretical perspectives on international relations and comparative politics. These perspectives included studies of alliance politics (Snyder, 1984; Walt, 1987; Christensen and Snyder, 1990), the effects of domestic politics (Evans, 1979; Skocpol, 1985; O'Donnell, Schmitter, and Whitehead, 1986; Hagan, 1987; Levy, 1989), game theory (Tollison and Willett, 1979; Axelord, 1984; Brams, 1985; Snidal, 1985; McGinnis, 1986), cognitive-psychological and cultural studies (Steinbruner, 1974; Holsti O., 1982, 1989; Hermann, 1985; Rosati, 1987), security issues of dependent states (Cardoso, 1973; Ferris and Lincoln, 1981; Mehta, 1985), the international political economy (Gilpin, 1975; Balassa, 1981; Johnson, 1982; Moon, 1985), and transnational relations (Nye, 1971; Keohane and Nye, 1974, 1989; Stein,

1982; Keohane, 1988). In short, a wide variety of factors involving military, economic, and sociopolitical forces were incorporated into their theoretical explanations of state behaviors.

As a whole, second-generation scholars of ISA used a variety of methodologies and theoretical causal mechanisms, and considered contingent and complex interactions among critical determinants that influence fluctuations of state behaviors. However, ISA largely relegated domestic political factors and social forces to a position of secondary importance; i.e., not enough attention was paid to Graham Allison's bureaucratic politics approach (1961) and Irving Janis's group-think model (1982).[6] With no clear conceptualization of security, its continued emphasis on politico-military aspects of security has hindered the development of the subject. The inability to agree on what is and is not international policy, as opposed to domestic policy, has been another pitfall. The problem is that the analytical foci have concentrated on international systemic factors at one time and domestic factors at the other, and have often shifted back and forth. What has become clear is that "the security problem is greater than the sum of the parts of first, second, and third-image analysis" (Kolodziej, 1992: 436). Thus, almost all aspects of societal contexts are included in their analyses of security and its policy problem. Another significant pitfall is an inadequate explanation of the importance of critical determinants: i.e., how, when, and under what conditions do causal factors influence state behaviors? The inherent theoretical difficulties resided in the failure to recognize and explain the complex interplay of international, domestic, and governmental factors of security policy change.[7]

The demise of the Cold War and the collapse of the Soviet Union created new security policy problems and new research puzzles for current third-generation scholars in the post-Cold War era.[8] What is significant is that there has been "a shift away from trying to build grand theory in favor of trying to build midrange theories that are empirically grounded, culturally sensitive, and often issue- or domain-specific" (Gerner, 1995: 30). No "pure and real security" is advocated in its spheres of the multidimensionality and interdisciplinary field. The boundaries of security have broadened into cultural, socio-psychological, environmental, and demographic issues. Increasingly, more scholars face difficulties in separating the boundaries of security and the distinctive spheres of "domestic" and "foreign." It is clear that economic interdependence, concerns of alliance politics, and regional and international organizations mean that governments are no longer free arbiters in making security policies. All of these suggest the need to establish multi-level and multi-variable explanatory frameworks with clear causal mechanisms for a fuller understanding of security policy phenomena.[9] Cumulative knowledge based on a variety of case studies and comparative systematic or contextual analyses is also required to improve causal claims of different theoretical analyses.

Attempting to fulfill such theoretical needs, third-generation scholars of security policy analysts (SPA) have paid greater attention to different aspects of domestic politics (Hagan, 1995; Doyle, 1996; Maoz, 1996; Stern and Verbeek, 1998), linkage politics (Putnam, 1988; Kaufman, 1994; Neack, 1995; Lohmann, 1997), regional and global economic interdependence and the world community (Muller, 1994; Strange, 1996; Tussie, 1998; Blackwill and Dibb, 2000), and political culture (Adler, 1992; Johnston, 1995; Finnemore, 1996; Huntington, 1996; Katzenstein, 1996; Legro, 1997). With multilevel and multicausal explanatory variables, the third generation of SPA has shifted their theoretical emphasis from international structural factors to domestic institutional determinants. They also have analyzed a set of domestic and international factors which constrain and facilitate the security policy of any given states.

The theoretical contributions of third-generation scholars of SPA have been enormous. Reexamination of linkage politics has contributed to a better understanding of security policy dynamics.[10] SPA has recently recognized the need for the refinement of theoretical explanatory power to combine multiple, interrelated sources of explanations drawn from different levels of analysis. A major theoretical contribution is the interdisciplinary analyses of security policy change, incorporating theoretical findings from cultural studies and domestic institutional analyses. Advocates of cultural studies maintain that the state's security policy behavior both generates and is influenced by widely shared public attitudes, values, and beliefs. However, they failed to specify which conceptual definitions of culture are most appropriate to SPA.[11] The most significant contribution is a comprehensive overview of domestic institutional dynamics (Rosati, 1993; Park, Ko, and Kim, 1994; Hagan, 1995; Moon, 1995; Stavridis and Hill, 1996; Ross, 1998) and international and domestic determinants (Skidmore, 1994; Mingst, 1995; Zakaria, 1995; Keohane and Milner, 1996; Schweller, 1998; Hauss, 1999) linked to the state's security policy behaviors. The critical determinants of security policy change such as regime types, political power structures, alliance patterns, and economic trade shares are accounted for in their analyses to explain the timing and the direction of the changes.

In sum, the field of SPA has tested and refined a diversity of theoretical frameworks, as Joseph Nye and Sean M. Lynn-Jones suggested to work on "the causes of war, the sources of cooperation, the formation of alliances, the implications of nuclear resolution, the security effects of economic interdependence, the domestic sources of foreign policy, the consequences of offensive or defensive doctrines, and the cultural and cognitive biases of decision-makers" (1988: 21). However, not enough theoretical integration of domestic institutional analysis has been applied to security policy analysis. Third-generation scholars also need to resolve the question of how certain critical factors, theoretical hypotheses, and even theories from different analytical levels can be integrated into more complete explanations. They also must provide the relative explanatory power of critical variables drawn from multi-level or multi-causal explanations and middle-range theories.[12]

## Theoretical Causal Claims

Different explanatory approaches of the three generational studies to security policy suggest at least four causal implications of the study of security policy change: security policy changes result from shifts in (1) the structural constraints of the international system, regardless of the characteristics of domestic politics, (2) the state's international position or its capability status, (3) domestic political alignments and regime types, and (4) institutional arrangements and bureaucratic processes. First-generation and most second-generation scholars have been concerned with the first two sets of causal mechanisms, while third-generation scholars of SPA give greater thought to the latter two sets or a combination of all causal claims. These generations highlight various critical determinants of security policy change, assessing the explanatory power of their own causal claims. I label those who deal with international sources of security policy change as international structuralists and those who concern themselves with domestic sources as domestic institutionalists.[13]

### *International Structuralism*

Neorealism and neoliberalism are the dominant theories in the international relations literature. Neorealists drive their causal claims from international systemic characteristics. Neorealists assume that the underlying international system is one of anarchy and "self-help" (Waltz, 1959, 1979, 1993; Tucker, 1977; Posen, 1984; Art and Jervis, 1986; Mearsheimer, 1990; Snyder, 1990; Van Evra, 1990; Buzan, 1991; Walt, 1991). Within the anarchic system, states are unitary-rational actors motivated by a desire for security in the international system. The anarchic structure as a unidirectional causal factor is the source of threats that determine the state's security policy behavior. They argue that international structural constraints such as the distribution of power and the character of threats override domestic sources of security policy-making.

Theoretical foci of neorealism are the nature and consequences of anarchy, balance of power politics, states' positions in terms of their relative and absolute capabilities in the international system, and alliance mechanisms. The chief theoretical assumption is that a state's security policy is reflective of changes in the international systemic factors and of changes in its relative position in the balance of power equilibrium.[14]   Neorealism suggests that regional structural factors determine the security policies of the two Koreas. Structural factors include the balance-of-power mechanism, alliance politics, and sources of threats in Northeast Asia. According to this view, South Korea, located in a geo-strategic setting where diverse interests of major powers intersect, has been reactive to its strategic calculations of interests and power politics. Neorealists emphasize the specification of the structural conditions under which certain types of changes occur. However, a primary problem is why states do not always follow systemic constraints and opportunities.

Refining neorealism, neoclassical realists incorporate both systemic and unit-level variables to explain the state's security policies; i.e., they assume an "intervening causality" of domestic politics (James and Oneal, 1991; Zakaria, 1995; Christensen, 1996; Schweller, 1998; Wholforth, 1998).[15]   They believe that domestic politics as independent variables "must be relegated to second place analytically because over the long run a state's security policy cannot transcend the limits and opportunities thrown up by the international environment" (Rose, 1998: 151). Thus, international systemic constraints may always be present, but intervening variables of domestic political structures and decision-makers' perceptions can have important roles in determining states' behaviors. In this respect, their theoretical foci combine both domestic and international variables as the sources of security policy change. This theory suggests that South Korea's security policy change is determined by the collective pressures driven from the international systemic factors and domestic institutional setting, although systemic factors shape the broad contours of its security policy. The theoretical assumption of neoclassical realism is that a state's security behaviors are contextual; i.e., with geo-structural transformations, its security policy is affected both by systemic constraints and subsequent or intervening domestic politics. The chief problem is when domestic politics matter more than international politics, and vice versa.

Neoliberals have pointed out the increasing complexity of economic interdependence, democratization waves, and transnational interactions as causes of states' behavior (Baldwin, 1971; Stein, 1982; Lipson, 1984; Keohane and Nye, 1989; Gibney, 1992; Doyle, 1996). Neoliberalism can be subdivided into commercial liberalism [linking free trade and world order], republican liberalism [linking democracy and world peace], and transnational liberalism [linking transnational institutions and world order] (Baldwin, 1993). Neoliberals accept the neorealists' view of anarchy that it inhibits cooperation, but argue that "institutions can alleviate the inhibitory effects of anarchy on the willingness of states to work together when they share common interests"

(Grieco, 1993: 303). These common interests stem from ever-increasing liberal principles of democracy and the market economy. The increasing salience of geo-economic factors and waves of democratization have led states to contribute to world peace or absolute gains rather than national self-interests. In addition, transnational contacts and coalitions built through international regimes defined as "norms, principles, rules, and decision-making processes" (Krasner, 1983; Keohane and Nye, 1989) have transformatory effects on states' mutually beneficial cooperation.

Their theoretical foci are the nature and consequences of geo-economic structural factors, international cooperation, absolute gains, international institutions and regimes, and alignment mechanisms. The primary theoretical assumption is that the state's security policy is reflective of changes in geo-economic and transnational factors and that the likelihood of policy change toward pluralistic order and peace will increase as the state becomes more economically vulnerable and sensitive.[16] According to this view, change in South Korea's security policy resulted from its economic interactions with other regional powers. In addition to economic interdependence, memberships in international organizations also explain South Korea's security policy patterns. However, the problem is that states often use international institutions as their means to reach self-interested goals, rather than absolute gains. There are also limitations in coping with free-riders and rogue states, which do not fulfill the demands of international regimes.

Logically, it is also possible to argue that geo-economic structural factors may not always be present in determining states' behaviors. Although international pressures transmitted by transnational institutions and economic interdependence alter states' preferences, domestic political pressures can often override systemic constraints for mutually beneficial cooperation. This analysis is labeled as neoclassical liberalism in SPA.[17] Neoclassical liberals also integrate both external and internal variables in their theoretical assumptions of security policy analysis. International economic constraints and incentives shape the overall trends of the state's security policy, but domestic-level intervening factors become salient in the security policy-making process. Thus, neoclassical liberals refute the sole causality of system-level variables on the state's security policies. The primary focus is "the interplay between internationalization and domestic institutions...[and] how governments respond to international pressures. Governments can influence the constraints imposed by the international economy both through unilateral and multilateral action" (Keohane and Milner, 1996: 23). In other words, states' security behavior is contextual; i.e., increased economic interdependence will lead to a change in its security concerns as well as in subsequent domestic goals and objectives in terms of international competitiveness and comparative advantages, and government can act to alter the international imperatives. Neoclassical liberalism connotes that South Korea's security policy is shaped by both geo-economic factors and domestic factors of institutional arrangements and the level of economic development. However, as in the case of neoclassical realism, the question is under what conditions the international geo-economic factors matter more than domestic political/economic factors, and vice versa.

## Domestic Institutionalism

Advocates of domestic institutionalism argue for institutional determinism and propose domestic factors as dominant causal forces.[18] Domestic institutionalists assume a unidirectional causality and hold that security policy is "the product of the state's domestic factors" (Hilsman, 1967; Allison and Halperin, 1972; Hagan, 1995; Skidmore and Hudson, 1993; Moon, 1995; Evangelista, 1997; Moravcsik, 1997; Wittkopf and McCormick, 1998). It has been noted that an unexplained theoretical inadequacy of systemic analysts lies in their treatment of the state as a "black-box." An overemphasis on structural determinants in international politics generates a lack of attention to domestic politics, particularly security policy-making institutions' responses to internal and external changes. Domestic institutionalists argue that there have been no sufficient explanations of how states perceive external threats and define their interests, why they choose certain alternative policies and reject others, and how they respond to external and internal crises or events.

The primary theoretical foci of domestic institutionalism are political types of government, institutional arrangements, the effects of bureaucratic politics, levels of socioeconomic development, and decision-making processes in resolving, or at least ameliorating, the state's security problems. More specifically, the security policy is reflective of state imperatives of "capital accumulation, state legitimacy, social stability, and government maintenance" (Moon, 1995: 198).[19] Thus, internal factors such as "political and economic ideology, national character, partisan politics, or socioeconomic structure determine how countries behave toward the world beyond their borders" (Rose, 1998: 148). Domestic institutionalists also incorporate political culture and individual leaders' world-views in their analyses of a state's security policy.

Security policies are produced by various interactions within domestic political structures, among participants, and through bureaucratic processes. Within domestic settings of bureaucratic politics, security policy is derived from the "pulling and hauling" among various participants. The decision-making structure and processes have received a close attention in descriptions and explanations of state behavior. The security policy changes as the domestic political opportunity structure changes; i.e., it will be markedly stable while the ruling regime is in power but quite variable at the moment of regime change.[20] If the decision-making system is centralized and has limited participation in its processes, policy implementation can be effective, but limited in terms of the formulation of various alternatives, and vice versa. In this vein, South Korea's security policy change is the product of its domestic institutional dynamics. However, the chief theoretical pitfall is "why states with similar domestic systems often act differently and why dissimilar states in similar situations often act alike" (Rose, 1998: 148). A more fundamental pitfall is a lack of appreciation of the international systemic constraints and incentives.

In brief, theoretical causal claims about the state's security policy changes as related to domestic and international variables are unidirectional and intervening. Innenpolitik theorists propose a unidirectional arrow flowing from domestic political factors to security policy, while neorealists and neoliberals point out unidirectional effects of geo-structural and geo-economic factors. Neoclassical realists and neoclassical liberals integrate domestic factors as intervening variables, although their causal systemic factors are different; i.e., geo-structural and geo-economic factors, respectively. The differences of causal claims among the existing theories are summarized in Figure 2.1.

**Figure 2.1. Theoretical Causal Claims**

| Theories | Causal Claims (Fluctuations of Variables) |
|---|---|
| Neorealism | Geo-Structural ⟶ Security Policy<br>Factors    Unidirectional |
| Neoclassical Realism | Geo-Structural ⟶ Security Policy<br>Factors    ↑<br>Domestic Factors<br>as Intervening Variables |
| Neoliberalism | Geo-Economic ⟶ Security Policy<br>Factors    Unidirectional |
| Neoclassical Liberalism | Geo-Economic ⟶ Security Policy<br>Factors    ↑<br>Domestic Factors<br>as Intervening Variables |
| Domestic Institutionalism | Domestic Political ⟶ Security Policy<br>Factors    Unidirectional |

**Theoretical Deficiencies and Further Research**

Theoretical causal claims that "black-box" domestic politics are significantly flawed, as are domestic institutional theories that "black-box" international politics. International systemic accounts are as insufficient as are domestic level explanations and they have to be complemented by "second-image reversed" concepts (Gourevitch, 1978). Rather than relying exclusively on one source of security policy change, integrating both system-level and state-level analyses is essential. Thus, studies in international relations "should seek contributions to forecasting which ones either individually or collectively cross the boundaries of paradigms, because we know that any single paradigm is in and of itself insufficient" (Bobrow, 1999: 7). Theoretical deficiencies of the existing theories in terms of their perspectives, emphasis on continuity, linkage politics, and causal determinants of states' behaviors are fourfold.

First, such critics argue that the existing theories often employ a hypothetical marketplace of ideas and approaches in ways that lead to a narrowing rather than a broadening of their perspectives.[21] Because of an overemphasis on some interesting trees, the forest is lost, and vice versa. The results are narrowly defined security policy problems, flawed policy analyses, and poor policy decisions. To enrich policy discussion, formulation, and implementation, advocates of particular approaches need to incorporate or acknowledge the other schools' legitimate insights into their own analyses. Charles W. Kegley Jr., for example, questions the validity of neorealist formulation for assessing international politics and advocates the development of a principled idealism combined with neoliberal perspectives. Hilary Putnam also attempts to redirect theory building by searching for a hybrid combination of both realist and liberal or idealist concepts in the post-Cold War era. In other words, they maintain that the nature and process of the shifts in security priorities from military domains of power to economic and diplomatic domains need to be accounted for by incorporating different theoretical perspectives.

Second, mainstream theorists in the field of international relations tend to emphasize static continuity, orderly interdependence, and mutually shared ideational interests in explaining the dynamics of world politics. Logically, this leads to the assumption that most academics "have a preference for stability, or at least a preference for orderly change" (Gilpin, 1981: 6). Theoretical limitations are evident in attempts to explain systemic dynamics in international politics, on the one hand, and policy change affected by political realignments in domestic politics, on the other. One manifestation of such theoretical weaknesses, as critics of mainstream international relations approaches argue, was a limited capacity to yield precise predictions regarding the demise of the Cold War, the emergence of a new world order, and the economic crisis in East Asia.[22] As a result, the study of policy change has neglected the "restructuring" of the state's policy context derived from the changes in domestic policy-making institutions and the international security environment. Thus, contemporary theories of neorealism and neoliberalism have lost their theoretical parsimony to explain and forecast systemic coherence and collapse.[23]

Third, although analyses of the logic of two-level games and linkage politics in neoclassical realism and neoclassical liberalism point out the close connection between domestic factors and international determinants of policy-making, generally "these two policy spheres are kept separate" (McGinns and Williams, 1993: 29).[24] Linkage is defined as "any recurrent sequence of behavior that originates in one system and is reacted to in another" (Rosenau, 1969: 44). In this respect, SPA needs to clarify different types of linkage politics and roles of international domestic actors that link the domestic polity and the international system. More fundamental questions are when and how, and under what conditions, "linkage politics" occur. The causal claims can be "reciprocal," since both systemic and regional changes and domestic political changes have significant implications on both domestic and international politics.[25] As a result, policy analysts should provide a better causal analysis of whether linkage politics occur simultaneously, sequentially, or independently. They also need to explain whether the causality or ordering between critical variables and security policy change is either permanent or temporal.

Fourth, the discussion above suggests that the existing theories about the relationship between security policy change and systemic transformations/institutional realignments are highly abstract and sketchy. Although there have been substantial efforts to explain the sources of the state's security behaviors, theoretical causal claims are generally limited to the changing factors of the international system.[26] Kal J. Holsti's analysis of "why nations realign" (1982) is also limited because his primary focus is on international constraints for security policy change. Recent studies also lack discussions of the conditions under which security policy changes occur and exclusively deal with one aspect of critical factors.[27] For a better understanding of security policy change, integration of levels of analyses is necessary, for the state's security policy behavior "can be explained only by a conjunction of external and internal conditions" (Waltz, 1993: 79).

In this study, only one aspect of linkages, interactions between external/internal variables and security policy change is examined. It also includes an analysis of contextual conditions that provide constraints on and/or opportunities in South Korea's security policy-making. Further research is required for the development of middle-range theories through exploration of the linkages between societies and social actors across national boundaries, between individuals' world-views and international systemic factors, and between transnational institutions, especially multinational corporations and domestic institutional arrangements. Theoretical importance also lies in forecasting linkage politics. Linkages can be multi-directional, resulting from non-linear structural changes that bring out "uncertainties," "discontinuities of expectations," and "theoretical anomalies" (Kuhn, 1970; Doran, 1999). Thus, an analysis of the past and the present should contribute to advancing theoretical parsimony and maturity, with what is likely to occur, when it will occur, and how it will occur also being specified. This study also explores and tests the causal mechanisms that provide the linkages between South Korea's security policy change and international systemic and domestic institutional factors.

# Notes

[1] Critics include Gaddis (1992/3), Lebow and Risse-Kappen (1995), Wholforth (1998), and Baker and Morrison (2000).

[2] The historical overview of international security studies is extensively discussed in Smith (1986), Nye and Lynn-Jones (1988), Murray and Viotti (1989), Walt (1991), Kolodziej (1992), Hudson and Vore (1995), Neack, Hey, and Haney (1995), and Barash (1999). This chapter discusses similar accounts for the generational change of foreign policy analysis (FPA) and security policy analysis (SPA), since FPA and SPA are not separate sub-fields of international relations theory.

[3] To Waltz (1959) and Claude (1962), the chance of war is least likely if power is equally distributed. Contrary to their claims, Wittman (1979) argues that the distribution of power has no effect on the likelihood of war, while Blainey (1988) maintains that war is least likely if power is unequally distributed. In this generational study, concepts such as balance of power, deterrence, first and second strike capabilities, limited nuclear war, nuclear rationality, and arms race stability were elaborated.

[4] A notable example is Graham T. Allison's analysis on the rational actor model, bureaucratic process model, and governmental politics model in *The Essence of Decision: Explaining the Cuban Missile Crisis* (1961).

[5] Spheres of influence are areas under which a big power influences its claims of national interests over other smaller states. During the Cold War, the two superpowers maintained their dominant influence and freedom in specified areas of the globe—the Communist and Capitalist blocs. See Schlesinger (1967), Keohane (1982), and Gaddis (1987).

[6] For these critics, see Smith (1986), Nye and Lynn-Jones (1988), and Hudson and Vore (1995).

[7] This leads to level-of-analysis and agency-structure problems. Scholars point out the need to specify the cause of state behaviors derived from the dynamic processes of either agents or structure or both and the relative importance of different levels of explanations. See Singer (1961), Dessler (1989), Hollis and Smith (1991), Wendt (1992), Ritzer and Gindoff (1994), and Rosati, Sampson, and Hagan (1994).

[8] One of the serious puzzles has been how to improve prediction, at least forecasting, of critical international events, such as the end of the Cold War and the East Asian financial crisis.

[9] For multi-level and multi-variable analysis of SPA, see Hermann, Kegley, and Rosenau (1987), Czempiel and Rosenau (1989), Hermann (1995), and Wohlforth (1998). These scholars advocate an integrated approach that combines different variables and levels of analysis.

[10] Robert Putnam's contribution of "two-level games" (1988) and George Tsebelis's "nested games" (1990) involved in the international-domestic bargaining process are the two most notable examples.

[11] Advocates of cultural studies and social constructivists support the idea that the state is not a natural entity but a cultural production; that is, it is socially produced. However, the explanatory power of social constructivism has limitations due to "the conceptual ambiguity of culture, lack of applicability and testability across cases, and subsequent limits on theoretical generalization" (Desch, 1998: 150). Because of these deficiencies, cultural analysis is not included in this study.

[12] Rather than explaining the causes of war and peace at the global level, middle-range theories call for "more specification of the dependent variables…[and] marriage between the empirically grounded indicators of foreign policy behavior and efforts at constructing foreign policy theories" (Hermann, 1995: 53).

[13] These theories are not mutually exclusive, but only analytically drawn from their perspectives. Recently, more scholars have posited their views in the integrated, middle ground of international structuralism and domestic institutionalism.

[14] The neorealist theoretical premise is derived from Thomas Hobbes' perception of human nature and the state of nature that assumes that everyone is in a state of war, all against all. Like Thucydides and Machiavelli, Hobbes proposed a strong civil social order as an alternative to the self-help society. In international politics, that state was referred to as the anarchic system and thereby neorealists proposed a balance-of-power mechanism as an alternative.

[15] Neoclassical realists "incorporate both external and internal variables...[and] argue that the scope and ambition of a country's foreign policy is driven first and foremost by its place in the international system. But the impact...is indirect and complex...because systemic pressures must be translated through intervening variables at the unit level" (Rose, 1998: 146). For analysis of classical realism and neoclassical realism, see also Smith (1986).

[16] Sensitivity "involves degrees of responsiveness within a policy of framework...[and] vulnerability can be defined as an actor's liability to suffer costs imposed by external events even after policies have been altered" (Keohane and Nye, 1989: 12-13). An example of sensitivity is the way South Korea was affected by the increased oil prices. Heavy involvement in foreign trade causes the problem of vulnerability.

[17] For analytical and theoretical aspects of neoclassical liberalism, see Katzenstein (1976), Risse-Kappen (1995), and Keohane and Milner (1996).

[18] Domestic institutional theorists stress the influence of domestic institutional factors on the state's security policy, and argue that internal factors are the determinants of the state's security policy change. Moravcsik (1997) and Rose (1998) also provide "innenpolitik" theorizing, or domestic institutionalism, in their study of security policy change.

[19] For state imperatives, see also Skocpol (1985) and Tilly (1985).

[20] A policy change can occur within a relatively stable institutional framework (King, 1992; Weir, 1992), as the result of institutional reform in response to external changes or the malfunctioning of existing institutions (Krasner, 1978; Baumgartner and Jones, 1993), as the result of large-scale political realignments (Skowronek, 1982), and as a combination of all of the above (Hall, 1992; Howlett, 1994).

[21] For these critics, see Putnam (1990), pp. 3-42 and Kegley (1993), passim.

[22] For recent claims on the these deficiencies, see Rosenau (1990), Gaddis (1992/3), Kegley and Wittkopf (1993), Lebow and Risse-Kappen (1995), Brown (1996), Wholforth (1998), and Dougherty and Pfaltzgraff (2000).

[23] Against the critics, Kenneth N. Waltz argues that neorealists attempt to resolve the problem based on problem-solving theory, as opposed to critical theory; that is, "problem-solving theory seeks to understand and explain, rather than predict, world politics" (Waltz, 1986: 341). However, the neorealists' methods based on the static structure of anarchy are not only limited in resolving the problem, but also in explaining the dynamics of international politics.

[24] For more on two-level games and linkage politics, see Putnam (1988), Mustanduno, Lake, and Ikenberry (1989), and Tsebelis (1990).

[25] For more on reciprocal causal claims, see Moravscik (1993), Keohane and Milner (1996), and Maoz (1996).

[26] Examples include works of Black and Thompson (1963), Harf, Hoovler, and James (1974), and Pirages (1987).

[27] James Rosenau's (1981) theory of adaptation is also accused of analyzing static aspects of the international system; recent studies that deal with particular aspects of security policy change include Schraeder (1994), Hagan (1995), Hill (1996), and Tehranian (2000).

# 3. Research Design: Security Dimensions and Contextual Determinants

In the study of security policies, it is essential to review what security means, who defines security policy problems and policy alternatives, and what causes security policy change. This chapter considers various meanings of security, security policy change, political institutions, and institutional capacity. It also spells out contextual determinants and methodological approaches. Depending on how security is interpreted by political institutions, security policy changes occur in a wide range of security dimensions, scopes, and levels. Institutions can be weak or strong, in response to systemic transformations in both domestic and international politics. Institutional capacity is concerned with the extent to which political institutions are capable of achieving security goals within the dynamic context of security policy change. Critical factors are also identified and described in a range of international and domestic settings. Finally, methodological approaches used to examine the sources of security policy change are discussed.

## Meanings of Security and Security Policy Change

Security, meaning freedom from external threat, underscores two contested objects of threats; i.e., "who" and "what" should be secured (Dupont, 1997). The "who" of security refers to whether one is discussing the security of individuals, groups, states, or international communities, while the "what" of security concerns sovereign-territorial, military, economic, socio-cultural, environmental, and transnational security.[1] These dual objects of threats connote "three referents of security: the ideas of the state [nationalism], the physical base of the state [population, resources, and technology], and the institutional expression of the state [administrative and political system]" (Buzan, 1991: 65). What has been stressed in security studies is the sovereign-territorial security of the state; that is, survival of the state.

Generally, the conventional meaning of security has been put forth as the protection of the territorial and political integrity of states from external threat or attack.[2] Strategic and military affairs have been dominant in traditional studies of both the conflicts between states and the causes of war and peace. This definition of security involves politico-military concerns that attempt to ensure national survival in a "self-help," anarchic international system. Security discourse is therefore stipulated as the study of external threats, distributions of power, war, and diplomacy confined essentially to a state-centric analysis. Balance-of-power or balance-of-threat has been offered as a solution to the anarchic security environment, stressing the geo-strategic power structure. For neorealists, for example, international structural constraints override domestic political concerns, internal politico-military relations, and characteristics of particular states. The regional alliance formation is the result of power politics and balance-of-power mechanisms.

Those who emphasize geo-economics point out the ways in which complex economic interdependence and liberal democracies can promote "perpetual peace" in international politics.[3] Security problems arise from trade frictions and breakdowns of the liberalized economic system and pluralistic democracy. The primary concern lies in maintaining harmony of international interests and consolidating multilateral cooperation and international institutions. The pluralistic multilateralism, arguably shared by states, will eventually promote a peaceful environment by increasing confidence- and security-building measures (CSBMs), agreement among nations on conventional arms reductions, and consensus on the dangers of nuclear proliferation. Advocates of a community-building approach through economic interdependence suggest a fairly optimistic picture of pluralism in East Asian international politics. Critics argue that the problem of multilateralism is in the lack of common security interests, lack of common historical backgrounds and political or cultural similarities, unfulfilled promises of arms control, and diminished American clout.[4] Security, for neoliberals, depends upon how firmly national or international communities maintain the complex and inter-linked patterns of relations, sustaining more benefits in order to outweigh the costs for members of the international community.[5]

There is another dimension of security, domestic regime security, which has been neglected in the study of security of the developing world.[6] Internal political institutions and state structures tend to be fragile in less-developed countries. These countries are fragile because of the limits on "free and fair competition, participation, and liberties" in political power acquisition and transition (Sorensen, 1998; Touraine, 1998). Due to the effects of weak domestic political structures, lack of societal consensus, and lack of regime legitimacy, less-developed states have had a tendency to "create an environment of insecurity and instability in which inter-state rivalries, encouraged as they are by the policies and actions of external forces, are relatively easily transformed into overt military hostilities" (Ayoob, 1984: 49). At the same time, major threats are derived from the international systemic constraints. Less-developed states have a dual problem of insecurity; that is, internal and external sources of threats. This situation is called the security and insecurity dilemma. The security dilemma "arises from the fear of defeat stimulated by the potential use of military means in the hands of other actors" (Buzan, 1991: 295). The security/insecurity dilemma involves "a weak state syndrome that contains a lack of social cohesion, absence of popular legitimacy, and lack of effective institutional capacities" (Job, 1992: 17-18). The post-Cold War security dilemma is broadly categorized as "the decrease in the security of others, decrease in the security of all, uncertainty of intention, no appropriate policies, and required insecurity" (Collins, 1997: 11). To a greater extent, South Korea during the Cold War had these dual insecurities of threats; concerns of domestic regime security have been lessened since the democratization of 1987.

The multiple meanings offered for security now question traditional conceptualizations and ask "whose security" or "to what kinds of security" the scholars are referring.[7] Do they refer to the well-being of individual states, the stability of the international system, the well-being of all human beings, or something else? These questions compel policy-makers as well as policy analysts to redefine security dimensions and priorities. Because of the lack of a sufficient understanding of, or realistic perspectives on, security, the term is often used to refer to the state and its relations with other states in international politics. What is most interesting is the fact that the meaning of security tends to be defined in the state's external or outward-directed terms.[8] For example, Cold War descriptions of security overtly stressed strong geo-strategic military and economic linkages for systemic stability, binding the security of the two major alliance blocs.

Extending the realm of security studies, I support the argument that politics and economics are hardly separable when it comes to the state's concern for security.[9] More specifically, security can be assured by sustaining "mature anarchy" and economic interdependence, shifted from "immature anarchy" and the breakdown of a multilateral economic community.[10] "Mature anarchy" is the situation where "the benefits of fragmentation are enjoyed without the costs of continuous armed struggle and instability" (Buzan, 1991: 176). Critical factors conducive to "mature anarchy" are a well-established economic order, mutual recognition of sovereign equality, stable regional security, and domestic political coherence. Segal identifies "four key conditions essential for the construction of durable regional security: a pluralist political system, growing interdependence, the creation of regional society, and a robust balance of power" (1997: 235). As a result, primary security policies during the post-Cold War era have focused on enhancing the maintenance of a balance-of-power system and economic interdependence as well as consolidating democratic political systems.

In summary, security is defined as the ability to maintain the domestic stability of political institutions and effective alliance and alignment mechanisms in the international system. Security policy is tied to the state's concerns about geo-strategic, geo-political, and geo-economic security policies that attempt to ensure national survival in the international system. It also deals with the insecurity dilemma within the borders of states that desire to assure their regime security. For example, South Korea's security policies were focused on the regional geo-strategic balance of power and regime security during the Cold War. Its security policies during the transitional phase and the post-Cold War era have been redirected toward the establishment of a regional security environment favorable to national unification and the consolidation of democratic government.

The discussions above imply that security policy change occurs as a response to the shifts in international structural factors and domestic institutional arrangements. Change, or Holsti's term "restructuring" (1982), occurs in the entire reorientation of the state's international relations, the pattern of alliance and alignment mechanisms, and the ways of achieving the desired condition or security goals. Policy reorientations can also be incremental or dramatic, reflective of external and internal fluctuations. Abrupt or piece-meal changes vary within the specific areas, issues of security policy, and situations of international and domestic contexts. As a whole, dimensions of security policy change involve "the level of change, the scope of change, and the time frame of change" (Hagan and Rosati, 1994: 266-269). By analyzing major trends of South Korea's security policy change, this study explores the specific conditions, scope, and time frames under which South Korea responds to contextual fluctuations.

Defining major security policy change, Hermann identifies four graduated levels of change: "adjustment/incremental changes, program changes, problem/goal changes, and international orientation changes" (1990: 5-6). Adjustment changes connote incremental adjustments of the state security commitment vis-à-vis the level of efforts and/or the scope of international interactions. Program changes result from shifts in ways or means of reaching security goals and assessing security problems. In contrast to adjustment changes, which "tend to be quantitative, program changes are qualitative and involve new instruments of statecraft" (Hermann, 1990: 5). In this vein, program changes include paradigm changes; that is, changes in a systemic understanding of the world derived from a consistent or coherent set of ideas, strategic doctrines, and theoretical models applied to analyze security policy problems and alternatives. Paradigms include anti-communism and realist or liberal worldviews. Changes in security problems and goals most often occur when new governments with different programs redefine the initial conditions of security problems and security goals in different ways.

International orientation change is the wholesale redirection of the state's external relations, which illustrates Holsti's notion of "dramatic foreign policy restructuring."[11]

The dramatic wholesale change of international orientation is rare. Thus, the scope of change constitutes a sector or sectors of the state's security relations and includes the patterns of externally directed politico-military, economic, and diplomatic relations. Variations of the scope are dependent upon changes in the state's security paradigms, programs, and goals. There is also a possibility of continuous or discontinuous patterns of relations across different sectors of the state's security commitment.[12] For example, states can have stable and/or discontinuous interactions with others on humanitarian aid issues, while having completely different stances on economic assistance issues. Incremental or dramatic changes also vary over specific areas of security relations and specific issues or security concerns.

Policy changes can be issue-specific, but at the same time temporally specific or long-lasting.[13] Some changes "are situationally specific and not generalizable to the entire issue area...[and] changes occur at the peak of an international crisis or at a critical stage in negotiations" (Hagan and Rosati, 1994: 268). Thus, the time frame of change is related to the degree of fluctuations in international and domestic contexts. Wholesale revisions in security policy are more likely to occur when there are abrupt transformations in domestic political regimes and international security structure; that is to say, Rosenau's "preservative adaptation" (1981).[14] Overall, in this analysis, security policy change is defined as restructuring in security policy orientations or paradigms, means or programs, and goals responding to the fluctuations in domestic institutional arrangements and international structural factors.

### Political Institutions and Institutional Capacity

Fundamental to this analysis is an understanding of who defines security-policy problems and goals. A policy problem is considered to be a "political condition" identified as "a gap between an existing and a desired set of circumstances" requiring a government's authoritative action (Anderson, 1978; DiMaggio, 1988; Robertson and Judd, 1989; Friedland and Alford, 1991; March, 1994). In other words, a policy problem arises when there is a gap between what the state is doing based on policy programs and what has come to be viewed as a desired condition. Since the security-policy problem is defined as a "political condition," it is impossible to understand policy outcomes of the state's security policy-making without locating policy-making institutions in a socio-political context.[15]

Various scholars have conceptualized policy-making institutions on legal, moral, and cultural grounds of policy-making. Largely, the political functions of institutions involve enactment of rules and regulations, provisions of normative and cognitive standards, protection from external threats, and preservation of individual wellbeing. Thus, a political institution has often been referred to as the state, government, public administrative apparatuses, and symbolic or normative order (Zucker, 1977; March and Olsen, 1989; Thelen and Steinmo, 1992; Ethington and McDonagh, 1995; Scott, 1995; Lowndes, 1996). Institutions have also been understood in a way that explains "causal inferences" between policy-making procedures and security policy change.[16] Depending on how institutions perceive external and internal threats and how they define the security-policy problem, the state's security policies reflect its perceptions and definitions. In view of this, security policy-making institutions use decision-making processes as well as behaviors to define the scope of alternative policy domains. Institutions also constitute the framework that determines how security policy decisions are made and implemented. A political institution is here defined as a formally constituted governing structure that provides opportunities and/or constraints, organizes political processes and behaviors, and influences political outcomes. In short, it is officials within political institutions who identify security policy paradigms, implement security programs, and formulate security goals and objectives.

Political institutions can be weak or strong in responding to changes in social and international affairs. An analysis of institutional weakness and strength is important in a number of ways. First, the analysis can demonstrate ways in which the state formulates and implements security policies. Second, it examines whether the state is capable of adapting internal and external changes. Third, it explains how the state attempts to achieve its security policy goals. Related to the state's ways of enhancing its goals, Thomas (1989) distinguishes two forms of power: despotic and infrastructural. The former is arbitrary or coercive power that imposes rules on civilians, while the latter is highly sophisticated and effective power that provides and extracts resources for and from citizens. Weak institutions lack infrastructural capacity and often face an internal insecurity dilemma, while at the same time they may be constrained by an external security dilemma. Thus, weak institutions tend to emphasize regime security and implement aggressive security policies toward rivals to offset domestic problems. External threats are also often used to generate internal strength and justify coercive power.

Institutional strengths and weaknesses are intimately related to the notion of the "autonomy" of institutional arrangements.[17] Strong states with coercive and infrastructural power are relatively autonomous vis-à-vis society and "implement effective goal-oriented social changes; i.e., more permanent alteration of social relations, shaping of national identity, and establishment of efficient appropriation through state bureaucracies" (Job, 1992: 21-22). Weak states can be autonomous with respect to their coercive power but lack the ability to transform society toward their goals. They also lack economic and military capabilities in relative terms compared to other states. A strong state's autonomy is "embedded" (Davis, 1995; Evans, 1995) in terms of insulation from social interference and bureaucratic autonomy. The strong state is also "sensitive" to international systemic forces, while weak states are more "vulnerable" to international systemic constraints. Weak states' policy-making machinery is dominated by a few power-holders, limiting other security policy alternatives and paradigms and lacking the ability to achieve security goals.

In this vein, institutional capacity involves the ability to reduce the gap between what is implemented (security policy behaviors) and what is desired (security policy goals). It includes two dimensions—"the ability to do what is required and the ability to do what is expected" (Gargan, 1997: 233-234). That is, institutional capacity is the ability to achieve the desired condition with the resources available. Institutional capacity depends in turn upon the two closely intertwined aspects of administrative bureaucratic capacity, or policy capacity, and political capacity, that capture procedural and structural features of institutions. The former refers to the extent to which the state is able to effectively and efficiently formulate and implement policy, while the latter refers to the ability to increase political support for enhancing policy goals. Thus, the state's institutional capacity varies with the structure of political support and the means of political control available and with effective implementation. Institutional capacity also involves the ability of the state to protect itself from external threats. The means of enhancing institutional capacity include the strengthening of military and economic capabilities, maintaining strategic alliances, and intensifying economic interdependence. Changes in external structural constraints and in the state's military and economic capabilities in the international distribution of powers all affect institutional capacity.

Security policy and security policy change are reviewed to the extent to which political institutions define security policy problems and attempt to reduce the gap between security expectations or goals and security requirements or programs. Institutional capacity is understood as the way that the state responds to the changes in contextual factors and tries to achieve its goals. These conceptual reviews are related to the extent to which states respond to external and internal transformations, why they formulate and implement certain security policies, and under what conditions they act as they do in international politics. This study explores the specific conditional factors that determine South Korea's security policy change and examines its institutional capacity when responding to external and internal fluctuations. It is to discover the importance of domestic political institutions and institutional arrangements in explaining changes in South Korea's security policies.

## Contextual Determinants

As discussed in Chapter 1, the dependent variable to be explained is South Korea's security policy change. It is defined as security policy restructuring in policy orientations, means or programs, and goals responding to fluctuations in domestic institutional arrangements and international systemic factors.[18]  In other words, security policy changes, or the shifts in a systemic understanding of the world and means to achieve security goals, are caused by systemic transformations in international politics and institutional realignments in domestic politics.  Security policy restructuring can be incremental or abrupt, and stable or discontinuous, reflective of the level or issue, scope, and time frame of change.  Security policy change occurs over different time contexts such as the Cold War era, transitional phase, and post-Cold War era.  Its levels and scope of change evolve with either domestic factors or international factors or both.

The causal factors are notably the independent variables that explain the dependent variables of the state's security policy change.  For analytical purposes, the contextual imperatives of security policy change are classified into two broad categories: those associated with the state's external factors and those residing in domestic politics.  Predominantly, international systemic factors have been the core concerns of analyses that debate how they influence a state's behavior.  Domestic sources of security policy change generally include national political pre-dispositions and military and economic capabilities.  However, none of these alone has been proven to explain all aspects of security policy.  Thus, this study seeks to embrace critical determinants of security policy in a wide variety of systemic conditions and domestic situations.  The independent variables are also incorporated to test theoretical causal claims of existing theories.  In addition, international and domestic sources of change are considered here in order to examine under what conditions domestic politics matter more than international politics, and vice versa.  As previously discussed, evaluative criteria include variations in the relative distribution of power, the US-ROK alliance system, formal diplomatic and trade relations, types of government, power sharing in the government and the National Assembly, and national military and economic capabilities.

Traditionally, external conditions are referred to as anarchy, but these conditional factors have different functions and structures.  Buzan and Little (1996) maintain that political unites are both functionally and structurally different under anarchic conditions.  In the similar vein, the determinants of external conditions include geo-structural factors, geo-strategic forces, geo-economics, and geo-political forces. Geo-structural factors are systemic configurations of regional security and economic structures, such as bipolarity or multipolarity and bipolar economic blocs or multipolar economic systems. Geo-strategic forces show the state's patterns of alliance formations in the regional security structure. Geo-economic forces and geo-political forces are related to the state's alignment mechanisms; i.e., the former involves economic interdependence and international financial alignments and the latter diplomacy and international institutions. Domestic determinants include types of government (democracy or authoritarianism), legal-institutional setting (the locus of security decision-making), the policy-making machinery (the functional web of policy-making structures), and national military and economic capabilities. Table 3.1 shows the contextual determinants of the state's security policy change.

**Table 3.1. International/Domestic Determinants of Security Policy Change**

| International Determinants | Geo-Structural Factors<br>--International Security Structure<br>--International Economic Structure<br>Geo-Strategic Factors<br>--Alliance Mechanisms<br>Geo-Economic Factors<br>--Economic Interdependence<br>--International Financial Alignments<br>Geo-Political Factors<br>--Diplomatic Alignment Mechanisms<br>--International Institutions |
|---|---|
| Domestic Determinants | Types of Government<br>--Democracy or Authoritarianism<br>Legal-Institutional Setting<br>--Locus of Decision-making<br>Policy-making Machinery<br>--Functional Web of Policy-making Structures<br>National Capabilities<br>--Size of GDP/GNP<br>--Military Expenditures |

## *International Systemic and Domestic Institutional Determinants*

The external setting, which provides systemic constraints and opportunities to the state, is the logical starting point for the study of security policy change.[19] Geo-structural and power relations suggest the possibility, if not the certainty, of substantial changes in a state's security policy.   Geo-structural factors involve both regional security and economic structures that illustrate balance-of-power politics in the international system.  Regional structures are "defined by two dimensions: the ordering principle—anarchy—and the distribution of capabilities—multipolar, bipolar, and, in the regional case, unipolar" (Lake, 1997: 60).[20]  The absence of authority over states (or anarchy) only influences the expected range of behavior and seldom dictates a particular response of the state.   Generally, regional security and economic structures are measured in military and economic terms that show the relative or asymmetrical distribution of states' capabilities and the concentration or dispersion of regional power equilibrium.

The regional security structure is the military power structure derived from the relative distribution of military capabilities on the levels of military expenditures, armed forces, and arms exports and imports among states.  These levels, fluctuating over time, show power polarity among regional states estimated by the U.S. Arms Control and Disarmament Agency, *World Military Expenditures and Arms Transfers* and the Stockholm International Peace Research Institute, *World Armaments and Disarmament Yearbook*.   The regional economic structure reflects states' comparative positions or relative wealth, which is the level of goods and services that states can purchase. States' percentage shares in world total trade and the relative purchasing power parity (PPP) values measure the wealth distribution among regional states. These data are calculated by the United Nations Development Program, *Human Development Report*, the World Bank, *World Bank Atlas*, and the Central Intelligence Agency, *The World Factbook*.  Gross domestic product (GDP) and gross national product (GNP) figures have the limitation of seldom indicating the true purchasing power of the state's currency at home.  Thus, the UN's International Comparison Project (ICP) has developed measures of GDP on an internationally comparable scale using PPP values rather than exchange rates as conversion factors.  The relative distribution of states' PPP values and trade shares display economic polarity among regional powers.

Geo-strategic factors represent alliance mechanisms which reflect Patrick Cronin's notion of "a latent security community" (1992).  An alliance is defined as "a formal or informal commitment for security cooperation between two or more states" (Walt, 1997: 157).  Alliances provide states with a capacity for flexibility and rapid reaction to threats by adding the strength of allies to one's own strengths (Organski and Kugler, 1980: 16).[21]   Alliances are generally maintained through military exercises, the presence of military forces, security alliance institutions, and foreign military aid. Military exercises are performed bilaterally or multilaterally and alliance institutions such as the US-ROK Combined Forces and the North Atlantic Treaty Organization are bilateral and multilateral institutions under which states perform combined military exercises for the maintenance of regional stability. The presence of forces indicates states' strategic commitment to allies. Military assistance has "projected the security interests of the donors, strengthened clients' hold on power in the face of internal challenges, and tipped regional balance of power" (Klare and Volman, 1996: 40).[22] Foreign military aid is financial assistance transferred for military equipment, supplies, and support services of the recipient countries. A substantial portion of arms transfers is provided through loans, grants, and credits. The data are calculated by the U.S. Arms Control and Disarmament Agency, *World Military Expenditures and Arms Transfers*, the U.S. Department of Commerce, *The Statistical Abstract of the United States*, and the Ministry of National Defense, *Defense White Paper*.

Geo-economic factors mirror the complexity of economic interdependence and financial alignment mechanisms. Economic interdependence encompasses openness to the international economy and "mutual and unequal dependence" (Keohane and Nye, 1989). A high intensity of trade and economic interactions across states is believed to be conducive to the reduction of the likelihood of war because states increase the expected costs associated with using armed force.[23] The percentages of trade shares (or shares of exports and imports) show the levels of economic interactions and economic alignment among states. The data are collected by the UN, *International Trade Statistics Yearbook*, the Bank of Korea, *Economic Statistics Yearbook*, and the Economic Planning Board, *Major Statistics of Korean Economy*. Financial alignment mechanisms, maintained through foreign direct investment and foreign economic aid, also measure the state's geo-economic commitments. Foreign direct investment, as opposed to portfolio investment, consists of international financial flows that involve not only a transfer of resources but also the acquisition of control through joint ventures, ownership, and merging.[24] Foreign economic aid, utilized as strategic instruments of donors' national interests, is the public transfer of goods and services for recipients' economic development and social welfare.[25] These financial resources are transferred via official development assistance, loans, grants, and other official flows set by the Development Assistance Committee (DAC) of the Organization of Economic Cooperation and Development (OECD). Annually calculated data are well documented by the OECD, *Geographical Distribution of Financial Flows to Developing Countries*, the International Monetary Fund

(IMF), *Financial Statistics Yearbook*, and the Ministry of Finance, *Fiscal and Financial Statistics*.

Geo-political factors represent diplomatic relations among states and memberships in international institutions. Diplomacy has been regarded as an important dimension that provides "a channel for furthering cooperative efforts and adjusting existing differences among states" (Black and Thompson, 1963: 20).[26] Diplomacy is also used to prevent adversaries making allies with one's own adversaries or allies and neutralize adversaries' activities in international politics. Formal diplomatic relations of the state are classified in terms of its relations with pro-Western, pro-communist, and developing countries. International institutions also generate constraints and opportunities in performing states' international interactions. International institutions are defined as "persistent and connected sets of rules that prescribe behavioral roles, constrain activity, and share expectations" (Keohane, 1989: 3).[27] States' responses to the conditions of geo-political forces are diverse with regard to their memberships in the UN organizations and intergovernmental institutions. Figures are gathered by the Ministry of Foreign Affairs, *Diplomacy White Paper*, the Institute of International Affairs, *Korean Defense Yearbook*, and the Ministry of National Defense, *Defense White Paper*.

While determinants of external factors can be the sources of security policy change and portray broad directions or patterns of the state's security policy, they are by themselves not sufficient to explain security policy dynamics. States do not always conform their behavior to international systemic guidelines of constraints and opportunities. The institutional attributes of domestic politics have been treated as given rather than as variables. Domestic factors help explain why states act differently in similar systemic circumstances and why states implement certain policies while eliminating other alternatives. An analysis of institutional determinants is aimed at exploring what sorts of security policy changes occur, the conditions under which they occur, and how they are likely to occur. Domestic determinants can be categorized into highly stable determinants (geographical size and resources), moderately stable determinants (political regimes and political processes), and highly unstable determinants (political culture and short-term attitudes of political leaders).[28] The domestic sources include political forms, legal-institutional setting, policy-making machinery, and national capabilities.

Types or forms of government, either authoritarian or democracy, refer to the political institutions that the state has used to formulate, implement, and evaluate its security policies. Democracy is referred to as constituting and limiting authority or having free and fair elections.[29] Analyses on political forms have offered the "garrison state syndrome thesis" (Maoz and Abdolali, 1989) and "democratic peace thesis" (Doyle, 1996; Owen, 1996; Russett,

1996). It has been argued that democracies are less likely to be involved in war-prone activities than authoritarian states and that democracies do not fight against other democracies.[30] Freedom status of political rights and civil liberties, issued annually by the Freedom House's *Freedom-at-Issue*, has been a useful measure of the political types of government. Countries whose combined average for political rights and for civil liberties fall between 1.0 and 2.5 are designated free, between 3.0 and 5.5 partly free, and between 5.5 and 7.0 not free. The data and evidence are also collected from the Asian Watch Committee, *Human Rights in Korea* and the Keesing's Contemporary Archives, *Record of World Events*.

The legal-institutional setting is a system of structuring and regulating policy-making machinery and legal/institutional controlling apparatuses. The institutional map of the state shows where decision-making agencies lie. The legal-institutional setting represents the locus of security policy-making and the degree of concentration and fragmentation of decision-making powers.[31] Security policy-making authority can be either authoritarian or democratic depending on the locations of authority and levels of obstacles from different branches in formulating security policies (Cowhey and McCubbins, 1995; Hill, 1996). The legal-institutional setting is derived from the legal enactment/revisions and the distribution of legislative powers in the National Assembly. The percentage distribution of legislative seats in the National Assembly is counted to examine political power diffusion or power sharing. The data are collected from the Election Management Committee, *History of Elections in Korea* and Sung-Chul Yang, *The North and South Korean Political Systems: A Comparative Analysis*.

The policy-making machinery is the functional web of decision-making structures that include bureaucratic agencies, think tanks, and academics. Bureaucracies perform day-to-day operations and are composed of persons who have professional skills in implementing security policies. Bureaucratic functions and bureaucrats' access to security policy-making illustrate the level of political influences of bureaucratic agencies and the operation of bureaucratic politics.[32] Changes of the policy-making machinery are measured by changes of bureaucratic agencies involved in security policy-making and by the professional background of administrative elites. Bureaucratic agencies include various agencies within the executive branch. Administrative elites include cabinet ministers and vice-ministers of the cabinet, other high-ranking bureaucrats, and provincial governors. The professional backgrounds of the administrative elites are categorized into percentages of academicians, bureaucrats, politicians, military, journalists, lawyers, and businesspersons.[33] The data are driven from the Ministry of Public Information, *The Governmental Elites of the Republic of Korea* and

Sung-Chul Yang, *The North and South Korean Political Systems: A Comparative Analysis.*

National capabilities are measured in terms of the state's economic size and military expenditures. National wealth measured by GDP/GNP, which refers to the state's domestic/national strengths in producing goods and services, is an example of economic capabilities. The national capability is used to analyze how security policy fluctuates as the country's economy increases or decreases. Both GDP/GNP and the distribution of GDP in terms of agriculture, industry, and service sectors are also used to calculate the state's wealth. Military spending represents the expenditure made by the government specifically to carry out the objectives of the military forces. Shifts of the absolute amount of military expenditures as percentages of GDP on force posture, weapon acquisition, and military maintenance are believed to be the indicator of security policy change. These figures are estimated by the UN, *Yearbook of National Accounts Statistics*; the Bank of Korea, *Economic Statistics Yearbook*; the National Unification Board, *Economic Comparison between North and South Korea*; and the U.S. Arms Control and Disarmament Agency, *World Military Expenditures and Arms Transfers.*

### Determinants of South Korea's Security Policy Change

In order to examine causal relations, critical determinants in domestic and international contexts are analyzed and compared to South Korea's security policy behaviors over the Cold War era (1954-1987), the transitional phase (1988-1992), and the post-Cold War era (1993-1998). The dependent variable to be explained is South Korea's security policy change, which refers to the restructuring of its security policy orientations, programs, and goals resulting from transformations of domestic institutional and international structural factors. South Korea's security policies are the governments' official security policies declared and stated in the Ministry of Defense, *Defense White Paper* and the Ministry of Foreign Affairs, *Diplomacy White Paper.* Its security policy is categorized as a defensive deterrence policy during the Cold War era and a governed interdependence policy during the transitional phase and the post-Cold War era. As noted in Chapter I, South Korea's security policies have changed from absolute anti-communism or non-alignment of the Syngman Rhee administration (1948-1960) to mutual antagonism or competitive diplomacy during the Park Chung Hee administration (1961-1979) and the Chun Do Whan administration (1980-1987), from mutual antagonism or competitive diplomacy to *nordpolitik* during the Noh Tae Woo administration (1988-1992), from *nordpolitik* to globalization during the Kim Young Sam administration (1993-1997), and from globalization to sunshine policy during the Kim Dae Jung administration (1998-present).

Both domestic institutional and international structural factors are examined to determine which critical determinants have more explanatory power in regard to South Korea's security policy changes. Regarding international systemic factors, the Northeast Asian system has shifted from bipolarity (1948-1971), to the bi-triangular geo-political system (1972-1987), and to the pluralistic or multiple bilateral system (1988-1998). From South Korea's perspective, it was bipolar between two military-political blocs from 1948 to the early 1970s and shifted toward a bi-triangular system during the 1970s and 1980s. The bi-triangular system was maintained through bilateral alliances among South Korea, the U.S., and Japan and was confronted by bilateral alliances among North Korea, the Soviet Union, and China. The Northeast Asian bi-triangular system began to shift toward a multiple, pluralistic system during the transitional phase. After the demise of the Cold War and the collapse of the Soviet Union, a multiple bilateral system has been maintained in the region. Table 3.2 illustrates overall fluctuations in international factors that determine South Korea's security policy change.[34]

**Table 3.2. Variations in South Korea's International Systemic Factors**

| International Systemic Determinants | Security Policy Change 1 (1961) | Security Policy Change 2 (1988) | Security Policy Change 3 (1993) |
|---|---|---|---|
| Geo-Structural Factors | ME (arms trade) | ME (arms trade) | ME (arms trade) |
| United States | 47.8b (160m) | 349b (16.6b) | 321b (28.9b) |
| USSR/Russia | 43.6b (280m) | 379b (28.4b) | 67.4b (3.8b) |
| China | 7.9b (50m) | 52.0b (3.9b) | 57.3b (1.8b) |
| Japan | .4b (10m) | 36.3b (1.4b) | 49.4b (2.1b) |
| South Korea | .3b (--) | 9.3b (.8b) | 13.0b (1.9b) |
| North Korea | 2.3b (--) | 6.9b (2.0b) | 5.7b (.3b) |
| Geo-Strategic Factors | US Forces Korea 58,000 | US Forces Korea 46,000 | US Forces Korea 39,000 |
| Geo-Economic Factors | Trade Shares (%) Exports/Imports | Trade Shares (%) Exports/Imports | Trade Shares (%) Exports/Imports |
| United States | 16.6/45.4 | 35.4/24.6 | 22.2/21.4 |
| Japan | 50.2/23.1 | 19.8/30.7 | 14.1/23.9 |
| | Trade Shares (m) | Trade Shares (m) | Trade Shares (m) |
| China | -- | 3,087m | 9,080m |
| USSR/Russia | -- | 204m | 1,576m |
| North Korea | -- | 1.1m | 186.6m |
| Geo-Political Factors | Countries 28 | Countries 134 | Countries 171 |

Note: b—billions of dollars and m—millions of dollars; 1970 and 1997 constant dollars for the figures of ME (military expenditures); and current prices and exchange rates for PPP values.
Sources: U.S. Arms Control and Disarmament Agency, *World Military Expenditures and Arms Transfers* (Washington, D.C.: Government Printing Office); UN Development Program, *Human Development Report* (Oxford: Oxford University Press); United Nations, *International Trade Statistics Yearbook* (New York: The UN Printing Office); Economic Planning Board, *Major Statistics of Korean Economy* (Seoul: EPB); Ministry of Unification, *Inter-Korean Trade Volume* (Seoul: MOU); and Ministry of Foreign Affairs, *Diplomacy White Paper* (Seoul: MFA).

The regional security structure is measured on the basis of the relative distribution of military capabilities or the relative levels of military expenditures, armed forces, and arms exports and imports among the U.S., USSR/Russia, China, Japan, and the two Koreas. To compare relative distribution of military capabilities at any given time, figures of current dollars in military expenditures and arms exports and imports are measured. In 1970 (1997) current dollars, the U.S. military expenditure amounted to $47.8 billion ($321 billion) and it traded $160 million ($28.9 billion) of arms with 2.5 million (1.8 million) armed forces in 1961 (1993). The Soviet Union/Russia spent $43.6 billion ($67.4 billion) and traded $280 million ($3.8 billion) of arms with 2.4 million (1.5 million) armed forces in 1961 (1993). China spent $7.9 billion ($57.3 billion) and traded $50 million ($1.8 billion) of arms with 3.0 million (3.0 million) armed forces in 1961 (1993). Japan spent $.4 billion ($49.4 billion) and traded $10 million ($2.1 billion) of arms with 240 thousand (242 thousand) armed forces in 1961 (1993). South Korea spent $.3 billion ($13 billion) with 650 thousand (750 thousand) armed forces in 1961 (1993), and it traded $1.9 billion of arms in 1993. North Korea spent $2.3 billion ($5.7 billion) with 350 thousand (1.2 million) armed forces in 1961 (1993), and it traded .3 billion of arms in 1993. In military terms, a bipolarity after the Korean War was maintained until it shifted to a unipolarity dominated by the U.S. since the early 1990s.

Along with changes in the regional security structure, regional economic relations followed bipolar economic blocs during the Cold War, but changed to multilateralism during the post-Cold War era. Percentage of trade shares in total world trade and purchasing power parity (PPP) or real GDP per capita values are used to measure the relative distribution of wealth among regional states. The U.S. during the Cold War accounted for about 15% of total world trade and more than a quarter of the world GDP. While the U.S. maintained a unipolar economic power, Japan increased its trade shares and percentage shares of the world GDP over the years. In the 1990s, the U.S. and Japan shared about 14% and 8% of total world trade, respectively.[35] In terms of per capita PPP values, the U.S. had $19,850 ($24,750), Japan $13,650 ($21,090), South Korea $5,680 ($9,810), Russia $6,270 ($5,240), China $2,470 ($2,120), and North Korea $2,000 ($1,750) in 1988 (1997). Economically, the U.S. and Japan became the dominant powers in the post-Cold War regional power equilibrium, which shifted from a unipolarity in the Cold War era.

Alliance or geo-strategic politics are maintained through bilateral mutual defense treaties in Northeast Asia; e.g., the US-ROK Mutual Defense Treaty of 1953. Military exercises have been consistently maintained between the two geo-strategic blocs. South Korea performed annual Team Spirit of the US-ROK Combined Forces (since 1976), annual US-ROK Eagle (since 1961), annual US-ROK Ul-gi Focus (since 1976), and biannual Rim of the Pacific Asian Countries (RIMPAC, since 1990) military exercises. The U.S., Canada, Japan, Australia, and Chile have exercised RIMPAC since 1976 and South Korea joined it in 1990. Security alliance mechanisms include the US-ROK Combined Forces established in 1978 and the Korean Peninsula Energy Development Organization (KEDO), an ad hoc consortium that was created as the result of the US-DPRK agreement in October 1994. It aimed to dismantle the North Korean nuclear program in exchange for economic aid and diplomatic recognition. Foreign military aid is always transferred bilaterally for the recipients' maintenance of military equipment, supplies, and support services. South Korea received more than $4,110 million in military aid from 1954 to 1978, and the U.S. retained at least 38,000 of its forces in South Korea. The U.S. has provided extended deterrence to maintain a regional balance-of-power mechanism. The US-ROK relations were asymmetrical and South Korea was reactive to the shifts of the U.S. global and regional security commitments. After the Cold War, the asymmetrical alliance system was transformed into a partnership of burden sharing. South Korea paid $70 million in 1990 and $175 million in 1998 for the support of the U.S. forces in South Korea and other maintenance costs.[36]

Geo-economic alignment mechanisms have been intensified and diversified since the end of the Cold War. Regional economic interdependence has increased with the advent of APEC in 1989 and the WTO in 1995. South Korea has normalized its economic relations with the U.S. (since 1948), Japan (since 1965), China (since 1979), Russia (since 1985), and North Korea (since 1988). The percentages of trade shares are derived from exports and imports that South Korea traded with the U.S., Japan, China, Russia, and North Korea. Trade volumes between South Korea and the U.S. and between South Korea and Japan have accounted for about 30 to 45% of South Korea's total trade since their economic normalization. However, in the 1990s, South Korea's trade shares with the U.S. and Japan decreased, while intra-regional trade with Asian Pacific countries increased, reaching 43.3% and 38.3% in terms of export and import shares, respectively, in 1998.[37] Trade with China, Soviet Union/Russia, and North Korea increased from $3,087 million, $204 million, and $1.1 million in 1988 to $9,080 million, $1,576 million, and $186.6 million in 1993, respectively. South Korea's trade with China increased up to 8%, with Russia 1.5%, and with North Korea .1% of total trade in 1998.[38] The public flow of goods and services transferred to South Korea has fluctuated over time. The total U.S. aid to South Korea was $202.4 million ($6.0 million) in 1961 (1987), and the total loans and foreign direct investment were $2,773 million in 1988. South Korea's foreign debt increased from $5,494 million in 1993 to $24,425 million in 1998.[39] Economic aid substantially declined in the 1980s. South Korea moved its developmental strategy from one of reliance on foreign economic aid to promotion of international trade and foreign direct investment. It changed into an aid donor, rather than an aid recipient, in the 1990s. But reversed financial flows in the 1990s caused South Korea's economic crisis in 1997.

South Korea had maintained its diplomatic relations with 6 countries in 1950, 28 in 1961, 134 in 1988, and 171 in 1993. It began to establish diplomatic relations with other developing countries in the 1960s. Until the middle of the 1980s, South Korea maintained predominantly pro-Western diplomatic alignments. In addition, South Korea's memberships in international institutions were also maintained along the line of geo-strategic security blocs until the middle of the 1980s. With the new international orientation, *nordpolitik*, South Korea signed the 1991 Basic Agreement with North Korea and both joined the UN simultaneously. A cross-recognition of the two Koreas had been suggested, but South Korea normalized its relations solely with Russia and China.

Domestic institutional factors, types of government, legal-institutional setting, policy-making machinery, and national capabilities are considered critical determinants to South Korea's security policy change. During the Cold War era, South Korea instituted military authoritarianism, but shifted to a market democracy through economic liberalization and democratization in the late 1980s. Political reforms took place at all levels of civil-military relations, bureaucratic politics, and legal-institutional setting. Table 3.3 shows overall patterns of changes in South Korea's domestic institutional factors.

**Table 3.3. Variations in South Korea's Domestic Institutional Factors**

| Domestic Institutional Determinants | Security Policy Change 1 (1961) | Security Policy Change 2 (1988) | Security Policy Change 3 (1993) |
|---|---|---|---|
| Types of Government | Political Rights/ Civil Liberties --/-- | Political Rights/ Civil Liberties 4/4  1987-1988 2/3  1988-1989 | Political Rights/ Civil Liberties 2/2  1992-1993 |
| Legal- Institutional Setting Percentage Distribution of Seats | Park Regime Ruling Parties/ Major Oppositions 55.7%—73.7%/ 23.4%—43.8% | 1988 Election DJP/PPD 125 (41.8%)/ 70 (23.4%) | 1992 Election DLP/DP 149 (49.8%)/ 97 (32.4%) |
| Policy- Making Machinery | Military Elites Park Regime 24.5% | Military Elites Noh Government 12.7% | Military Elites Kim Government 3.9% |
| National Capabilities South Korea North Korea | GNP 2.1b 1.9b | GNP 179.8b 25.3b | GNP 330.8b 23.0b |
| South Korea North Korea | ME 300m 2,300m | ME 9.3b 6.9b | ME 13.0b 5.7b |

Note: DJP—Democratic Justice Party; PPD—Party for Peace and Democracy; DLP—Democratic Liberal Party; and DP—Democratic Party. 1961 data of the two Koreas are GDP figures; m—millions of dollars and b—billions of dollars; and 1970 and 1997 constant dollars for the figures of ME (military expenditures).
Sources: Freedom House, *Annual Survey of Freedom Country Scores* (Washington, D.C.: Freedom House); Election Management Committee, *History of Elections in Korea* (Seoul: EMC); Ministry of Public Information, *The Government Elites of the Republic of Korea* (Seoul: MPI); and U.S. Arms Control and Disarmament Agency, *World Military Expenditures and Arms Transfers* (Washington, D.C.: Government Printing Office).

South Korea's political forms had been authoritarian during the Cold War and the first free and fair presidential election was held in 1987. Compared to former presidents who were elected by the delegates of the Supreme Council for National Reconstruction (SCNR), President Noh Tae Woo received 36.6% of the direct popular vote in December 1987. During the authoritarian regimes, oppressive measures were applied to sustain regime security. Thus, the status of political rights and civil liberties remained above 4 until 1987-1988, and its

1988-1989 status was 2 in political rights and 3 in civil liberties, which are designated free.[40] During the Cold War, bipolar ideological struggles and absolute anti-communism in foreign relations had immensely influenced South Korea's security policy, both in national security and regime security. For example, the Park regime's "total defense" as a guiding ideology emphasized anti-communism, military self-help, and an economic catch-up mentality. However, after the democratization of 1987, political rights were guaranteed by the new Constitution.    South Korea shifted from an authoritarian developmental state to a market-democracy.  The 1992-1993 status was 2 in political rights and 2 in civil liberties, which designate a high level of freedom.[41]

The legal-institutional settings serve as enduring sources of constraints and imperatives on South Korea's security policy.  These include the National Security Law, Martial Law, and Anti-Communist Law, which were modified and finally eliminated during the late 1980s.  The primary government agencies that have implemented South Korean security policies include the president's Secretariat, the Agency for National Security Planning or the former KCIA, the National Security Council, the Ministry of Foreign Affairs, the National Unification Board, the Ministry of National Defense, and the Economic Planning Board.    Particularly during the military authoritarian regimes, standard operating procedures were closed, public participation was prohibited, and relatively few bureaucrats dominated security policy decisions, while such procedures were pluralistic during the post-Cold War era.  With regard to standard operating procedures, public participation, and intergovernmental relations, different types of governmental institutions have implemented different security policy alternatives.  Greater participation in policy-making processes and National Assembly oversight over the use of national security for regime survival have led to more flexible and expanded choices of security policy goals and objectives.  Thus, security policy-making is no longer the executive domain of ROK military elites in the post-Cold War era.

The most rudimentary reforms were institutionalized in the new democratic Constitution, and the legal basis for politicization of national security and the military was abolished.  Another major departure was party politics.  During the Cold War, there were always a dominant ruling party and a number of weak opposition parties.  The ruling parties during the Park Chung Hee regime had at least 55.7% of the seats in the National Assembly, and its maximum was 73.7%.  However, after the 1988 election, the ruling party failed to win a majority in the National Assembly.  The ruling Democratic Justice Party (DJP) had 125 seats (41.8%) out of 299 seats, while the major opposition party had 70 seats (23.4%).  In the 1992 election, the ruling party also lacked a majority of seats in the National Assembly.  Still another important change was the military withdrawal from politics.  During the authoritarian regimes, the percentages of administrative elites from a military background were 24.5%, but they were reduced to less than 10% in the 1990s. The percentage from a military background in the administrative branch decreased from 12.7% during the Noh Tae Woo government to 3.9% during the Kim Young Sam administration. In addition, the average percentage of military retirees in cabinet ministries fell to 9.5% during the post-Cold War era from about 35% during the Cold War era. Since the transitional phase, political liberalization and decentralization have been implemented in the legal-institutional setting and the policy-making machinery.

South Korea's GDP was about $1.4 billion in 1954 and about $476 billion in 1997.[42] Economically, South Korea, with a greater margin, started to surpass the North Korean economic capability during the early 1970s. There is some controversy as to when South Korea surpassed North Korea in its GNP size, but the former has had greater economic strength since the mid-1970s at the latest.[43] South Korea's GDP was $2.1 billion, while that of North Korea was $1.9 billion, in 1961. South Korea's GNP reached $330.8 billion, while North Korea had $23.0 billion, in 1993. Compared to the North's GNP, the South's lead was 14.4:1 in 1993, increasing from 7.1:1 in 1988. In terms of the distribution of GDP, the agricultural industry accounted for 40 to 45%, the manufacturing industry 25 to 30%, and the service industry 20 to 25% of the South Korean economy during the 1950s and 1960s, while the agricultural industry accounted for 5 to 7%, the manufacturing industry 35 to 40%, and the service industry 47 to 53% during the 1990s.[44]

Since the late 1980s, South Korean military expenditures have remained at 3.4% to 5% of GDP, compared to 6.5% to 9% of GDP during the 1960s and 1970s.[45] South Korea spent $300 million and $13.0 billion, while North Korea spent $2,300 million and $5.7 billion in 1961 and 1993, respectively. South Korea's military expenditures began to surpass those of North Korea in the late 1980s. The South's lead in military spending was 2.5:1 in 1997, increasing from 2.1:1 in 1993. Although the percentage of military spending as a percentage of its GDP has steadily declined, South Korea has constantly attempted to improve naval and air capabilities. Despite the fact that the North still has a comparative advantage in the military vis-à-vis the South in relative and absolute terms, South Korea's total defense burden was about five times lower than North Korea's in the 1990s.[46]

**Methodological Considerations**

Thus far, this chapter has presented a variety of contextual determinants that may be useful in explaining South Korea's security policy change. It is now important to elucidate the methodological considerations employed in this study. The methodologies used here are: historical-comparative analysis, multilevel approach, theory-testing, and descriptive statistics.[47] These approaches are employed to clarify the framework of comparative analysis laid out in Figure 1.1 in Chapter 1. In order to examine the explanatory power of the existing theories, shown in Figure 2.1 of Chapter 2, the research strategy also involves a systematic comparison of variations in independent and dependent variables. Thus, the historical-comparative approach explores historically continuous and discontinuous patterns of South Korea's security policy as influenced by internal and external factors. One of the primary problems in the field of international relations is that mainstream theories tend to emphasize the static or continuous impact of the international security structure on a state's security policies. Without investigating historical patterns of changes over time, it becomes impossible to explore why, when, and how the state's security policies fluctuate.

The historical-comparative approach or longitudinal comparison provides an analytic ground to test hypotheses generalized by theoretical causal claims concerning South Korea's security policy dynamics. The three specific approaches or perspectives to be examined are: neorealist views on the international power politics and regional balance-of-power mechanism, neoliberal perspectives on the regional economic interdependence, and domestic institutionalists' approaches on the political system and institutional arrangements. These approaches have provided the basis for generating theoretical hypotheses regarding South Korea's security policy dynamics. Hypotheses from (1) to (3) are drawn from international structuralism, and (4) and (5) from domestic institutionalism. Hypothesis (6) is laid out to examine the relative explanatory power of international structuralism and domestic institutionalism.

The hypotheses put forth are as follows:

(1) Variations in South Korea's security policy are determined by the prevailing balance-of-power mechanism; i.e., changes in its relative military and economic levels impact its security policy dynamics.

(2) Changes in regional power politics determine South Korea's alliance and alignment politics.

(3) Alterations in South Korea's economic interactions and trade relations have a decisive effect on changes in its international security orientation.

(4) South Korea's security policy change occurs as the result of changes in its domestic institutional arrangements, such as alterations in

percentage shares of political parties' holdings in the National Assembly and administrative elites in the government.

(5) As South Korea's military and economic capabilities increase, its security policy priority will be shifted to concerns for economic interactions rather than those for politico-military balance-of-power.

(6) Changes in South Korea's systemic posture, as measured by its relative levels of military and economic power vis-à-vis other regional states, have a greater impact on its security policy change than those in domestic institutional arrangements.

In order to assess the changing nature of security policies, I compare critical determinants of South Korea's security policies during the Cold War era (1954-1987), transitional period (1988-1992), and post-Cold War era (1993-1998). This strategy is logically compatible to the comparative analysis of the most similar vs. different systemic characteristics addressed by Przeworski and Teune (1970). Thus, a structured comparison of critical determinants, based on longitudinal analysis, enables one to examine which factors have more significant impacts on South Korea's security policy changes. As George and McKeown (1985) suggest, Mill's logical methods of agreement and of difference (1950) are combined to provide more powerful theoretical explanations. The method of agreement is used when the outcome of the dependent variable is the same in several cases, while the method of difference is utilized when the outcome differs in several cases over time and space. These methods are applied to compare similarities and differences in international and domestic determinants that cause South Korea's security policies to fluctuate. This study is to examine how a change in domestic and/or international politics is related to a shift in South Korea's security policy.

For the design and implementation of a historical-comparative approach, I utilize an integrated level of analysis, combining system-level and state-level analyses, as Waltz (1959) suggested.[48] The integrated level of analysis or interactive approach is designed to analyze the sources of security policy change.[49] Traditionally, studies that emphasize international sources of change have only reluctantly recognized theoretical and empirical findings that highlight domestic sources of change. This inquiry attempts to provide a better understanding of the politics of security policy change by demonstrating the explanatory power of both international structural determinants and domestic institutional determinants. Variables relevant to system-level and state-level analyses are used to test hypotheses drawn from different theoretical insights. The integrated level of analysis enables one to examine the comparative dynamics of domestic institutional and international systemic determinants to South Korea's security policy change.

According to Walt, security analysts engage in three major activities: "theory-building or creation, theory-testing, and theory application or policy analysis" (1991: 221). Theory-building develops logical causal claims that explain particular outcomes in international politics. Theory application is a specific policy analysis through particular theoretical lenses used to clarify security policy problems. Theory-testing is used to verify, falsify, and refine existing theories by examining their causal claims and specifying whether causal variables are unidirectional or intervening. Most research involves some form of theory-testing analyses, but this study more specifically explores theoretical causal claims of international structuralism and domestic institutionalism, laid out in Figure 2.1 in Chapter 2. Thus, it will help to examine the relative explanatory power of theoretical causal claims that explain South Korea's security policy dynamics.

In order to examine the relative importance of international systemic and domestic institutional factors, evaluative criteria are compared over the Cold War era, transitional phase, and post-Cold War era. Evaluative criteria employed in this study are variations in the relative distribution of power, US-ROK alliance system, formal diplomatic and trade relations, types of government, power sharing in the government and the National Assembly, and national military and economic capabilities. Following the international rivalry and power politics theses advocated by neorealists, the relative distribution of capabilities or power in the Northeast Asian system (Min, 1978; Kim, 1988; Kwak and Olsen, 1996) and the formal alliance mechanism (Koh, 1984; Nam, 1986; Oh, Cha, and Hwang, 1990) are suggested as critical determinants. Diplomatic patterns and trade relations are also proposed as critical factors by advocates of transnationalism and neoliberalism (Gibney, 1992; Shin H., 1993; Lee M., 1995). Domestic institutionalists support political types of government as well as power sharing in the government and the National Assembly for the primary determinant of South Korea's security policy change (Hagan, 1987, 1995; Moon and Lee, 1995; Hahm and Plain, 1997). Most scholars agree that national economic and military capabilities have had direct impacts on the security policies of the two Koreas (Baek, 1985; Hamm, 1992, 1999; Yang, 1994).

Descriptive statistics summarize the association between variables and bring out the salient features or patterns of the data. They permit depiction of the data graphically. Changes in the dependent variable are compared to fluctuations of the independent variables in terms of frequency, percentages, and cumulative distributions. The degree and direction of associations are examined by analyzing variations between dependent and independent variables. The real task is to show statistically how variables are associated in given situations. It requires an assessment of the validity and reliability of measurements and associations. To enhance validity and reliability of the study, theories that support the associations between variables are incorporated into the existing analyses, rather than simply rejecting or accepting hypotheses. In this study, potential problems of indexing variables lie in assessing validity (construct and external validity) and reliability.[50] Construct validity refers to whether an investigator uses the correct measures that accurately operationalize the concepts in a study. It has been a common critique of case studies that they are subjective and interpretive due to "history, selection biases, instrumentation of measurements" (Campbell and Stanley, 1963: 5-6). But I will establish construct validity by utilizing multiple data sources on the variables. External validity emphasizes the importance of integrating the theoretical findings of cases into a previous theoretical framework. By incorporating historical or contextual evaluation into statistical analysis and theory-oriented interpretation, external validity will be enhanced. Reliability refers to demonstrating the operations of a study so that it can be repeated by other researchers. When operationalizing the variables, the difficulties lie in minimizing the measurement errors and subjective interpretations of the variables. A possible way to reduce these problems is in documenting the data and sources of references so that other researchers can obtain the same results.

A clear and consistent estimation of data is an important factor in security policy analysis. If the nature and quality of available data impose some constraints, then a reasonable degree of objectivity and insight become difficult to obtain. Specifically, in this study, the difficulties involve the amount, comparability, and soundness of the data available in the public domain. These data include figures on military expenditures, arms transfers, armed forces, GNP/GDP, and trade among regional states, especially in the cases of the former communist countries and North Korea. The exceptional scarcity, secrecy of the data, and errors of under- or over-estimation are the factors that lead to the incompleteness of data analysis. To reduce this uncertainty, I use the methods of analogy, extrapolation, and trend analysis. These methods are used to identify major trends and compare continuities and discontinuities of the data between the past and the present. Thus, the goal is to explore overall patterns of South Korea's security policy change.

# Notes

[1] For the objects of security, see Ullman (1983), Mathews (1989), Haftendorn (1991), Cassidy (1993), Lipschutz (1995), Wover (1995), and Katzenstein (1996).

[2] See Snyder (1961), Waltz (1979), Walt (1987), Tellis (1995), Frankel (1996), and Kim W. (1997) for neorealist conceptions of security.

[3] Baldwin (1971), Lipson (1984), Gibney (1992), Russett (1993), and Doyle (1996) propose intensified transnational interdependence in economics and politics as a solution for world peace.

[4] These critics include Clad (1992), Cronin (1992), and Lee (1994).

[5] International regime theorists or transnationalists include Nye (1971), Stein (1982), Keohane (1989), Keohane and Nye (1989), and Risse-Kappen (1995). They point out that the rise of transnational relations functions as a systemic constraint for states within the international economic community.

[6] The concept of regime security is elaborated by Azar and Moon (1988), Hagan (1995), Moon (1995), and Evangelista (1997).

[7] For detailed discussions on the multidimensionality of security and the issues of "core values" and "whose security," see Buzan (1991), Walt (1991), and Kolodziej (1992).

[8] Under this rubric, national security "refers to the security of the nation-state, i.e., an externally focused interest derived from the presumption of a unified, self-identifying, and ordered society within the state's borders" (Job, 1992: 17). Interestingly, Huntington (1996) goes beyond states' boundaries and considers ethnic civilizations as different units of analysis. However, he also lacks clear boundaries for the context of security in his classification of global civilizations.

[9] For this fused approach of neorealist politco-military and neoliberal economic concerns, see Gilpin (1987), Shin H. (1993), Stubbs and Underhill (1994), Betts (1995), Owen (1996), and Huh (1997).

[10] Differences between mature and immature anarchy are made by Buzan (1991), Cossa and Khanna (1997), Han (1997), Papayoanou (1997), and Segal (1997).

[11] According to Holsti, a security policy change or a change of a grand strategy involves "the dramatic, wholesale alteration of a nation's pattern of external relations" (1982: ix).

[12] Boyd and Hopple (1987), Goldmann (1988), and Sampson (1994) elaborate on the state's changing or continuous patterns of relations in international politics through case studies.

[13] For an analysis of issue-specific security policy change, see Kegley and Wittkopf (1993), Dixon and Gaarder (1994), and Greffenius (1994).

[14] Rosenau lays out four possible patterns of security policy change or what he calls "adaptation": preservative adaptation or convulsive behaviors (responsive to both external and internal demands and changes), acquiescent adaptation or deliberative behaviors (responsive to external demands and changes), intransigent adaptation or spirited behaviors (responsive to internal demands and changes), and promotive adaptation or habitual behaviors (unresponsive to both internal and external demands and changes). See Rosenau (1978, 1981).

[15] Political institutions are the part of contextual determinants employed in this study. However, the primary concern is how fluctuations within political institutions affect South Korea's security policy change, rather than political institutions *per se*.

[16] Causal explanations have been largely three-fold: structural, process-oriented, and behavioral explanations (Skocpol, 1985, 1992; Hall, 1986; Levi, 1988; North, 1990; Eisner, 1993; Weaver and Rockman, 1993; Crawford and Ostrom, 1995). That is, structural arrangements, bureaucratic processes, and political leaders' worldviews and behaviors change the state's policy behaviors.

[17] Regarding the role of political institutions, scholars variously explain the relationship between a political institution's autonomy and its capacity. The political institution is viewed as an autonomous agent (Nordlinger, 1981), a partially independent or relatively autonomous actor

(Krasner, 1984), and an embedded actor within state-society context (Evans, 1995).  See also Almond and Powell (1966), Tilly (1985), Scalapino (1986), and Migdal (1988).

[18] For more on contextual determinants of security policy change, see Buzan and Jones (1981), Katzenstein (1989), Rosenau (1992), and Rosati, Sampson, and Hagan (1994).

[19] Primary sources of data are included in the later part of this chapter.

[20] Barry Buzan defines the regional structure as "a group of states whose primary security concerns link together sufficiently closely that their national security cannot realistically be considered apart from one another" (1991: 190).  On the discussion of regional security structure, see also Volgy and Schwarz (1994), Morgan (1997), Shirk (1997), and Huntington (1999).

[21] An alliance can be bilateral or trilateral; thus, it involves a group of two or three powers, whereas a coalition or alignment is formed by four or more states.  See Riker (1962), Organski (1968), Midlarsky (1983), and Sheehan (1996).

[22] For issues on military assistance, see Pierre (1982), Klare (1993), and Grimmett (1994).

[23] The theory of international trade is founded on the principle of comparative advantage.  No matter whether a country "is absolutely more or less efficient in producing all goods, it will gain from trade..., since virtually every country in the world has a comparative advantage in something [and hence comparative disadvantage in something else], every country in the world should gain from trade" (Riedel, 1996: 69).    The relationships between economic interdependence and conflict are in Grieco (1988), Axelord and Keohane (1993), Harris (1995), and Deng (1997).

[24] The amount of international financial flow is about $3 billion a day.  Since foreign direct investments involve commercial flows of multinational corporations, exact data are virtually impossible.  Despite the lack of accurate data, the overall trends are examined in this study.

[25] For details, see McKinlay and Mughan (1984), Hayter (1985), Wood (1986), and Hook (1995, 1996).

[26] Diplomatic relations of cooperation and competition are well illustrated by game theorists like Stein (1982), Powell (1991), Snidal (1993), and Risse-Kappen (1995).

[27] Regime theorists and advocates of transnationalism specify conditional factors that generate states' particular behaviors constrained by international institutions.    See Krasner (1983), Kratochwil (1989), and Czempiel and Rosenau (1992).

[28] This study only deals with highly and moderately stable determinants. For this classification, see Lentner (1974) and Hill (1996).

[29] This meaning of democracy is almost universally accepted by scholars.  See Diamond (1991), Huntington (1991), Schmitter and Karl (1991), and Chee (1993).

[30] Critics of the democratic peace thesis include Mearsheimer (1990), Clifton and Campbell (1991), Morgan and Campbell (1991), Layne (1994), Spiro (1994), and Mansfield and Snyder (1995).

[31] See Wilkenfeld (1973), Hagan (1995), Maoz (1996), and Evangelista (1997).

[32] For the analysis of bureaucratic politics, see Allison (1961), O'Donnell (1979), Kozak (1988), and Welch (1992).

[33] Yang (1990), Yang (1994), and Hwang (1997) estimate changing patterns in the administrative elites.

[34] The years of 1961, 1988, and 1993 highlight South Korea's major security policy change.

[35] See UN, *International Trade Statistics Yearbook* (New York: The UN Printing Office).

[36] See Ministry of National Defense, *Defense White Paper* (Seoul, MND).

[37] See IMF, *Direction of Trade Statistics Yearbook* (Washington, D.C.: IMF).

[38] See Ministry of Unification, *Inter-Korean Trade Volume* (Seoul: MOU) and Economic Planning Board, *Major Statistics of Korean Economy* (Seoul: EPB).

[39] See Ministry of Finance, *Fiscal and Financial Statistics* (Seoul: MOF).

[40] See Freedom House, *Annual Survey of Freedom Country Scores* (Washington, D.C.: Freedom House).

[41] *Ibid.*

[42] See Bank of Korea, *Economic Statistics Yearbook* (Seoul: BOK).

[43] For the economic comparison between North and South Korea, see Koh (1984), Yang (1994), and National Unification Board, *Economic Comparison between North and South Korea* (Seoul: Research Center for Peace and Unification).

[44] See UN, *Yearbook of National Accounts Statistics* (New York: The UN Printing Office).

[45] See US Arms Control and Disarmament Agency, *World Military Expenditures and Arms Transfers* (Washington, D.C.: Government Printing Office).

[46] See Ministry of National Defense, *Defense White Paper* (Seoul: MND).

[47] For discussions of methodological approaches employed in this study, see Przeworski and Teune (1970), Ragin and Zaret (1983), George and McKeown (1985), Skocpol (1985), McMichael (1990), and Thelen and Steinmo (1992).

[48] Security policy analysis can be performed through system-, state-, political culture-, group-, and individual-level analyses. This study combines system- and state-level analyses. On the levels of analysis, see Rosenau (1971), Rosati, Sampson, and Hagan (1994), Gerner (1995), Ikenberry (1996), and Hughes (1997).

[49] For the interactive approach, see Gourevitch (1978), Putnam (1988), Moravscik (1993), and Muller and Risse-Kappen (1993).

[50] For the review on reliability and validity of case studies, see Yin (1993, 1994).

# 4. From Anti-Communism to Mutual Antagonism

South Korea's security policy changed from anti-communism to mutual antagonism during the Cold War. Its major goals were to achieve "political legitimacy, economic development, and deterrence" (Koh, 1984: 8-20; Institute of International Affairs, *Korean Defense Yearbook*, 1989). Both political legitimacy and economic development were inseparably bound up with the defensive deterrence strategy against the North's military aggression and perceived communist expansionism. Sources of South Korea's security policy change can be found both in the international power structure and in the domestic institutional setting. To date, theoretical explanations have been twofold. First, South Korea's international relations have been greatly affected by the major powers' strategic calculations in the context of their power competition that determined the route of South Korea's own destiny.[1] Second, domestic institutional accounts have hypothesized that the substance of South Korea's security policy has been shaped by its institutional arrangements.[2]

The purpose of this chapter is to examine whether South Korea's security policy change is resulted from international systemic or domestic institutional factors. It looks into the relative explanatory power of internal and external determinants of security policy change within the context of the Cold War era from 1954 to 1987.[3] This chapter will also examine hypotheses proposed by security theories of international structuralism and domestic institutionalism. Finally, it will explore critical determinants of security policy change in the Cold War order, and assess the institutional capacity of South Korea's security policy-making institutions.

## International Systemic Determinants

The international attributes provide systemic constraints and opportunities that determine South Korea's security policies. Analytic explanations of international structuralism stress the "ordering principles" of international anarchy—the absence of a centralized world government (Waltz, 1959, 1979). Logically, external structural settings condition South Korea's security policy and its security policy changes. However, anarchy is a much more complex phenomenon than Waltz recognizes. Buzan and Little (1996) postulate functionally and structurally different political units under the anarchic system.[4] In a similar account, the Northeast Asian system is not necessarily "self-help" all the time. Defining features of the Northeast Asian regional system include structural, strategic, economic, and diplomatic factors under a fragmented and competitive system.

After World War II, bipolar ideological blocs in Northeast Asia competed to strengthen each side's spheres of influence. The U.S. and the Soviet Union, globally and regionally, maintained antagonistic politico-military, economic, and diplomatic alliance formations. However, following President Nixon's visit to China in February 1972, the U.S. and China normalized diplomatic relations. The U.S., China, and Japan formed a "trilateral diplomacy" or "geo-political triangular" that was designed to prevent Soviet expansionism (Griffith, 1975; Gong and Leng, 1995). Regionally, North Korea established a double-standing alliance strategy, or so-called "equi-distance policy," with the Soviet Union and China, while South Korea relied on the US-ROK alliance and economic/diplomatic ties with Japan.[5] The two Koreas, however, had no formal diplomatic relations with either side's adversaries during the Cold War. The regional bi-triangular system, as shown in Figure 4.1, was maintained until the late 1980s.

**Figure 4.1. Bi-triangular Northeast Asian System during the Cold War**

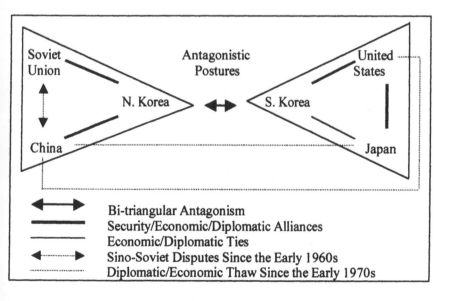

### Geo-Structural Factors—Regional Security and Economic Structures

Both regional security and economic structures demonstrate states' relative distribution of military and economic capabilities, and thereby reflect a balance-of-power mechanism in Northeast Asian power politics. The regional security structure is gauged by the relative distribution of military capabilities or the relative levels of military expenditures, armed forces, and arms transfers distributed among the U.S., the Soviet Union, China, Japan and the two Koreas. The regional economic structure reflects states' comparative positions in terms of national wealth measured by their relative shares in total world trade.

In the distribution of military expenditures, the United States and the Soviet Union retained a bipolar order.[6] As shown in Tables 4.1 and 4.2, the U.S. spent higher amounts than the Soviet Union during the 1950s, but the trend was reversed in the mid-1960s. For a more accurate approximation of data, Tables 4.1 and 4.2 are separated and measured by 1970 and 1987 constant dollars.[7] China spent about $20 billion since the late 1960s, while Japan reached $24.3 billion in 1987 from $10.5 billion in 1972. North Korea spent a lot more than South Korea in earlier decades, but both spent relatively equal amounts in the 1980s. In military expenditures, a balanced level was maintained between the U.S. and the Soviet Union and between the two Koreas.

**Table 4.1.    Military Expenditures of Major Powers in Northeast Asia: 1954-1970**

| Year | US | SU | CH | JP | SK | NK |
|------|------|------|------|-----|-----|-----|
| 1954 | 42.7 | 28.0 | 2.5 | .4 | .9 | 1.1 |
| 1956 | 41.7 | 26.7 | 5.5 | .4 | .6 | 1.9 |
| 1958 | 45.5 | 30.2 | 5.8 | .4 | .5 | 2.5 |
| 1960 | 45.3 | 36.9 | 6.7 | .4 | .2 | 3.0 |
| 1962 | 52.3 | 49.9 | 9.3 | .5 | .2 | 2.5 |
| 1964 | 51.2 | 48.7 | 12.8 | .6 | .5 | 3.0 |
| 1966 | 67.5 | 69.7 | 15.9 | .9 | .7 | 2.9 |
| 1968 | 80.7 | 85.4 | 17.8 | 1.1 | .8 | 4.8 |
| 1970 | 77.8 | 72.0 | 23.7 | 1.3 | 1.0 | 4.9 |

Note: US—United States, SU—Soviet Union, CH—China, JP—Japan, SK—South Korea, and NK—North Korea. 1970 constant dollars (billions).
Sources: U.S. Arms Control and Disarmament Agency, *World Military Expenditures and Arms Transfers* (Washington, D.C.: Government Printing Office); for the data of the U.S., the Soviet Union, China, and Japan from 1954 to 1970, Paul Kennedy, *The Rise and Fall of the Great Powers* (New York: Vintage Books, 1989), p. 384; and for the data of North and South Korea in the 1950s, Taik-young Hamm, *Arms Race and Arms Control between North and South Korea* (Seoul: The Center of Northeast Asian Affairs, 1992), pp. 35-36.

**Table 4.2.    Military Expenditures of Major Powers in Northeast Asia: 1971-1987**

| Year | US | SU | CH | JP | SK | NK |
|------|-----|-----|------|------|-----|-----|
| 1971 | 135 | 162 | 19.3 | 9.3 | 1.3 | 5.0 |
| 1973 | 140 | 178 | 20.5 | 11.1 | 1.3 | 3.8 |
| 1975 | 151 | 208 | 21.5 | 12.1 | 2.1 | 3.7 |
| 1977 | 177 | 256 | 21.2 | 14.5 | 3.3 | 4.4 |
| 1979 | 183 | 265 | 24.8 | 16.6 | 3.6 | 4.8 |
| 1981 | 213 | 275 | 22.0 | 17.8 | 4.4 | 5.3 |
| 1983 | 246 | 284 | 21.6 | 19.9 | 4.7 | 5.6 |
| 1985 | 282 | 294 | 21.1 | 22.0 | 5.1 | 5.7 |
| 1987 | 296 | 303 | 20.7 | 24.3 | 5.6 | 5.8 |

Note: US—United States, SU—Soviet Union, CH—China, JP—Japan, SK—South Korea, and NK—North Korea. 1987 constant dollars (billions).
Source: U.S. Arms Control and Disarmament Agency, *World Military Expenditures and Arms Transfers* (Washington, D.C.: Government Printing Office).

Armed forces represent military personnel on active duty, including paramilitary forces; reserve forces are excluded in the figures of military personnel.[8]  As shown in Table 4.3, the U.S., the Soviet Union, and China maintained large armed forces during the Cold War, but the U.S. reduced one third of its military personnel after the Vietnam War.  Huge military forces in China are due to the size of its population.  South Korea's greater population was also partly responsible for large military forces as compared to the North's until the late 1970s.  North Korea steadily increased its armed forces and surpassed South Korea in the late 1970s.  That is, South Korea maintained its armed forces between 570,000 and 720,000, while North Korea increased its forces over time, reaching at 840,000 in 1987.  Since the Korean War, the two Koreas have maintained about one million or more soldiers on active-duty across the demilitarized zone (DMZ).  Interestingly, there was an inverse relationship between armed forces and military expenditures of the two Koreas.  When the North spent more in military expenditures, the South had more military personnel.  When the North had more military forces, the South increased its military expenditures to balance its military strength with the North.

**Table 4.3. Armed Forces of Major Powers in Northeast Asia: 1954-1987**

| Year | US | SU | CH | JP | SK | NK |
|------|------|------|------|-----|-----|-----|
| 1954 | 3.33 | 5.00 | 4.00 | .18 | .70 | .30 |
| 1956 | 2.84 | 5.10 | 3.50 | .21 | .61 | .35 |
| 1960 | 2.51 | 2.43 | 3.00 | .23 | .65 | .35 |
| 1964 | 2.69 | 3.11 | 2.75 | .24 | .60 | .36 |
| 1968 | 3.55 | 3.19 | 3.10 | .25 | .62 | .41 |
| 1970 | 3.07 | 3.32 | 3.10 | .25 | .65 | .44 |
| 1976 | 2.10 | 4.20 | 4.30 | .24 | .63 | .47 |
| 1978 | 2.10 | 4.20 | 4.50 | .24 | .60 | .63 |
| 1980 | 2.08 | 4.30 | 4.65 | .24 | .64 | .72 |
| 1984 | 2.22 | 4.30 | 4.10 | .24 | .62 | .78 |
| 1987 | 2.28 | 4.40 | 3.53 | .24 | .63 | .84 |

Note: US—United States, SU—Soviet Union, CH—China, JP—Japan, SK—South Korea, and NK—North Korea. Military personnel on active-duty throughout the world (millions).
Sources: U.S. Arms Control and Disarmament Agency, *World Military Expenditures and Arms Transfers* (Washington, D.C.: Government Printing Office); for the figures of the Soviet Union, China, and North Korea, S. H. Steinberg and John Paxton, *The Statesman's Yearbook: Statistical and Historical Annual of the States of the World* (New York: St. Martin's Press); for the figures of Japanese Self-Defense Forces in the 1950s and 1960s, James H. Buck, *The Modern Japanese Military System* (Beverly Hills, CA: Sage, 1975), p. 76 and p. 240; and for North and South Korea's armed forces in the 1950s, Taik-young Hamm, *Arms Race and Arms Control between North and South Korea* (Seoul: The Center of Northeast Asian Affairs, 1992), pp. 14-17.

Arms transfers represent international transfers of conventional military equipment, supplies, and support services.[9] Tables 4.4 and 4.5 contain data on total flows of arms exports and imports, based on actual deliveries of major conventional weapons. These data are separated for a clearer approximation of data. During the Cold War, the Soviet Union transferred 25 to 40% of world arms exports, while the U.S. supplied 35 to 55% of world arms exports.[10] Since the early 1960s, the Soviet Union has surpassed the U.S. in arms exports. In the 1980s, the U.S. arms transfers decreased to only 25% of the total world arms trade. More than 90% of the arms trade transferred by the Soviet Union, the U.S., and China consisted of exports. Until the early 1970s, in the case of Japan and the two Koreas, about 90% of arms transfers were imports. South Korea ranked among the top 12 arms recipients and surpassed North Korea in arms transfers in most years during the 1970s and 1980s.[11] This was due to economic growth and continued increase in military research and development expenditures.[12] Overall, the U.S. and the Soviet Union dominated world arms transfers, forming bipolar trading blocs; sources of arms transfers for the two Koreas were their strategic allies.

**Table 4.4. Arms Transfers of Major Powers in Northeast Asia: 1954-1970**

| Year | US | SU | CH | JP | SK | NK |
|------|------|------|-----|----|-----|----|
| 1954 | 300 | 5 | -- | 20 | -- | -- |
| 1956 | 280 | 100 | -- | 5 | -- | -- |
| 1958 | 800 | 140 | 80 | 10 | -- | -- |
| 1960 | 510 | 160 | 50 | -- | -- | -- |
| 1962 | 160 | 540 | -- | 20 | -- | -- |
| 1964 | 1623 | 1763 | 10 | 38 | 85 | 40 |
| 1966 | 2513 | 2236 | 223 | 54 | 195 | 90 |
| 1968 | 3421 | 1848 | 166 | 50 | 386 | 87 |
| 1970 | 3570 | 1826 | 210 | 79 | 163 | 65 |

Note: US—United States, SU—Soviet Union, CH—China, JP—Japan, SK—South Korea, and NK—North Korea. From 1954 to 1962, only arms exports are included; 1968 constant dollars (millions)—the SIPRI data. From 1963 to 1970, arms transfers include exports and imports; and 1972 constant dollars (millions)—the ACDA data.
Sources: Stockholm International Peace Research Institute, *World Armaments and Disarmament Yearbook* (London: Taylor & Francis) and U.S. Arms Control and Disarmament Agency, *World Military Expenditures and Arms Transfers* (Washington, D.C.: Government Printing Office).

**Table 4.5. Arms Transfers of Major Powers in Northeast Asia: 1971-1987**

| Year | US | SU | CH | JP | SK | NK |
|------|-------|-------|------|------|------|-----|
| 1971 | 8942 | 6799 | 629 | 213 | 553 | 481 |
| 1973 | 11603 | 18948 | 686 | 192 | 389 | 540 |
| 1975 | 9429 | 12307 | 552 | 180 | 371 | 320 |
| 1977 | 11930 | 16483 | 367 | 262 | 717 | 280 |
| 1979 | 9031 | 25458 | 480 | 434 | 1056 | 450 |
| 1981 | 10903 | 21662 | 651 | 1077 | 814 | 970 |
| 1983 | 13706 | 23273 | 1936 | 1242 | 895 | 544 |
| 1985 | 12406 | 19617 | 1352 | 1167 | 562 | 764 |
| 1987 | 13226 | 21825 | 1380 | 805 | 580 | 830 |

Note: US—United States, SU—Soviet Union, CH—China, JP—Japan, SK—South Korea, and NK—North Korea. Arms transfers include exports and imports. 1987 constant dollars (millions).
Sources: U.S. Arms Control and Disarmament Agency, *World Military Expenditures and Arms Transfers* (Washington, D.C.: Government Printing Office) and Anne Gilks and Gerald Segal, *China and the Arms Trade* (New York: St. Martin's Press, 1985), pp. 192-195.

The regional economic structure mirrors states' relative economic positions in the regional power equilibrium. The relative wealth distribution in terms of states' percentage shares in total world trade connotes concentration or dispersion of economic capabilities.[13]   As Table 4.6 indicates, the U.S. remained a unipolar economic power, while Japan increased its trade shares over the years.[14]   The U.S. traded about a quarter of the world's goods and services and dominated markets of the Western Hemisphere as a buyer and supplier, principal international investor, and foreign aid donor. The average ratio of the U.S. international trade to its GNP was about 6.9% while Japan had 20% or more during the Cold War. In other words, U.S. trade relations with other states were less "vulnerable" and "sensitive" compared to those of Japan and South Korea (Hirschman, 1969; Keohane and Nye, 1973). The average U.S. trade accounted for 14.6% of total world trade from 1950 to 1987. South Korea's trade shares in total world trade increased over the years (as did China's), while North Korea had less than 0.1% of total world trade. In terms of world GDP and world trade, the U.S. remained dominant, while Japan increased its shares in both categories during the Cold War era.

**Table 4.6.   Relative Shares of Northeast Asian States in World Trade: 1954-1987**

| Year | US | SU | CH | JP | SK |
|------|------|-----|-----|-----|-----|
| 1954 | 16.2 | -- | -- | 3.2 | .1 |
| 1958 | 14.0 | 3.7 | 1.6 | 2.6 | .2 |
| 1962 | 13.1 | 1.2 | .7 | 3.6 | .2 |
| 1966 | 15.7 | 1.4 | .8 | 4.7 | .3 |
| 1970 | 15.2 | 1.3 | .5 | 6.2 | .5 |
| 1974 | 13.6 | 1.5 | .8 | 7.6 | .7 |
| 1978 | 13.2 | 1.7 | .8 | 7.0 | 1.1 |
| 1982 | 12.9 | 2.3 | 1.1 | 7.5 | 1.1 |
| 1986 | 14.6 | 1.9 | 1.8 | 8.2 | 1.5 |
| 1987 | 14.2 | 1.7 | 1.8 | 8.0 | 1.7 |

Note: Percentages; US—United States, SU—Soviet Union, CH—China, JP—Japan, SK—South Korea, and NK—North Korea. For the figures from 1954 to 1958, the UN data are used and from 1959 to 1987, the IMF data are used. North Korea is omitted from the calculation because it accounted for less than 0.1% of total world trade. From 1954 to 1957, figures for the Soviet Union and China are unavailable.
Sources: UN, *International Trade Statistics Yearbook* (New York: The UN Statistical Office) and IMF, *Direction of Trade Statistics Yearbook* (Washington, D. C.: IMF).

In summary, published statistics on the aggregate data are notoriously unreliable and need to be carefully examined. However, we can nonetheless take note of trends and relative levels of distributions in the Northeast Asian power equilibrium. Statistical data show that the Northeast Asian geo-structure was militarily bipolar, structured by the U.S. and the Soviet Union, and economically unipolar, dominated by the U.S. during the Cold War. As neorealists have described, a major driving force of states' foreign relations has been a structure that facilitates competition, alliance, and alignment among regional states. South Korea adopted a reactive security policy as a client state following the U.S. security and economic leadership in the Asia-Pacific. South Korea also attempted to strengthen its relations with the U.S. and Japan on order to safeguard its national survival. The relative distributions in military and economic capabilities certainly support the view that states search for security through power politics, such as a balance-of-power and extended deterrence strategy. In order to reach its goal of deterrence, South Korea adjusted and changed its security programs of anti-communism and non-alignment to those of mutual antagonism, extended deterrence, and military modernization. The security policy change, initiated by the Park administration, did not result from variations in the geo-structural conditions but was determined by the "ordering principles" of international balance-of-power politics. Thus, its security policy change was a confirmation of the policy of systemic constraints or the realization of geo-structural power politics in Northeast Asia. However, a remaining question is why South Korea did not confirm the structural changes of the bi-triangular Northeast Asian system that occurred during the détente of the 1970s.

*Geo-Strategic Factors—Security Alliance Mechanisms*

The Cold War Northeast Asian geo-strategic factors include regional alliance mechanisms that incorporate security alliance treaties, military exercises, the presence of military forces, and foreign military aid. An alliance is an organization or a commitment of a number of states to take certain cooperative actions against adversaries. What Patrick Cronin (1992) calls "a latent war community" is generally formalized by the signing of a treaty and the formation of security alliance institutions to oversee international commitments. Alliance institutions can be bilateral or multilateral. However, there were no collective security institutions in Northeast Asia during the Cold War. Alliances were bilateral among North Korea, the Soviet Union, and China on the communist side, and bilateral between South Korea and the U.S. on the capitalist side. Strategically, the alliance was bi-triangular, formed by the 1953 US-ROK Mutual Defense Treaty and by the Mutual Friendship Treaties among North Korea, the Soviet Union, and China.[15] Security alliance treaties were established to maintain a regional balance-of-power and lasted intact throughout the Cold War.

In accordance with the defense treaty, military exercises were performed within the two geo-strategic blocs. Bilateral military exercises as well as security meetings between the U.S. and South Korea have been intensified since the 1960s. Annual US-ROK Eagle (since 1961), annual US-ROK Ulgi Focus (since 1976), and annual US-ROK Team Spirit (since 1976) are some examples. The US-ROK Security Committee Meeting (SCM) and the US-ROK Military Committee Meeting (MCM) have been held annually since 1968 to deal with security matters.[16] In addition, the US-ROK Combined Forces were established in 1978, and controlled both operation-at-war and operation-at-peace. Military exercises were aimed at meeting the geo-strategic goal of deterrence against the North's military adventurism. The Park administration's goal was the maintenance of peace via close security ties with the U.S., and thus military exercises symbolized the U.S. role as a guarantor of South Korea's security.

The U.S.-extended deterrence to South Korea also provided a security guarantee through the presence of forces. The stationing of forces abroad is a clear indication of international commitment to one's allies. The U.S. forces in South Korea had three major objectives: (1) to deter the use of force by North Korea either alone or in combination with China and/or the Soviet Union, (2) to meet force with force if deterrence failed, and (3) to provide peace and stability in East Asia (Nam, 1986: 76-77; Institute of International Affairs, *Korean Defense Yearbook*, 1989). However, the role of the U.S. forces in South Korea shifted along with the U.S. global strategic commitment from the "two-and-a-half-wars" to the "one-and-a-half-wars" strategy.[17] Until the early 1970s, the policy of the U.S. was to defend Europe against a Soviet attack and to defend Southeast Asia as well as Korea against an all-out Chinese attack, as well as to meet a contingency in the Middle East. After the Vietnam War, the one-and-a-half-war strategy sought a Euro-centered defense, while leaving its deterrence framework in East Asia and in the Middle East largely intact. Shifts in the U.S. global commitment had a direct impact upon the U.S. role in Northeast Asia.

Regionally, U.S. troop commitment to South Korea was not unlimited and the US-ROK treaty did not provide any time frame for U.S. commitment. During the Vietnam War, President Nixon (on Guam in July 1969) announced that the U.S. would keep all its commitments but would withdraw many of its contingent forces. The Nixon Doctrine aimed to give new meaning to America's involvement in regional security from that of acting as a paternalistic world police force to a partnership of "burden sharing." Burden sharing had been implemented by increasing military sales and reducing the size of the U.S. forces, while facilitating South Korea's military modernization.

Thus, a phased reduction was regarded as essential for implementation of the Nixon Doctrine.[18] As shown in Table 4.7, the U.S. forces were reduced to 50,000 in 1959 from 70,000 in 1957 and to 41,000 in 1972 from 61,000 in 1969. Another reduction occurred during the Carter administration, from 42,000 in 1978 to 39,000 in 1979, but U.S. forces were increased to 45,000 by 1987.[19] Without a doubt, the South did not want to live without the U.S. security guarantee, because the South could not achieve security by its own means as long as the North was allied with the Soviet Union and China.[20] Thus, change in American foreign policy objectives was a deciding factor regarding South Korea's security concerns. Since the U.S. forces "operated as a restraint on North Korean adventurism, the withdrawal of the U.S. forces led to South Korea's militarization and an arms race between the two Koreas" (Kang, 1985: 62).

**Table 4.7. U.S. Forces in South Korea: 1954-1987**

| Year | USFISK | Year | USFISK | Year | USFISK |
|------|--------|------|--------|------|--------|
| 1954 | 223,000 | 1966 | 52,000 | 1978 | 42,000 |
| 1956 | 75,000 | 1968 | 67,000 | 1980 | 39,000 |
| 1958 | 52,000 | 1970 | 54,000 | 1982 | 39,000 |
| 1960 | 56,000 | 1972 | 41,000 | 1984 | 41,000 |
| 1962 | 57,000 | 1974 | 38,000 | 1987 | 43,000 |
| 1964 | 63,000 | 1976 | 39,000 | 1987 | 45,000 |

Note: USFISK—U.S. forces in South Korea.
Sources: Craig Murphy and Gareth Evans, *U.S. Military Personnel Strength by Country of Location since World War II, 1948-1973* (Washington, D.C.: Congressional Research Service, 1973); U.S. Department of Commerce, *The Statistical Abstract of the United States* (Washington, D.C.: Government Printing Office); and Kwan Chi Oh, Young-Gu Cha, and Dong-Jun Hwang, *The Evolution and the Future of South Korea-US Military Cooperation* (Seoul: Se-Kyung, 1990), p. 56.

Foreign military aid is defined as financial assistance transferred for military equipment, supplies, and support services of recipient countries. Military aid had been regarded as a bulwark to South Korea, since President Truman stated that the U.S. would "support free peoples...resisting attempted subjugation by armed minorities or by outside pressures" (*Congressional Quarterly*, 1969: 39). U.S. aid was transferred by grants under the Military Assistance Program (MAP) and included military personnel training, military equipment, and conventional weapons.[21] In accordance with the US-ROK treaty of 1953 and the Agreed Minutes on Economic and Military Cooperation of 1954, South Korea received the highest amount of $460 million in 1957, but after that year the amount of military aid began to decline.[22]   The U.S. saw "military assistance programs as key instruments in the implementation of the Nixon Doctrine" (Levin and Sneider, 1981: 47).   However, since the Kennedy administration, more emphasis was given to foreign military sales rather than military assistance.   As shown in Table 4.8, the U.S. provided $4,110.6 million from 1954 to 1978, and officially U.S. aid ended in 1977.   Consequently, South Korea implemented its Force Modernization Plan (1971-1975) and Force Improvement Plan (1976-1980) to strengthen its forces.[23]   South Korea's militarization was established to compensate for the reduction in U.S. military assistance.

**Table 4.8. U.S. Foreign Military Assistance to South Korea: 1954-1980**

| Year | USFMA | Year | USFMA | Year | USFMA |
|------|-------|------|-------|------|-------|
| 1954 | 3.4   | 1964 | 140   | 1974 | 104   |
| 1956 | --    | 1966 | 172   | 1976 | 64    |
| 1958 | 331   | 1968 | 263   | 1978 | 3     |
| 1960 | 287   | 1970 | 155   | 1979 | --    |
| 1962 | 137   | 1972 | 218   | 1980 | 1.6   |

Note: Millions of dollars; USFMA—U.S. foreign military assistance to South Korea.
Sources: Congressional Quarterly, *Global Defense: U.S. Military Commitments Abroad* (Washington, D.C.: Congressional Quarterly Service, 1969), p. 40; Taik-young Hamm, *Arms Race and Arms Control between North and South Korea* (Seoul: The Center of Northeast Asian Affairs, 1992), pp. 35-36; and Sun-Ho Lee and Kwang-Sun Jung, *Internationalization of Korean Defense* (Seoul: Palbokwon, 1996), pp. 202-203.

South Korea's geo-strategic relations were bilateral and dependent on the United States' global and regional commitment.   South Korea was reactive to U.S. geo-strategic recalculations and commitments, which were occasionally reassessed in relation to the international strategic setting.   As in the case of geo-structural factors, the Euro-centered one-and-a-half-war strategy, political rapprochement with China, and reassessment of the U.S. global role led to change in the U.S. commitment to South Korea.   Thus, its security alliance "was not the result of accumulated U.S. national interests…but an accident of particular Cold War circumstances" (Nam, 1986: 177).   To a great extent, Northeast Asian geo-strategic determinants influenced South Korea to strengthen its extended deterrence with the U.S.   In particular, the reduction of U.S. forces and military aid caused South Korea's militarization.

South Korea's security goal was to have the ability to deter a second North Korean military attack.   One means to achieve this end was the US-ROK security alliance system, including the U.S. force commitment in South Korea, bilateral military exercises, and military assistance programs. Fluctuations in these geo-strategic factors had a direct impact upon changes in South Korea's security policy programs, which shifted to military modernization. In the event of an extreme occasion, Seoul made it clear that "it would develop its own nuclear capability if the U.S. nuclear umbrella and military commitment were removed from South Korea."[24] Despite the vacillation of U.S. policies toward South Korea, however, there had been both a sustained commitment to the regional balance-of-power system and clear-cut action to maintain stability and order in Northeast Asia. Apparently, asymmetrical geo-strategic relations between South Korea and the U.S. support international rivalry and power politics, as advocated by neorealists. In their view, small states like South Korea are dependent upon the strategic calculations of superpowers like the U.S. However, South Korea did not follow the route of strategic rapprochement that the U.S., China, and Japan had formulated in the 1970s. Interestingly, North Korea did not take any action toward regional rapprochement.

### *Geo-Economic Factors—Trade and Financial Alignment Mechanisms*

Geo-economic alignment mechanisms reflect levels of economic and financial interactions among states. Both percentage shares of trade and financial alignment such as foreign economic aid mirror the complexity of regional economic interdependence. Trade shares among states encompass the degree of openness to the international economy and "mutual and unequal dependence," and financial relations measure states' geo-economic commitments to the recipients. During the Cold War, South Korea's geo-economic relations were aligned with the U.S. and Japan, following the geo-structural links in Northeast Asia. Among systemic constraints and incentives that have accompanied South Korea's security policy change, one of the most startling factors can be found in the role of trade shares and economic aid.

Percentages of trade shares represent the level of South Korea's economic interactions and the degree of "mutual and unequal dependence" with other regional states.[25] As Table 4.9 indicates, exports to the U.S. and Japan reached 89.2% of South Korea's total exports in 1954. Since 1975, exports to these two countries dropped to 55% or less, but remained more than 40% of its total exports. Exports to Japan were the highest at 66.2% in 1959, but since then steadily decreased. Up until 1974, South Korea's exports to the U.S. and Japan accounted for 60% or more of its total exports. The overall average ratio of exports to GNP was less than 10% in the 1950s, but increased to 15% in 1970, 59.4% in 1975, and 67.4% in 1985. During the Cold War, the U.S. and Japan were the principal sources of South Korea's exports.

**Table 4.9. South Korea's Trade Shares with the U.S. and Japan:1954-1987**

| Year | United States | | Japan | |
|------|---------|---------|---------|---------|
|      | Exports | Imports | Exports | Imports |
| 1954 | 56.3 | 22.1 | 32.9 | 38.2 |
| 1958 | 17.6 | 55.3 | 60.7 | 13.2 |
| 1962 | 21.9 | 52.2 | 42.3 | 25.9 |
| 1966 | 38.3 | 35.4 | 26.5 | 41.0 |
| 1970 | 47.3 | 29.5 | 28.1 | 40.8 |
| 1974 | 33.5 | 24.8 | 30.9 | 38.3 |
| 1978 | 31.9 | 20.3 | 20.6 | 40.0 |
| 1982 | 28.6 | 24.6 | 15.5 | 21.8 |
| 1986 | 40.0 | 20.7 | 15.6 | 34.4 |
| 1987 | 38.7 | 21.4 | 17.8 | 33.3 |

Note: Percentages.
Sources: UN, *International Trade Statistics Yearbook* (New York: The UN Statistical Office); Bank of Korea, *Economic Statistics Yearbook* (Seoul: BOK); and Ki Hoon Kim, "The Role of the United States in the Economic Development of Korea," in *Forty Years of Korea-U.S. Relations, 1948-1988*, eds., Tae-Hwan Kwak and Seong Hyong Lee (Seoul: Kyung Hee University Press, 1990), pp. 161-162.

From the beginning of its industrialization, South Korea was successful because of a favorable market access provided by industrialized countries, especially the U.S. The U.S. market share for South Korean exports climbed from less than 20% in 1961 to more than 50% in 1968, and it fluctuated between 25% and 50% during the 1970s and 1980s. On the contrary, exports to Japan were only maintained between 14% and 38.5% after 1963.[26] However, the exporting of goods to Japan created a need for an economic normalization to facilitate South Korea's economic take-off. From South Korea's perspective, Japan was important as a market for primary products and the U.S. remained as the primary market for manufactured products (Castley, 1997: 167-178; Numazaki, 1998: 66-70). Some 50% or more of South Korea's total exports were dependent upon the U.S. and Japanese markets.

South Korea imported more from Japan than from the U.S. by 1965; then the trend reversed until the early 1980s. South Korea's imports from Japan increased at the time of the Normalization Treaty in 1965 and accelerated thereafter.[27] However, imports from the U.S. declined after the mid-1960s. Both the U.S. and Japan accounted for three-quarters of South Korea's imports in the 1960s, falling to two-thirds after the first oil crisis (1973-1974) and to around 50% in the 1980s. Thus, it was not until the 1980s that other countries in Europe and Asia became important trading partners.

South Korea's imports from the U.S. and Japan also chronologically evolved. That is to say, South Korea imported goods and services for the light and labor-intensive manufacturing industry in the 1960s, the capital-intensive and heavy industry in the 1970s, and the knowledge-intensive and high-tech industry in the 1980s.[28] The U.S. and Japan were the major sources of South Korea's imports, accounting for 50% or more of total imports. As a result, South Korea was dependent upon the U.S. and Japanese markets and highly vulnerable to them.

Both the U.S. and Japan were important trading partners and sources of transactions. Japan was the major market and the U.S. the major supplier until the early 1960s. By the late 1960s, the roles completely reversed; i.e., the U.S. was the major market and Japan the main supplier. Since trade with the U.S. and Japan accounted for a relatively high portion of South Korea's GNP, economic relations were vulnerable and sensitive. Thus, economic interdependence was asymmetrical in terms of "the intensity of relations" and "relative power resources of states" (Keohane and Nye, 1973). Despite the fact that its market shares decreased over the years, South Korea was continuously dependent upon the U.S. and Japanese markets. In short, geo-economic interdependence was one of the reasons that changed South Korea's security concerns and economic normalization with Japan.

The asymmetrical nature of economic interdependence is more clearly evident in the area of foreign economic aid. Economic aid is defined as the public transfer of goods and services for the recipient's economic development and social welfare. South Korea relied heavily on U.S. economic aid until 1972, and U.S. economic aid "constituted about 75% of total imports during the period from 1954 to 1960 in South Korea" (Krueger, 1979: 67). The U.S. began to reduce the level of foreign aid substantially in the late 1950s and the early 1960s, as shown in Table 4.10. In its search for foreign capital, South Korea normalized economic relations with Japan and shifted its economic development policy from an inward-looking to an outward-looking strategy.[29] From 1964 to 1987, Japanese economic aid accounted for $ 2761.8 million, and Japan's public loans to South Korea consisted of 29.1% of its total loans, while commercial loans were 70.9%. The U.S. provided about $4 billion in grants from 1948 to 1982; 50% of its total loans were public loans. These generous levels of grant aid were linked to U.S. geo-strategic considerations that aimed to build South Korea into a bulwark against the North's military aggression and communist expansionism. Gradual reduction of the U.S. grants and steady increase of its commercial aid were due mainly to the rapid growth of the Korean economy during the 1960s and the 1970s.[30] Japanese economic aid was related to its own economic interests and aimed to tighten trade ties. The U.S., by contrast, played the role of "bloc leader" (Holsti, 1970) and promoted both security and economic interests. As noted, the U.S. preoccupation with politico-military concerns was evident in its patterns of military and economic aid to South Korea.[31]

**Table 4.10. Foreign Economic Aid to South Korea: 1954-1987**

| Year | US | Japan | Year | US | Japan |
|------|-------|-------|------|-------|-------|
| 1954 | 153.8 | -- | 1971 | 184.0 | 128.9 |
| 1955 | 236.7 | -- | 1972 | 230.0 | 117.3 |
| 1956 | 326.7 | -- | 1973 | 116.0 | 163.0 |
| 1957 | 383.0 | -- | 1974 | 34.0 | 179.0 |
| 1958 | 321.2 | -- | 1975 | 108.0 | 97.4 |
| 1959 | 231.2 | -- | 1976 | 143.0 | 41.4 |
| 1960 | 248.0 | -- | 1977 | 90.0 | 106.6 |
| 1961 | 202.4 | -- | 1978 | 76.0 | 102.3 |
| 1962 | 242.8 | -- | 1979 | 54.0 | 100.5 |
| 1963 | 236.4 | -- | 1980 | 47.0 | 125.6 |
| 1964 | 253.8 | .4 | 1981 | 37.0 | 373.5 |
| 1965 | 134.0 | 67.8 | 1982 | 12.0 | 81.9 |
| 1966 | 181.5 | 111.8 | 1983 | 8.0 | 80.3 |
| 1967 | 203.4 | 65.2 | 1984 | 8.0 | 69.7 |
| 1968 | 191.2 | 125.7 | 1985 | 7.0 | 84.6 |
| 1969 | 219.0 | 108.0 | 1986 | 5.0 | 123.2 |
| 1970 | 176.0 | 91.3 | 1987 | 6.0 | 216.4 |

Note: Millions of dollars. Figures are based on the total gross Official Development Aid (ODA). Sources: OECD, *Geographical Distribution of Financial Flows to Developing Countries* (Paris: OECD); Bank of Korea, *Economic Statistics Yearbook* (Seoul: BOK); Anne O. Krueger, *The Developmental Role of the Foreign Sector and Aid* (Cambridge, MA: Harvard University Press, 1979), passim; and Ki Hoon Kim, "The Role of the United States in the Economic Development of Korea," in *Forty Years of Korea-U.S. Relations, 1948-1988*, eds., Tae-Hwan Kwak and Seong Hyong Lee (Seoul: Kyung Hee University Press, 1990), p. 155.

The decline of U.S. aid in the 1960s compelled South Korea to look elsewhere for foreign capital. During this critical period of economic development and the second Five-Year Plan period (1967-1971), the level of domestic investment and savings was insufficient to finance development.[32] Without foreign capital sources, South Korea could not make a structural transition into light industries, heavy industries, and knowledge-intensive industries. In fact, it was "foreign capital that enabled South Korea to choose a development strategy" (Suh, 1978: 78). With $800 million of Japanese grants and loans over a ten-year period beginning in 1966, the Normalization Treaty marked a critical turning point. This structural transition was also accompanied by a diversification of economic alignments with other developing states after the early 1960s. Thus, the success of economic growth lay partly in the South's export-oriented strategy financed by foreign economic aid and the market excess provided by the U.S. and Japan.[33]

A particularly striking point is that strategic calculations about politics and economics were not equally applied to regional major powers. The primary motive of normalization with Japan was economic, while antagonism toward communist China was geo-strategic. It was "a realist calculation of national economic interests" that dictated the normalization process with Japan (Cha, 1996: 145). However, this same logic was not applied to China, although Japan normalized its economic relations with China in the early 1970s. Rather, economic interactions were intensified with other developing states in Asia and Latin America. The neoliberal argument that the spread of economic and diplomatic interdependence is conducive to regional stability did not hold as an alternative for South Korea.

## *Geo-Political Factors—Diplomacy and International Institutions*

Geo-political alignment mechanisms are generally maintained through formal diplomatic relations and memberships in international institutions. Diplomacy has provided a channel for cooperation among states, but often is used as a means of manipulating and compelling rivalries in the international arena. The underlying basis of South Korea's diplomatic relations was formed by its ideological rivalry with North Korea. Heavily influenced by the U.S. in the bipolar hegemonic blocs, anti-communism was the national ideology. President Rhee repeated his rhetoric for a northern military expedition and recognized no policy options but one of total war for national unification. South Korea's primarily aligned countries were all within the Western Hemisphere until the early 1960s. As Table 4.11 shows, South Korea began to establish diplomatic relations with other developing countries and communist countries in the 1960s. Diplomatic relations with communist countries were minimal and these countries did not oppose either North Korea or South Korea. By 1969, 23 African states and 21 Latin American states were formally aligned with South Korea.[34] In the 1970s, South Korea improved its relations with other Asian and Middle Eastern countries. Thirteen Asian countries and seven Middle Eastern countries formally aligned with South Korea (Park, 1985: 234-240). In 1971, the number of countries aligned with South Korea was more than two times higher as compared to the number of countries aligned with North Korea; this resulted from the South's competitive diplomacy.[35] By 1987, however, there was an approximate parity in diplomatic recognition; i.e. South

Korea had 122 aligned countries and North Korea aligned with 101 countries (Seo, 1992: 515).

**Table 4.11. South Korea's Diplomatic Relations: 1954-1987**

| Year | West | Communist | Developing |
|------|------|-----------|------------|
| 1954 | 6 | -- | -- |
| 1956 | 8 | -- | 1 |
| 1958 | 10 | -- | 3 |
| 1960 | 16 | -- | 4 |
| 1962 | 24 | 2 | 31 |
| 1964 | 28 | 3 | 40 |
| 1966 | 30 | 3 | 44 |
| 1968 | 30 | 3 | 45 |
| 1970 | 30 | 4 | 49 |
| 1972 | 30 | 4 | 52 |
| 1974 | 31 | 7 | 58 |
| 1976 | 31 | 8 | 62 |
| 1978 | 31 | 8 | 71 |
| 1980 | 31 | 8 | 81 |
| 1982 | 31 | 8 | 82 |
| 1984 | 32 | 8 | 86 |
| 1986 | 32 | 8 | 89 |
| 1987 | 32 | 9 | 91 |

Note: Numbers of countries. Developing countries include those countries in Asia, Latin America, and the Middle East.
Sources: Categorization of countries and figures are from Jae-Jin Seo, *Comparative Analysis on the National Capabilities of North and South Korea* (Seoul: The Center of National Unification Studies, 1992), pp. 509-524 and Ministry of Foreign Affairs, *Diplomacy White Paper* (Seoul: MFA).

South Korea's diplomatic relations evolved from pro-Western diplomacy to competitive diplomacy from the 1960s. Its competitive diplomacy aimed to isolate and neutralize North Korea's aggressive activities in world affairs. Seoul campaigned to portray Pyongyang as irrational, aggressive, and brutish.[36] Competition between the two Koreas was also strong pertaining to their memberships in international institutions. The Rhee administration joined more UN institutions than it did intergovernmental organizations. Anti-communism functioned as a determining factor in South Korea's membership patterns in the 1950s. President Rhee, relying on the UN diplomacy, promoted

South Korea as "the only lawful country" in the Korean peninsula that was acknowledged by the Western countries.[37] In 1948, the UN recognized the Republic of Korea as the validly elected lawful government in which elections were permitted.[38] In the 1960s and 1970s, South Korea joined 34 diplomatic institutions; among these, 27 were intergovernmental institutions. By 1985, the South had joined 17 UN organizations, while the North had joined 10 (Seo, 1992: 544).

In addition to UN diplomacy, Presidents Park and Chun attempted to gain international recognition of political legitimacy in the Korean peninsula by diversifying diplomatic relations. The underlying purpose of South Korea's diplomacy was to have its political legitimacy recognized by the UN and other aligned countries. President Rhee's non-alignment policy was adjusted to one of alignment with countries that were not hostile to the Republic of Korea. Another change in its policy of anti-communism occurred in August 15, 1970, upon announcing *de facto* recognition of the North and advocating a cross-recognition of the two Koreas by the four major powers, namely, the United States, the Soviet Union, China, and Japan (Kihl, 1984: 174-175; Kang, 1985: 64-65). Presidents Park and Chun modified UN diplomacy to one of international diplomacy, which was often implemented via competitive diplomacy and mutual antagonism against the North.[39]

In general, changes in South Korea's diplomacy resulted from a realistic calculation of its geo-political situations. A part of its policy change was to follow the international trend; that is, many less-developed and developing countries began to influence the issues and decisions of international organizations.[40] Expansion of international trade and stable acquisition of national resources such as oil were also reasons for changes in the international alignment mechanism. In addition to consideration of geo-economic factors, South Korea expanded its diplomatic ties with other developing countries in order to explore and diversify overseas markets. But there was "no correlation between political and economic relations in analyzing South Korea's relations with the Third World" (Park, 1985: 245-246). Instead, economic and trade relations carried more weight than power politics concerning non-aligned countries. In this sense, a neoliberal perspective would describe South Korea's new alignment policy toward developing countries. However, at the same time, South Korea's competitive diplomacy was motivated by its desire to win the support of the Third World in security matters and to isolate North Korea from the rest of the world (Kihl, 1984: 197). It was both geo-political situations and regional power politics that affected South Korea's security policy change.

## Domestic Institutional Determinants

Advocates of domestic institutionalism propose to explore domestic institutional settings that have been neglected in explaining South Korea's security policy dynamics. Due to an over-emphasis on international systemic factors, the institutional attributes of domestic politics have been treated as givens rather than variables by the wholistic assumption of unitary-rational actors in international politics. A fundamental question is why South Korea did not always follow international systemic constraints and why it chose certain alternative policies and rejected others. Domestic institutionalists have argued that domestic factors are the primary sources of security policy change. Domestic institutional settings include governmental types, location of legal-institutional authorities, policy-making machinery, and national capabilities.

   The settlement of World War II resulted in the division of the two Koreas; i.e., Korea was liberated, but the consequence was not independence. From its beginning, the nature of bipolar ideological struggle and the catastrophic Korean War led South Korea to form a security regime. Politically, its system was authoritarian, resembling a "bureaucratic authoritarian" state or a "hard authoritarian" state, following an authoritarian pattern of modernization.[41]   During the Syngman Rhee regime (1948-1960), centralized bureaucratic institutions controlled by aristocratic scholars, land-owners, local gentry, and bureaucrats imposed hierarchical rules that precluded democratic participation. From 1961 to 1987, military intervention in politics undermined civilian control of the military—an essential feature for democracy. The authoritarian government also rationalized the legitimate use of the state's pervasive power in directing the backward economy and strategically prioritizing industrial necessities.   In brief, the government directed an "unbalanced development" between politics and economics.[42]   This system is known as "state capitalism" or "governed-market system" (Hofheinz and Calder, 1982; Armsden, 1989; Wade, 1991; Woo-Cumings, 1997). South Korea, as shown in Table 4.12, was an authoritarian developmental state.

**Table 4.12. South Korea's Modernization Paths during the Cold War**

|  | Rhee Administration (1948-1960) | Park and Chun Administrations (1961-1987) |
|---|---|---|
| Political Formation | Aristocratic Authoritarianism | Military Authoritarianism |
| Economic Formation | Backward Economy (Inward-Oriented Economy) | Governed-Market System (Outward-Oriented Economy) |

## Types of Government—Authoritarian/Military Regimes

Political types of government refer to political institutions, democratic or authoritarian, that the state has used to formulate, implement, and evaluate its security policies. Minimal conditions that evaluate or form the indices of democratization can include "basic freedom, participation, administrative code, and publicity" (Saward, 1994: 16-17). Democracy may also incorporate such principles as "consensus, participation, access, responsiveness, majority rule, parliamentary sovereignty, party government, pluralism, federalism, presidentialism, and checks and balances" (Schmitter and Karl, 1991: 83-85). It is safe to say that political systems vary in degree rather than in kind. South Korea, in principle, had some of these democratic characteristics, but it did not have a peaceful transfer of power through a free and fair election until 1987. Its political forms had been characterized as aristocratic authoritarianism (1948-1960) and military authoritarian regimes (1961-1987).

According to the Freedom House's *Freedom-at-Issue*, which measured states' freedom status regarding political rights and civil liberties, South Korea was a "not free" or a "partially free" country during the Cold War. The more strongly civil and political rights are reinforced in a country, the more democratic it becomes. However, in the 1950s and 1960s, South Koreans were not free from torture or coercion, indefinite detention and curfew by the state, or political censorship of the press and mail (Asian Watch Committee, *Human Rights in Korea*, 1986). They also did not have rights such as peaceful political opposition, multi-party elections by secret and universal ballot, or political and legal equality for women.[43] This authoritarian governance continued until the late 1980s. From 1972-1973 to 1987-1988, South Korea remained within the range of 4 to 6 in the political rights and civil liberties category of Freedom House.

Born of the Korean War, anti-communism had become at once an official ideology and a *raison d'etre*. Any challenge to the ruling regime was countered by repressive measures. Repressive measures under the name of security laws, martial laws, and presidential decrees functioned as devices for the ruler's imperative. The arrest of opposition leaders and political critics for alleged ties with communists was one example.[44] The state policed all political activities and its repression was legitimized, as if coercion was necessary for national survival. Growing hostility and consolidation of the two Koreas also sharply restricted any ideological alternatives. Thus, both Koreas attempted to ensure their political survival by coercive measures and their national survival by competitive diplomacy, extended deterrence, and militarization.

Legitimacy and security were twin pillars of authoritarian regimes during the Cold War, and establishing legitimacy was considered to be one way to create permanence in their political institutions. Legitimacy is defined as "the degree to which institutions are valued for themselves and considered right and proper" (Lipset, 1959: 71). Under the Rhee administration, it was hoped that domestic legitimacy would be gained by achieving internationally recognized legitimacy through UN Resolution 195 (III). In addition to that, the Park Chung Hee regime (1961-1979) and the Chun Do Whan regime (1980-1987) sought to gain political legitimacy through economic development. They also expanded diplomatic networks, creating alignments with nations friendly to South Korea. During the Cold War, external threats were often used to justify domestic coercion and military authoritarianism. South Korea maintained a relationship of hostile reliance or mutual antagonism toward North Korea.

As noted, geo-structural and geo-strategic relations affect South Korea's international relations to some extent, but not completely. If the preeminent interest of the state is to maximize the possibility of national survival, South Korea could increase this possibility by instituting formal diplomatic and economic, if not strategic, relations with China. It was domestic political formation that restrained South Korea's security policy alternatives. Authoritarian regimes with pro-Western and pro-capitalism policies pursued competitive diplomacy, hostile reliance against the North, and extended deterrence in order to maintain domestic political legitimacy for regime survival. Domestic goals of regime security and political legitimacy were sought via international moves of pursuing both hostile reliance against communist countries and international recognition of its legitimacy. In this sense, the lack of legitimacy of its authoritarian regimes led South Korea to adopt overt hostile security policies, as domestic institutionalists argue.

### Legal-Institutional Setting—Legal Enactment and Party Holdings

All governments, democratic or authoritarian, incorporate some forms of legal and institutional controlling apparatuses. The legal-institutional framework is a system of structuring and regulating machinery that locates security policy-making authorities. Legal enactment and revisions are determinants of how a government's security policy is made. The institutional setting also represents the degree of concentration or fragmentation of decision-making powers. Thus, the distribution of party holdings (both ruling and opposition parties) in the National Assembly illustrates the levels of checks and balances in formulating and implementing security policies. During the Cold War, South Korea's institutional structure was highly centralized, both in legal/constitutional terms and in a more basic behavioral sense.

The fundamental legal apparatuses that the South Korean governments utilized were the Constitution, the Anti-Communist Law, the National Security Law, and measures and decrees such as martial laws and presidential decrees.[45]

The Constitution, established in July 17, 1948, was amended eight times during the Cold War, as shown in Table 4.13. Every constitutional amendment was the result of an extension of a presidential term or a political upheaval, and there was no peaceful transition of political power by the constitutional process. The purpose of every constitutional revision was to extend, facilitate, or acquire political powers for the authoritarian regimes. President Park initiated Yushin reform in 1972 to extend his rule and President Chun continued in power by amending the constitution to create a seven-year single-term presidency in 1980. Using the sixth amendment, a system of referendum was adopted in order to gain legitimacy for the revised Constitution. However, the referendum's value "had been largely void, given the curb on free speech and political activities, coupled with open interference by governmental power" (Yoon, 1990: 107). All in all, authoritarian governments attempted to use constitutional amendments to perpetuate their rule.

**Table 4.13. Constitutional Amendments from 1952 to 1980**

|       | Dates          | Passed by             | Major Changes                                                                                                      |
| ----- | -------------- | --------------------- | ----------------------------------------------------------------------------------------------------------------- |
| 1st   | July 7, 1952   | National Assembly     | Presidential election by direct popular vote with a bicameral legislature.                                        |
| 2nd   | Nov. 29, 1954  | National Assembly     | Unlimited term for the presidency.                                                                                |
| 3rd   | June 15, 1960  | National Assembly     | Parliamentary system.                                                                                             |
| 4th   | Nov. 19, 1960  | National Assembly     | Political retaliation against high-ranking officials during the Rhee administration.                              |
| 5th   | Dec. 26, 1962  | SCNR                  | State authority came under the Supreme Council for National Reconstruction.                                       |
| 6th   | Oct. 21, 1969  | Referendum            | Third term revision for the presidency.                                                                           |
| 7th   | Dec. 27, 1972  | Referendum            | Yushin reform—unlimited power of the president and indirect election by the National Conference for Unification.  |
| 8th   | Oct. 27, 1980  | Referendum            | Seven-year single-term presidency.                                                                                |

Sources: Edward R. Wright, "The Constitution and Governmental Structures." In *Korean Politics in Transition* (Seattle, WA: University of Washington Press, 1975), pp. 49-69; Dae-Kyu Yoon, *Law and Political Authority in South Korea* (Boulder, CO: Westview Press, 1990), pp. 89-108; and Sung-Chul Yang, *The North and South Korean Political Systems: A Comparative Analysis* (Boulder, CO: Westview Press, 1994), pp. 423-450.

The Anti-Communist Law and the National Security Law of 1948 were revised under the Rhee administration. President Rhee deployed police in the National Assembly to secure the amendment of the National Security Law and to control opposition groups. Foreseeing a slim chance of reelection, the Rhee administration also amended the Constitution to create a direct popular vote in 1952 and eliminated the two-term restriction of the presidency.[46] The authoritarian regime was "able to manipulate [South Koreans'] anti-communist feeling as a device for securing legitimacy and for eliminating his opponents" (Sohn, 1989: 17). Revisions of laws were primarily aimed to manipulate elections and control political oppositions for regime survival.

Under the Park administration, preexisting security laws became not only tougher, but new laws were enacted. President Park's legal controlling apparatuses included the Central Intelligence Law of 1962, Political Purification Law of 1962, National Protection Law of 1962, Law on the National Conference for Unification of 1972, Law on National Referendum of 1972, Law on National Assembly of 1973, Public Security Law of 1975, and Civil Defense Law of 1975.[47] The Park administration expanded the power of the president to a great extent. Political opposition was seldom tolerated and rights provided by the Constitution were not guaranteed. Constitutional amendments, legal enactment, and martial decrees were created to maintain and strengthen the power of authoritarian military rule.[48] President Park, using political and legal apparatuses, constitutionally became the national leader, situated above the executive, legislative, and judicial branches.

President Chun maintained most of the legal apparatuses enacted by the Park administration. The Anti-communist Law and the National Security Law were repealed, but replaced by the new National Security Law of 1980. Closely paralleling President Park's National Conference for Unification, President Chun enacted the Special Committee for National Security Measures (SCNSM) in 1980.[49] The SCNSM "acted as the ultimate decision-making body for the entire state...and ruled South Korea through the use of coercive instruments and by monopolizing the state apparatus" (Kihl, 1984: 82-83). The National Security Law was applied to those who criticized the Chun administration and challenged the political legitimacy of President Chun's rule. Imitating policies of Presidents Rhee and Park, legal apparatuses were also administered in order to reach the political goal of regime security.

The legal controlling apparatuses, including the Constitution itself, "were the South Korean version of an authoritarian political order exhibiting anti-democratic features" (Yang, 1994: 449). Constitutional amendments, martial laws and presidential decrees were implemented to achieve the goals of regime security and political legitimacy. Military regimes had frequently politicized national security issues, and whenever the politicization of national security issues failed to bring forth order, the military intruded into politics.

Military intervention into politics was justified under the name of national survival, the legal basis being national security laws. Overall, it was "the politics of military authoritarian regimes that was above law" (Yoon, 1990: 70).

Another of South Korea's political controlling apparatuses was the National Assembly. The South Korean political party system was not characterized by the two-party or multi-party system. There were always a dominant ruling party and a number of weak opposition parties. The names of ruling parties disappeared, but its members continued to survive politically under different party labels.[50] President Rhee's Liberal Party, President Park's Democratic Republican Party, and President Chun's Democratic Justice Party were some examples. As shown in Table 4.14, there were 12 elections for the National Assembly; the percentage distribution of party holdings between the ruling parties and opposition parties was uneven. Except for the first and second National Assembly, ruling parties always had the majority of holdings in the National Assembly and had few challenges from opposition parties. The party head, president, managed and controlled the nomination of party candidates of every electoral district. A top-down hierarchy was a salient characteristic of South Korea's party politics.

**Table 4.14. Distribution of Legislative Seats by Two Major Parties:**
**1948-1987**

| Republic | National Assembly | Number of Seats (%) |
|---|---|---|
| Rhee Regime (1948-1960) | 1st NA (1948-1950)—200* | 55 (27.5)  vs. 29 (14.5)** |
|  | 2nd NA (1950-1954)—210* | 24 (11.4)  vs. 24 (11.4)** |
|  | 3rd NA (1954-1958)—203* | 114 (56.2) vs. 15 (7.4)** |
|  | 4th NA (1958-1960)—233* | 126 (54.1) vs. 79 (33.9)** |
| Chang Regime (1960-1961) | 5th NA (1960-1961) Representatives—233* | 175 (75.1) vs. 4 (1.7)** |
|  | Councilors—58* | 31 (53.4)  vs. 4 (6.9)** |
| Park Regime (1961-1979) | 6th NA (1963-1967)—175* | 110 (62.9) vs. 41 (23.4)** |
|  | 7th NA (1967-1971)—175* | 129 (73.7) vs. 45 (25.7)** |
|  | 8th NA (1971-1972)—203* | 113 (55.7) vs. 89 (43.8)** |
|  | 9th NA (1974-1979)—219* | 146 (66.7) vs. 52 (23.7)** |
|  | 10th NA (1979-1980)—231* | 145 (62.8) vs. 61 (26.4)** |
| Chun Regime (1980-1987) | 11th NA (1981-1985)—276* | 151 (54.7) vs. 81 (29.3)** |
|  | 12th NA (1985-1988)—276* | 148 (53.6) vs. 67 (24.3)** |

Note: NA—National Assembly; *Total Seats in the National Assembly; **Seats (percentages) of the ruling party vs. those of the major opposition party.
Sources: Election Management Committee, *History of Election in Korea* (Seoul: EMC) and Sung-Chul Yang, *The North and South Korean Political Systems: A Comparative Analysis* (Boulder, CO: Westview Press, 1994), pp. 499-504.

Virtually little room existed for power diffusion or power sharing; that is to say, South Korea "had remained essentially as a one-party state" (Stokes, 1982: 6). Political power was concentrated in the ruling party and the executive branch, and the ultimate power was with the presidency. The 1972 Constitution and the 1980 Constitution gave an extraordinary concentration of power to the president, giving him authority to consider all important security policy matters. The ability of the National Assembly to restrain the presidency "was diluted by the provision that the president had the power to dissolve the Assembly and by the further fact that the electoral system made it exceedingly difficult for political parties other than the president's own to gain control of the Assembly" (Koh, 1984: 119). Consequently, authoritarian regimes were free from legal and institutional restrictions and had monolithic power over security policy-making.

South Korea's legal and institutional framework resembles a "bureaucratic authoritarian" (O'Donnell, 1979) and a "hard authoritarian state" (Johnson, 1982) that suppressed opposition parties by the party in power and the government. With almost exclusive power in rulemaking, ruling parties enacted and revised national security laws in their favor for regime security. By claiming political instability as a threat to national survival, military regimes intensified the use of force in domestic politics. Thus, illegitimate political infrastructures and external threats led South Korea to form an authoritarian security regime, armed with monopolized legislative power held by the ruling parties in the National Assembly. As in the case of political types, antagonistic security policies such as competitive diplomacy and mutual antagonism toward the North were implemented to legitimize the authoritarian security regime. In short, external threats and antagonistic security postures were necessary to justify authoritarian regimes and perpetuate their rule.

### *Policy-Making Machinery—Bureaucracies and Administrative Elites*

Policy-making machinery is the functional web of decision-making structures that include bureaucratic agencies, think tanks, and academics. Bureaucracies perform day-to-day operations and are composed of persons who have professional skills in implementing security policies. The bureaucratic structure and processes illuminate who makes security policy and how, and show the direction or routes of bureaucratic politics. Changes in policy-making machinery are measured by changes of bureaucratic agencies involved in security policy-making and the professional background of administrative elites. Changing patterns of bureaucracies and the distribution of elite groups in administrative agencies enable one to examine the sources of security policy decisions.

In the beginning of the republic, South Korea's executive branch had a cluster of twelve cabinet-level ministries, two offices, ten agencies, and two independent boards, together embracing over 500 bureaus, sections and field offices scattered around the country and abroad. In 1987, it had seventeen ministries with about 1000 bureaus and agencies.[51] Among them, top political organs of security policy-making included the President's Secretary Service, Korean Central Intelligence Agency (KCIA), National Security Council (NSC), Military Intelligence Agency, Counter-Espionage Operations Command, Capital City Military District Command, National Unification Board, Ministry of Foreign Affairs, and Ministry of National Defense. Significant constraints and secrecy regarding the flow of information among these agencies were a marked characteristic. In addition to the use of secrecy as a self-protective device, there was a high degree of competition among bureaucratic agencies.[52]

Policy formulation and implementation were handled exclusively by the president and his top executive aides. During the Rhee regime, security policy-making agencies were the Presidential Secretariat, Ministry of Foreign Affairs, and Ministry of National Defense. The NSC, during the Park administration, was a pivotal agency that was composed of the president, prime minister, director of the KCIA, Minister of Foreign Affairs, Minister of National Defense, and top echelons of the Presidential Secretariat in the Blue House. President Park also utilized military and intelligence agencies to provide information on security matters. The NSC was empowered by the Constitution to give advice to the president on issues of foreign, military, and domestic policies bearing on national security with priority over any other issues and agencies.[53] While keeping other agencies intact, President Chun reorganized the Presidential Secretariat and the KCIA into the Agency for National Security Planning (ANSP).[54] Interactions among bureaucratic agencies were minimal and standard operating procedures were hierarchical. Overwhelmingly, these agencies had formed a consensus regarding anti-communism and national security (Koh, 1984: 61-65).

Regarding security matters, the president and his few policy-making elites performed "the markedly ad hoc and crisis-oriented nature of security policy-making, impeding formality and standard operating procedures" (Koh, 1984: 118). The decision-making system was considered a prerogative of the military elites who dominated bureaucratic politics. Only a few institutions with strategic access to the president retained security policy-making roles. It is not surprising that other alternatives (with the exception of hostile reliance and competitive diplomacy) were largely inapplicable and even irrelevant to South Korea's security concerns. Preoccupied with the issue of military confrontations along the DMZ, the political stability of domestic politics was inexorably related to the issue of national security. In short, concerns for domestic political legitimacy, national security, and regime security were highly correlated in South Korea's security policy. That is, political instability and a lack of political legitimacy led the nation to form a centralized authoritarian regime, which in turn formulated and implemented hostile security policies.

Changes in policy-making machinery had gone hand in hand with changes in the political elite structure. Political elites are defined as top position-holders who are able to affect national policy outcomes regularly and substantially.[55] Political elites or administrative core elites in the executive branch consisted of ministers, vice-ministers of the cabinet, high-ranking bureaucrats in the security planning agencies, provincial governors, and city mayors. Professional backgrounds of administrative elites are closely associated with those who control political power. As Table 4.15 illustrates, during the Rhee regime bureaucrats topped the list, followed by academicians and lawyers. However, during military regimes, bureaucrats, military elites, and academicians controlled a three-way oligopolistic elite system. Total percentages of administrative elites with backgrounds in bureaucracy, military, and academia were 87% in the Park regime and 91% in the Chun regime. Among these, the number of elites from a military background significantly increased from 5.1% in the Rhee regime to 24.5% and 21.5% in the military regimes.[56]

**Table 4.15. Administrative Elites' Professional Background: 1948-1987**

| Professional Background (Previous Occupation) | Rhee Regime (1948-1960) | Park Regime (1961-1979) | Chun Regime (1979-1980) |
|---|---|---|---|
| Academicians | 18.4 | 14.1 | 11.7 |
| Bureaucrats | 43.0 | 48.4 | 57.8 |
| Politicians | 1.9 | 1.2 | -- |
| Military | 5.1 | 24.5 | 21.5 |
| Journalists | 1.3 | 1.9 | 2.2 |
| Lawyers | 14.6 | 7.4 | 5.4 |
| Business | 5.1 | 1.9 | 0.9 |
| Others | 3.8 | 0.6 | 0.5 |

Note: Percentages. Others include local land-owners, farmers, religious leaders, police-persons, and entertainers.
Sources: Jae-In Yang, *Korean Political Elites* (Seoul: Daewangsa, 1990), pp. 203-205; Sung-Chul Yang, *The North and South Korean Political System: A Comparative Analysis* (Boulder, CO: Westview Press, 1994), p. 531; and Jong-Sung Hwang, "Analysis of the Structure of the Korean Political Elite," *Korea Journal* 37 (1997), pp. 107-110.

A centralized, monopolistic decision-making structure was salient in the policy-making machinery. In particular, the military constituted a significant portion of the administrative agencies, and thereby security policy issues inevitably dealt with the issue of national survival and regime security.[57] South Korea's bureaucratic politics were dominated by "the military as the institution and government" (Perlmutter, 1981). Thus, domestic institutionalists' argument, that military-led administrations have more hostile security policies than pluralistic administrations, is valid in South Korea's case. Within the oligopolistic system, communication lines among bureaucratic agencies were limited, and decision-making procedures were top-down. Most security policies were determined by the president and his close aides in the NSC. Antagonistic security postures were the result of this centralized process of policy-making machinery, empowered by the Constitution under the military regimes.

### National Capabilities—GDP and Military Expenditures

Both economic and military capabilities are factors in the analysis of how South Korea's security policy fluctuates as its power of the purse changes. National capabilities of the two Koreas are also compared in order to examine shifts in their capability differences. As indicated earlier, figures and numbers are not exclusive of other factors in a comprehensive comparative analysis, but highlight overall trends and patterns of national capabilities related to South Korea's security policy change. Both gross domestic product (GDP), referred to as a state's domestic strength in producing goods and services, and the distribution of GDP in terms of agriculture, industry, and service sectors are measured to examine the relation between security policy dynamics and economic capabilities. In the same vein, shifts in the relative amount of military expenditures, compared to the North's, are analyzed to pinpoint their relative importance to the South's security policy change.

South Korea's GDP was $1.4 billion in 1954 and increased to $136.3 billion in 1987. As shown in Table 4.16, statistical indicators of South Korea's economic growth since 1962 are quite striking.[58] The average real GDP growth rates were 4.3% in the 1950s, 7.7% in the 1960s, 8.8% in the 1970s, and 6.1% in the 1980s.[59] Except for the year 1980, South Korea marked double-digit growth rates for about 20 years from 1962 to 1987. The real GDP growth rate for 1969 was a stunning 13.8% and for 1973 was 12.8%. The year 1963 was the turning point that marked a 9.1% of growth rate from 2.1% in 1962. Economically, South Korea began to surpass North Korea in economic capability from the late 1960s.[60] Compared to the North's GDP, the South's lead was 7.0:1 in 1987.

**Table 4.16. GDP Comparison between the Two Koreas: 1954-1987**

| Year | S. Korea | N. Korea | Year | S. Korea | N. Korea |
|------|----------|----------|------|----------|----------|
| 1954 | 1.4 | .4 | 1971 | 9.5 | 4.1 |
| 1955 | 1.4 | .4 | 1972 | 10.7 | 4.6 |
| 1956 | 1.4 | -- | 1973 | 13.6 | 6.3 |
| 1957 | 1.7 | 1.0 | 1974 | 18.7 | 7.3 |
| 1958 | 1.9 | -- | 1975 | 21.3 | 9.4 |
| 1959 | 1.9 | -- | 1976 | 29.1 | 9.7 |
| 1960 | 2.0 | 1.5 | 1977 | 37.3 | 10.6 |
| 1961 | 2.1 | 1.9 | 1978 | 52.3 | 13.3 |
| 1962 | 2.3 | 2.1 | 1979 | 62.7 | 12.4 |
| 1963 | 2.7 | -- | 1980 | 62.8 | 13.5 |
| 1964 | 2.9 | 2.3 | 1981 | 70.0 | 13.6 |
| 1965 | 3.0 | -- | 1982 | 74.8 | 13.6 |
| 1966 | 3.6 | 2.5 | 1983 | 82.7 | 14.5 |
| 1967 | 4.2 | -- | 1984 | 91.3 | 14.7 |
| 1968 | 5.2 | 4.0 | 1985 | 94.8 | 15.1 |
| 1969 | 6.5 | 5.7 | 1986 | 108.6 | 17.4 |
| 1970 | 8.1 | 4.3 | 1987 | 136.3 | 19.4 |

Note: Billions of Dollars. 1987 constant dollars.
Sources: UN, *Yearbook of National Accounts Statistics* (New York: The UN Printing Office); Bank of Korea, *Korean Statistics Yearbook* (Seoul: BOK); and National Unification Board, *Economic Comparison between North and South Korea* (Seoul: Research Center for Peace and Unification).

In terms of the distribution of GDP, as in Table 4.17, the agricultural sector accounted for 40 to 50%, the industrial sector 10 to 20%, and the service sector 20 to 25% of the South Korean economy up until the mid-1960s, while the agricultural sector accounted for around 10%, the industrial sector 35 to 45%, and the service sector 40 to 50% during the 1980s. As a percentage of the total GDP, the manufacturing sector's contribution within the industrial sector rose from 15% in 1963 to 22% in 1973, and to 31% in 1980. Transformations in the composition of industries were accompanied by shifts in the product cycles and the Five-Year Plans initiated by President Park from 1962. As previously discussed, South Korea's industrial structure changed from primary products in the 1950s, to light industries in the 1960s, to heavy industries in the 1970s and 1980s, to knowledge-intensive industries in the mid-1980s. Since the first Five-Year Plan (1962-1966), foreign capital and domestic savings substantially financed South Korea's industrialization and its transformation of industries.[61]

During the Rhee administration, economic development was of secondary importance as long as the U.S. provided economic aid.[62] Import-substitution and foreign aid maximization strategies were implemented. But the Park regime shifted to an export-oriented development strategy after the first Five-Year Plan. Foreign capital and investment were vital for the transition of South Korea's economy. Thus, internal economic needs motivated South Korea's diversification efforts toward foreign assistance and international alignment mechanisms. President Chun followed the same route that President Park initiated for economic development, transforming Korea's economy into the growth of knowledge-intensive industries. In doing so, the government intervened to influence or control all sectors of the industry. Factors that motivated economic development were the military regimes' efforts to gain political legitimacy and regime security. As previously discussed, internal economic needs for foreign capital and market access, geo-strategic factors of the US-ROK alliance system, and geo-economic factors of foreign aid and trade relations were all primary factors that affected South Korea's routes to modernization.

**Table 4.17. South Korea's Composition of Industries: 1954-1987**

| Year | Agri. | Ind. | Ser. | Year | Agri. | Ind. | Ser. |
|------|-------|------|------|------|-------|------|------|
| 1954 | 39.2 | 13.4 | 47.4 | 1971 | 31.1 | 30.3 | 38.6 |
| 1956 | 46.2 | 13.5 | 40.3 | 1973 | 27.4 | 33.4 | 39.2 |
| 1958 | 41.0 | 14.7 | 44.3 | 1975 | 24.5 | 32.5 | 43.0 |
| 1960 | 39.5 | 15.7 | 44.8 | 1977 | 22.8 | 34.6 | 42.6 |
| 1962 | 39.9 | 16.3 | 43.8 | 1979 | 20.3 | 36.1 | 43.6 |
| 1964 | 50.5 | 15.5 | 34.0 | 1981 | 14.9 | 38.5 | 46.6 |
| 1966 | 39.2 | 25.4 | 35.4 | 1983 | 13.6 | 39.1 | 47.3 |
| 1968 | 31.8 | 28.7 | 39.5 | 1985 | 12.8 | 41.9 | 45.3 |
| 1970 | 30.4 | 31.0 | 38.6 | 1987 | 10.5 | 40.5 | 49.0 |

Note: Percentages; Agri. (agriculture), Ind. (industry), and Ser. (service); Service industries include GDP shares of public administration and defense.
Sources: UN, *Yearbook of National Accounts Statistics* (New York: The UN Statistical Office); National Statistical Office, *Korean Statistical Yearbook* (Seoul: NSO); and Bank of Korea, *Economic Statistics Yearbook* (Seoul: BOK).

Military spending represents the expenditure made by the government specifically to carry out objectives of its military forces. The average of the South's military expenditures accounted for 5.5% of its GDP, while the North's was 17.9% of its GDP. From 1960 to 1987, the South's military spending ranged from 22.8% to 37.0% of its government expenditures and from 4% to 6% of its GNP, while the North spent 20% or more of its GNP on the military (Hamm, 1992:34-47). As shown in Table 4.18, the South spent 6.1 times less than the North on military expenditures in the 1960s and 1.9 times less in the 1970s; the two Koreas spent nearly equal amounts in the 1980s.[63] To balance its military power, the South has steadily increased military expenditures since the 1960s. In the 1970s, the authoritarian regime also implemented military modernization plans to compensate for the reduction of U.S. military assistance.

**Table 4.18. Military Expenditures of the Two Koreas: 1954-1987**

| Year | S. Korea | N. Korea | Year | S. Korea | N. Korea |
|------|----------|----------|------|----------|----------|
| 1954 | 900 | 1140 | 1972 | 1420 | 3220 |
| 1956 | 600 | 1900 | 1974 | 1680 | 3870 |
| 1958 | 500 | 2500 | 1976 | 2900 | 3990 |
| 1960 | 180 | 3000 | 1978 | 3840 | 4560 |
| 1962 | 200 | 2500 | 1980 | 4000 | 4800 |
| 1964 | 500 | 3000 | 1982 | 4570 | 5410 |
| 1966 | 670 | 2930 | 1984 | 4780 | 5680 |
| 1968 | 840 | 4750 | 1986 | 5500 | 5780 |
| 1970 | 1000 | 4920 | 1987 | 5630 | 5800 |

Note: Millions of dollars. 1987 constant dollars.
Sources: U.S. Arms Control and Disarmament Agency, *World Military Expenditures and Arms Transfers* (Washington, D.C.: Government Printing Office) and Taik-young Hamm, *Arms Race and Arms Control between North and South Korea* (Seoul: The Center of Northeast Asian Affairs, 1992), pp. 65-68.

During the Cold War, Pyongyang had at least a two-to-one advantage over Seoul in army artillery, naval vessels, and combat aircraft.[64] South Korea also lacked the facilities and technology to produce conventional weapons. Thus, military modernization, implemented through the Force Modernization Plan (1971-1975) and Force Improvement Plan (1976-1980), was the result of perceived external threats and variations in geo-strategic factors. South Korea's economic growth was also conducive to a relative increase in military expenditures. Militarization had both positive and negative impacts. It exacerbated North-South rivalry and prolonged aggressive military antagonism. Arguably, militarization also facilitated and lengthened military rule in South Korea. A large number of arms transfers as a percentage of GNP is a facilitating factor in the occurrence of coup d'etat and helps prolong military rule (Maniruzzaman, 1992: 750-752).[65] However, a balance-of-power mechanism, which means that neither side's military forces can defeat those of the other without the third party's assistance, has been maintained between the two Koreas. With the U.S. security guarantee and extended deterrence, a rough balance has prevailed in the Korean peninsula during the past three decades. Despite antagonistic military postures between the two Koreas and periodic outbursts of violence along the DMZ, statistical data on military capabilities indicate that neither side possessed an overwhelming superiority over the other.

South Korea's economic capability remained the essential underpinning of its military capability, and growing national capability has been the source of its security policy change. The goal of economic ascent was inextricably linked to other goals of political legitimacy and deterrence. Thus, modernization was "an indispensable requirement for effective conduct of South Korea's security which necessitated not only arms but also an industrial base and a capability to manufacture its own weapons" (Koh, 1984: 230). Both constant military threats along the DMZ and geo-structural/geo-strategic factors were determining factors of South Korea's defensive deterrence policy. In summary, South Korea attempted to maintain a balance-of-power mechanism in the Korean peninsula and to develop its economy to justify the authoritarian military regime.

**Critical Factors of Security Policy Change in the Cold War Order**

Among the most interesting and important theoretical questions raised by contemporary literature are those which have to do with the relative explanatory power of international structuralism and domestic institutionalism. In this chapter, correlation of internal and external determinants of South Korea's security policy change has been examined within the context of the Cold War era (1954-1987). Generally, South Korea throughout the Cold War era followed the ordering principles of international power politics, namely, systemic constraints derived from the bipolar hegemonic security blocs dominated by the U.S. and the Soviet Union. During the Cold War, the bi-triangular antagonism in Northeast Asia formed by the U.S., Japan, and South Korea on the capitalist side and the Soviet Union, China, and North Korea on the communist side paved South Korea's path to defensive deterrence policy.

South Korea's security policy change from anti-communism to mutual antagonism occurred when there were variations in both international systemic and domestic institutional factors. Reductions in the U.S. forces and its military and economic aid to South Korea had decisive effects upon the South's efforts to strengthen its economic and military capabilities. A high degree of trade dependence upon the U.S. and Japan as well as internal economic needs for foreign capital created a need for diversification in South

Korea's economic and diplomatic alignment mechanisms. Geo-structural/geo-strategic factors and constant external military threats from the North led the South to form an authoritarian military regime. The authoritarian regimes made constitutional revisions and enacted security laws in order to monopolize political power in the government and the National Assembly, which were primarily dominated by the military. In order to justify its authoritarian rule, South Korea adopted mutual antagonism and competitive diplomacy policies toward North Korea. As a result, the conditional factors that determined South Korea's security policy behaviors were both bi-triangular antagonism and an authoritarian military regime during the Cold War era. South Korea attempted to strengthen its military and alliance with the U.S. for defensive deterrence, to develop the economy for regime security and political legitimacy, and to diversify diplomatic and trade relations with other developing countries, while intensifying economic alignments with the Western countries in order to establish economic development and international legitimacy.

The principal source of South Korea's security policy change was the configuration of international systemic determinants. Geo-structural factors were conducive to the maintenance of a balance-of-power mechanism, and determined South Korea's overall direction of competition, alliance, and alignment in Northeast Asia. In a geo-strategic sense, South Korea's alliance pattern was asymmetrical, relying on the global and regional commitments of the U.S. The asymmetrical nature more clearly prevailed in South Korea's trade relations and in linkages of economic interdependence with the U.S. and Japan. Changes in South Korea's diplomatic alignment mechanism resulted from the realistic calculation of its geo-strategic situations. But the underlying basis of South Korea's diplomatic relations was its ideological rivalry against communist countries. Consequently, international factors generated systemic constraints and opportunities pertaining to its security policy change.

But South Korea did not always follow international systemic constraints and opportunities during the Cold War era. Institutional analysis of domestic political settings demonstrated South Korea's alliance and alignment patterns that were not necessarily derived from international systemic factors. Its behaviors toward China and North Korea were also constrained by domestic institutional factors. As mentioned above, domestically, both political instability and the lack of political legitimacy caused the emergence of the military security regime, which in turn implemented antagonistic policies against the communist countries. South Korea's institutional controlling apparatuses were often utilized to strengthen regime security and to prolong authoritarian rule. External threats were also politicized to justify internal repressive measures and used to secure the military regime. Economic and military modernization was essential to meet internal economic needs, to gain political legitimacy, and to maintain a balance-of-power mechanism in the Korean peninsula.

Overall, variations in international systemic and domestic institutional factors provoked South Korea's security policy change. As shown in Figure 4.2, South Korea's security policy goals changed to deterrence, economic development, and political/international legitimacy. South Korea shifted its security programs to mutual antagonism, competitive diplomacy, extended deterrence, military modernization, and economic alignment. Its security policy was also adjusted by its alignment with nations friendly to South Korea, its recognition of the *de facto* existence of North Korea, and its attempt to gain international legitimacy from its allied and aligned countries. In other words, when South Korea was forced to balance international and domestic concerns in a "double-edged process" (Putnam, 1988), authoritarian governments were reactive to the systemic logic for national survival, while internally attempting to prolong regime survival via repressive measures.

**Figure 4.2. South Korea's Security Policy Change during the Cold War**

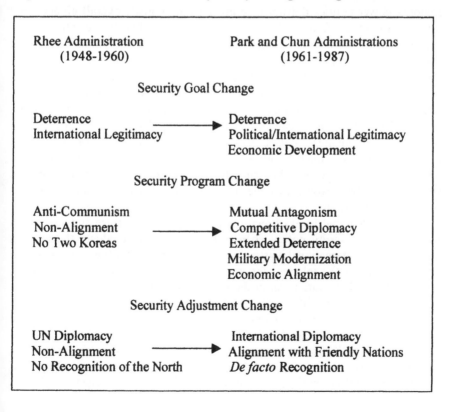

| Rhee Administration<br>(1948-1960) | Park and Chun Administrations<br>(1961-1987) |
|---|---|
| **Security Goal Change** | |
| Deterrence<br>International Legitimacy | Deterrence<br>Political/International Legitimacy<br>Economic Development |
| **Security Program Change** | |
| Anti-Communism<br>Non-Alignment<br>No Two Koreas | Mutual Antagonism<br>Competitive Diplomacy<br>Extended Deterrence<br>Military Modernization<br>Economic Alignment |
| **Security Adjustment Change** | |
| UN Diplomacy<br>Non-Alignment<br>No Recognition of the North | International Diplomacy<br>Alignment with Friendly Nations<br>*De facto* Recognition |

To a large extent, external military threats and superpower rivalry had led South Korea to retain international structuralists' prescriptions that incorporate strengthening military capabilities, economic development, competitive diplomacy, and effective formation of extended deterrence. Thus, neorealism, which recognizes a state's security policy behavior as underlying international systemic and power politics, includes South Korea as an example of its theoretical premise. But strategic calculations of politics and economics were not equally applied to regional major powers, although diversification of diplomatic and economic alignments resulted from the realist calculation of national economic interests. In this vein, neoliberal views on regional interdependence were not applied to South Korea's security policy in the regional alignment mechanism except for relations with Japan and other developing countries. South Korea's relationship with Japan was based on economic logic, while maintaining geo-strategic relations with China. Economic trade relations carried more weight than international power politics in its alignment policy toward developing countries.

Consequently, international rivalry and power politics explain South Korea's security policy change only in part. This is so because changes in regional power politics did not determine South Korea's overall alliance and alignment politics. Détente during the 1970s minimally affected inter-Korean relations and South Korea's international alliance and alignment relations. South Korea's mutually antagonistic behaviors toward North Korea and China were dependent more upon domestic political situations than upon regional power politics, as the state was more preoccupied with concerns of regime security and political legitimacy. Lack of theoretical analysis of domestic politics has left South Korea's security policy change unexplained. As domestic institutionalists suggest, weak domestic political structures and a lack of regime security limited South Korea in improving external relations. The above discussions suggest that an integrated approach of system-level and state-level analysis would provide a better understanding of South Korea's security policy change.

An integrated level of analysis can pinpoint the nature and sources of South Korea's security policy change, but it does not evaluate the relative importance of international systemic and domestic institutional factors. In order to compare the relative importance of critical determinants, evaluative criteria (that include variations in the relative distribution of power, US-ROK alliance system, formal diplomatic and trade relations, types of government, power sharing in the government and the National Assembly, and national military and economic capabilities) are employed. Comparative analysis of these criteria indicates international systemic determinants as intervening variables, as shown in Figure 4.3. From the beginning of the Republic, international power politics structured by the bipolar hegemonic blocs determined South Korea's security policy behaviors of defensive deterrence. Variations in the US-ROK alliance and in economic alignment caused shifts in South Korea's security programs such as mutual antagonism, competitive diplomacy, extended deterrence, and military/economic modernization that were implemented to maintain a regional balance-of-power mechanism. External conditions were also conducive to the emergence of an authoritarian regime, which monopolized political power and in turn adopted antagonistic postures. The authoritarian military regime shifted South Korea's security goals to those of deterrence, political legitimacy, and economic development; these were often utilized to ensure regime security as well as national survival. The discussions above indicate that neither neoclassical realists nor neoclassical liberals offers a better explanation since South Korea's domestic factors were not intervening variables of international systemic factors, respectively, geo-structural and geo-economic factors. In brief, South Korea's security policy change is associated more with variations in international systemic factors than with variations in domestic institutional factors. As Kihl puts it,

> both regime formation and regime types in divided Korea owe much to the pressure generated in the external context...[and] are the consequence of international politics in World War II, the Korean War, and the system of security alliances entered into by each Korea with the outside powers. The policy behavior of the respective Korean regimes also reflects the imprint of external pressures. (1984: 236)

**Figure 4.3.    Causal Determinants of South Korea's Security Policy Change during the Cold War**

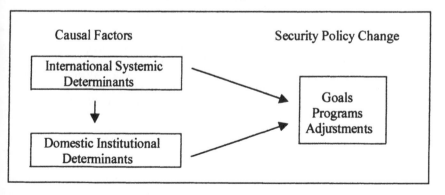

For South Korea in the Cold War order, rapid economic growth appeared to be a solution that could be implemented under the slogan of "rich nation and strong army." Despite remarkable economic growth, however, the overriding strategic goals of deterrence and development "had constrained South Korea to forge special ties of an asymmetrical alliance with the U.S. and of economic dependence on both the U.S. and Japan" (Koh, 1984: 231). A lack of political legitimacy had further undercut South Korea's institutional capacity in improving its relations with North Korea and other communist countries. Rigid hostile postures were applied to secure regime survival. As a result, South Korea, lacking "infrastructural capacity"—both administrative bureaucratic capacity and political capacity (Thomas, 1989; Job, 1992; Gargan, 1997)—faced both an internal insecurity dilemma and an external security dilemma. The internal insecurity dilemma resulted from the lack of political legitimacy and regime security of the authoritarian military regime, while the external security dilemma arose from the North's military aggression and the communists' expansionism. In sum, South Korea as a weak institution emphasized and utilized external threats to ensure regime security and implemented aggressive security policies toward rivals in order to reach its security goals.

## Notes

[1] For power competition and rivalry thesis or international structuralism in Northeast Asian power politics, see Kim (1979), Gilbert (1988), Mack (1993), Kwak and Olsen (1996), Roy (1997), McDougall (1997), and Kim (1998).
[2] Domestic institutional accounts of security policy in Northeast Asia are explained by Kwon (1974), Koo (1975), Kihl (1984), Koh (1984), Moon (1995), Hagan (1995), and Cotton (1995).
[3] In this chapter, South Korea's security policy change is examined from the post-Korean War period to the pre-transitional period. See Chapter 1, Figure 1.1.
[4] Buzan and Little formulate four broad types of international anarchy, such as a European Union type of political unions (structurally and functionally differentiated), a Watsonian system (structurally undifferentiated but functionally differentiated), a classical heterogeneous system (structurally differentiated but functionally undifferentiated), and a Waltzian, or Westphalian, system (structurally and functionally undifferentiated) [1996: 430].
[5] Another example of the equi-distance policy or equally-balanced policy toward two different countries can be found in the Japan's foreign economic policy toward the Soviet Union and China during the 1970s. This policy is different from neutrality, since states can be aligned and become allies, while some of them remain adversaries. See Zagoria and Kim (1976), Kihl (1984), and Yang (1994).
[6] Regarding the definition of military expenditures, the U.S. Arms Control and Disarmament Agency in *World Military Expenditures and Arms Transfers* sets the following guidelines: (1) civilian-type expenditures are excluded; (2) grant military assistance is included in the expenditures of the donor country; (3) purchases of military equipment for credit are included at the time the debt is incurred; and (4) military expenditures of communist countries are based on Central Intelligence Agency (CIA) estimates.
[7] The military expenditure data are of uneven accuracy, and correct estimation is extremely difficult due to the exceptional scarcity, ambiguity, secrecy, and errors of under- or over-

estimation of data. However, the primary goal is to identify overall trends and the relative distribution of military expenditures.

[8] Figures for armed forces in communist countries are rarely consistent among security data sources. To determine consistency, armed forces data of the Soviet Union, China, and North Korea are collected from S. H. Steinberg and John Paxton, *The Statesman's Yearbook: Statistical and Historical Annual of the States of the World* (New York: St. Martin's Press) and Taik-young Hamm, *Arms Race and Arms Control between North and South Korea* (Seoul: The Center of Northeast Asian Affairs, 1992).

[9] There are two sources available for aggregate data on arms transfers: Stockholm International Peace Research Institute (SIPRI) and U.S. Arms Control and Disarmament Agency (ACDA). The SIPRI provided more accurate figures for the 1950s, while the ACDA data are used for the figures from 1963 to 1987. See Brzoska (1982) and Laurence (1992).

[10] The total volume of arms transfers to developing countries (in U. S. constant dollars) rose from $1.6 billion in 1963 to $7.7 billion in 1973, to $23.1 billion in 1979, and to $33.3 billion in 1984. Throughout the Cold War, the total volume of arms transfers to the developing countries amounted to $150 billion, which was three times larger than the total volume of economic aid to these countries. The figures are derived from U.S. Arms Control and Disarmament Agency, *World Military Expenditures and Arms Transfers* (Washington, D.C.: Government Printing Office).

[11] See Stockholm International Peace Research Institute, *World Armaments and Disarmament Yearbook* (London: Taylor & Francis).

[12] See Brzoska and Ohlson (1986), p. 23.

[13] UN, *International Trade Statistics Yearbook* provides individual countries' trade performance; e.g., exports and imports of the world to and from countries, and the International Monetary Fund, *Direction of Trade Statistics* presents the aggregated data on trade flows between major areas of the world.

[14] In terms of world GDP shares, the U.S. had about 50% of world wealth in the 1950, 31.8% in 1970, and 25.9% in 1987, while Japan reached 13.8% of world wealth in 1987. See UN, *Yearbook of National Accounts Statistics* (New York: The UN Statistical Office).

[15] North Korea signed formal diplomatic treaties with the Soviet Union in 1948 and China in 1949, and the two communist giants continued to be the principal sources of economic and military aid to North Korea. In 1961, the Soviet Union and China signed mutual defense treaties with North Korea. See Koh (1984), p. 11 and p. 205.

[16] After the North's Blue House raid and the capture of the Pueblo in 1968, the SCM and the MCM were established to continuously affirm the readiness that is required to meet an armed attack from the North. See Ha (1984) and Nam (1986).

[17] For the changed U.S. global strategies, see Forester and Wright (1965), Berry (1990), Jordan, Taylor, and Korb (1993), and Institute of International Affairs, *Korean Defense Yearbook* (Seoul: IIA).

[18] Seoul tried to cultivate political factors within Washington to ensure the United States' continued commitment to South Korea. The result was Koreagate (also known as the Park Tong-Sun incident) in South Korea. For more details, see Han (1985), p. 157.

[19] President Park decided to "go nuclear" when President Carter announced, in May 1977, a phased withdrawal of the U.S. forces in three stages by 1982. See Kihl (1984) and Koh (1984).

[20] This was so, because the U.S. forces in South Korea numbered 500 in 1949, the year before the Korean War broke out. The U.S. forces were 128,000 from 1945 to 1948. See Oh, Cha, and Hwang (1990), p. 56.

[21] From 1950 to 1968, 28,525 South Korean military personnel were trained under the International Military Education and Training (IMET) program. See *Congressional Quarterly* (1969), p. 44.

[22] American military assistance accounted for about 60% of the total military expenditures of South Korea from 1955 to 1960. In 1961, the share of US military aid reached 90% and then slowly declined to a level of 70% in 1970 and dropped to the 10% level by the mid-1970s. With the Military Assistance Service Fund (MASF) in connection with the Vietnam War, the share of military aid was maintained at a level of 60% from 1961 to 1968. See Ha (1984), pp. 118-119.

[23] See Institute of International Affairs, *Korean Defense Yearbook* (Seoul: IIA).

[24] Due to the North's military aggression and armed superiority over the South, withdrawal of U.S. forces would leave the South's national survival at stake. Thus it should not be surprising that the South considered acquiring an independent nuclear deterrent capability during the late 1970s, since the independent nuclear option would compensate for the loss of the security alliance program. However, the nuclear issue was highly controversial at that time. See *Dong-A Daily News*, March 29, 1978 and Institute of International Affairs, *Korean Defense Yearbook* (Seoul: IIA).

[25] Total exports comprise exports of national merchandise wholly or partly produced or manufactured in the country, and total imports are the combined total of imports for direct domestic consumption and withdrawals from bounded warehouses or free zones for domestic consumption. For these definitions, see UN, *International Trade Statistics Yearbook* (New York: The UN Statistical Office).

[26] The primary reason was the Japanese restrictive neo-mercantile policy. See Kuznetts (1977) and Shin (1998).

[27] Commodities that South Korea imported from Japan were mostly materials and tools necessary for the production of export goods. See Castley (1997), pp. 91-100 and passim.

[28] For the analysis of South Korea's chronological industrialization and trade relations with regional powers, see Amsden (1989), Wade (1991), Blomqvist (1997), Islam and Chowdhury (1997), and Shin (1998).

[29] Todaro (1992) differentiates an outward-oriented (export-promotion) from an inward-oriented (import-substitution) strategy of development. From the first Five-Year Plan (1962-1966), South Korea initiated the export-led development strategy. See also Amsden (1989), Kwon (1990), Wade (1991), Gereffi and Ellison (1991), and Islam and Chowdhury (1997).

[30] Average growth rates reached nearly 10% in real terms from 1962 to 1987, whereas the rate between 1953 to 1960 was only 4.2%. See Economic Planning Board, *Major Statistics of Korean Economy* (Seoul: EPB).

[31] Hook (1995) also finds similar patterns of foreign aid among the Development Assistant Countries.

[32] Low savings rates were due to the poverty of a large segment of the population. From 1954 to 1960, savings rates were less than 10%. See Krueger (1979) and Castley (1997).

[33] For the international political economy of economic growth in East Asia, see Woo-Cumings (1997, 1998) and Shin (1998).

[34] By 1977, South Korea opened new diplomatic missions in 21 African states and 25 Latin American states. See Park (1985), pp. 224-234 and pp. 240-244 and Ministry of Foreign Affairs, *Diplomacy White Paper* (Seoul: MFA).

[35] South Korea aligned with 84 countries, while North Korea had 39 aligned countries in 1971. See *ibid.*

[36] Hart (1999) explains salient features on this aspect by examining South Korea's public education system. North Korea had similar accounts.

[37] President Rhee considered North Korea to be illegitimate since it had no recognition from the UN, but only from communist countries.

[38] For the only such lawful government in Korea, see the UN, General Assembly Resolution 195 (III), December 12, 1948 and UN, *Official Records of the General Assembly*, Third Session, Part I, 1948, pp. 961-962.

[39] President Park also suggested a policy of peaceful coexistence between the two Koreas on August 15, 1970. North-South dialogues and Red Cross talks were held in the early 1970s, but ended in a stalemate, due to the refusal of the two Koreas to make any changes in their fundamental strategies for unification. During these meetings, although it agreed on "unification preceded by peace," the North continued to propose the withdrawal of foreign forces, reduction of military forces to 100,000 or less, and stoppage of the arms race, while the South enumerated three principles of peaceful unification which included signing a mutual non-aggression pact, opening each side's doors, and holding a free and fair general election. See Koh (1985), pp. 87-99.

[40] Group 77 and OPEC are examples.

[41] South Korea's political system was similar to what O'Donnell (1979) calls "bureaucratic authoritarianism" for Latin American states; Johnson (1982) considers East Asian states as either "hard" or "soft" authoritarian states. South Korea as a latecomer followed the industrialization process that Gerschenkron (1962) and So and Chiu (1995) suggested; that is, the more backward a state's economy, the more likely was its industrialization to start at a relatively high rate of growth, initiated by the developmental state.

[42] For the analysis on balanced and unbalanced development in East Asia, see Chee (1993), Kim E. (1993), and Kim S. (1994).

[43] See Keesing's Contemporary Archives, *Record of World Events* (London: Longman), Department of State, *Country Reports on Human Rights Practice* (Washington, D.C.: Government Printing Office), and Humana (1986).

[44] For authoritarian regimes' coercive behaviors toward dissidents, see Keesing's Contemporary Archives, *Record of World Events* (London: Longman); Lee (1975), pp. 19-32; and Sohn (1989), pp. 15-21.

[45] For South Korea's chronological changes in legal-institutional settings, see Yoon (1990), pp. 89-108.

[46] Under the 1948 Constitution, the president was to be elected by the National Assembly. Due to the lack of majority seats, President Rhee declared a national emergency and imprisoned ten National Assembly persons for their alleged alliance with communism. Meanwhile, within this terrifying political atmosphere, constitutional amendments were passed. See Yang (1994), pp. 552-553.

[47] President Park was elected by the National Conference of Unification (NCU) and empowered to dissolve the National Assembly. These laws were enacted to manipulate elections and eliminate political oppositions. See Sohn (1989), p. 17 and p. 90.

[48] For example, the *Yushin*, or "revitalizing" reform, was initiated to tighten President Park's power in 1972. The officially stated reason was to maintain law and order and protect South Korea from North Korea's military aggression. However, President Park was insecure with the result of the 1971 presidential election. President Park received 51.2%, while Kim Dae Jung, the current President, received 43.6% of the vote. With the new constitutional revision, President Park was elected by electoral colleges, the NCU, winning the votes of all but two of the 2,359 delegates in December 23, 1972. The *Yushin* system collapsed after the assassination of President Park by Kim Jae-Kyu, director of the KCIA, in 1979. See Kihl (1984), pp. 59-65.

[49] In 1980, martial laws were invoked to repress the Kwangju democratic movement. President Chun was elected by the NCU with 2,524 votes out of 2,525. See Yang (1994), p. 432.

[50] For the historical patterns of changes in South Korea's party labeling, see Pae (1986) and Yang (1994).

[51] For bureaucratic restructuring, see Koh (1984) and Yang (1994).

[52] Each ministry and agency "was seen in competition for presidential favor...[and] there was no direct communication between agencies" (Winn, 1976: 21).

53 The NSC functioned as "the major guarantor of Korean security and source of intelligence coordination" (Winn, 1976: 15).

54 The strategic role of the ASNP and the KCIA "stemmed not only from its capacity to collect, interpret, and transmit foreign policy related information, but also from its unique function...[that] had served as an indispensible tool of political power and governance for the president" (Koh, 1984: 119).

55 Higley and Burton (1989), Lachmann (1990), and Hwang (1997) differentiate core or power elite from peripheral or task elite. Core elites are those who ranked highest within each elite group or the appointees to the most strategically important governmental agencies. This study examines changes in the core elite structure in the executive branch.

56 During the 1960s, the percentage of elites from a military background reached 32.7%. Before the Park regime, a civilian-military coalition was maintained in bureaucratic politics. See Kwon (1974) and Han (1993).

57 About 90% of top military elites were the presidents' personal aides, and their foremost concerns were to sustain their political privileges by stressing external threats and relying on a hostile strategy against the North. See Han (1993) and Shin M. (1993).

58 After the Korean War, about 70% or more of South Korea's industry was destroyed and its per capita GNP was $67 in 1953, but reached $2,813 in 1987. See Economic Planning Board, *Major Statistics of Korean Economy* (Seoul: EPB).

59 South Korea had negative growth rates after the Korean War and during the second oil crisis.

60 There is a controversy as to when South Korea surpassed North Korea. Although the data show that the South started to have greater economic capability in the late 1960s, most scholars point to the mid-1970s as the starting point. North Korea's annual growth rates were 7% between 1947-1965 and 6% between 1966-1978. Its growth rates started to decline in the mid-1970s. See White (1982), pp. 337-338 and Koh (1984), pp. 40-53.

61 Foreign savings accounted for 10.2% and domestic savings 6.7%, but since 1966 there was a substantial increase in domestic savings reaching to 15% during the second Five-Year Plan (1966-1970) and an increase thereafter up to 35% in the 1980s. See Economic Planning Board, *Major Statistics of Korean Economy* (Seoul: EPB).

62 The U.S. aid was massive during the Rhee regime and provided more than "one-third of the total Korean government budget and 75% of total fixed capital formation, as well as 8% of GNP" (Steinberg, 1989: 126).

63 North Korea spent 1.1 times more than South Korea on military expenditures in 1987. See U.S. Arms Control and Disarmament Agency, *World Military Expenditures and Arms Transfers* (Washington, D.C.: Government Printing Office).

64 See Stockholm International Peace Research Institute, *World Armaments and Disarmament Yearbook* (London: Taylor & Francis).

65 Actually, military coup d'etat occurred in 1961 and 1980, and military regimes remained in control until 1987 in South Korea.

# 5. From Defensive Deterrence to Governed Interdependence

A wholesale revision of South Korea's security policy took place following its democratization in 1987. Unexpectedly, the Noh Tae Woo administration (1988-1992) issued a "Special Declaration in the Interest of National Self-esteem, Unification, and Prosperity" on July 7, 1988.[1] The declaration of *nordpolitik* marked a major turning point in South Korea's security policy involving inter-Korean relations and those with other communist countries. Basic principles were fourfold: (1) the promotion of normalization with the communist countries, (2) the facilitation of the North's entry into the world economy, (3) the intensification of regional economic interdependence, and (4) the relaxation of military tensions and the normalization of the inter-Korean dialogues for peaceful unification (Ministry of National Defense, *Defense White Paper*, 1989). This new international approach transformed South Korea's security policy from a defensive deterrence to a governed interdependence, as laid out in Chapter 1.

Some questions are: What caused South Korea's dramatic security policy change in its international orientation? To what extent did democratization and shifts in the international system affect South Korea's security policy dynamics? In order to answer these questions, this chapter will examine the relative explanatory power of international systemic and domestic institutional determinants within the context of the transitional phase from 1988 to 1992.[2] Following the format elaborated in Chapter 3, internal and external factors will be analyzed to determine the extent to which South Korea's security policy shifted in terms of its international orientation, goal/problem, program, and adjustment changes. After an examination of theoretical hypotheses, this chapter will summarize critical determinants of security policy change and will evaluate the institutional capacity of South Korea's security policy-making institutions.

## International Systemic Determinants

The "ordering principles" of international anarchy and the bi-triangular antagonistic system had conditioned South Korea's security policy and its security policy change. The Northeast Asian bi-triangular system had transformed its systemic alignment and alliance mechanisms as early as the 1970s. Although informal and minimal, there were indirect contacts and trade relations among South Korea, the Soviet Union, and China during the 1970s. But during the détente, South Korea's primary goal was to enhance competitive diplomacy and mutually hostile postures against North Korea. With the 1986 Asian Games and 1988 Olympic Games, South Korea began to have formal and informal contacts and trade with the Soviet Union, China, and eastern European communist countries. *Nordpolitik* as initiated by the Noh administration was an attempt to stop "the vicious cycle" of mutual antagonism, the arms race, and a diplomatic isolation policy toward the North (Park, 1993: 220). *Nordpolitik* ultimately caused diplomatic and economic normalization among the communist countries, which started with Hungary in 1989, the Soviet Union in 1990, and China in 1992. Although the bi-triangular competition was largely intact from the South Korean perspective, antagonistic postures were lessened and economic/diplomatic relations were normalized among the regional major powers during the transitional phase.[3] As shown in Figure 5.1, the bi-triangular Northeast Asian system was shifting toward a multiple, pluralistic system of the post-Cold War.

**Figure 5.1. Structural Transformation of the Bi-triangular System during the Transitional Phase**

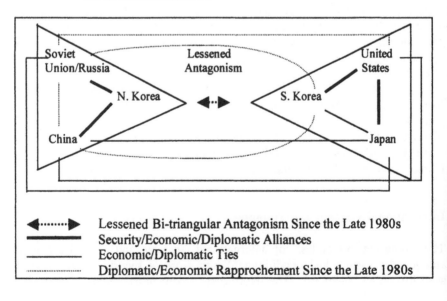

*Geo-Structural Factors—Regional Security and Economic Structures*

Regional security and economic structures indicate the relative distribution of military and economic capabilities among the U.S., the Soviet Union/Russia, China, Japan, and the two Koreas. The regional security structure reflects regional military power equilibrium, as measured by the relative levels of military expenditures, armed forces, and arms transfers among regional powers. The regional economic structure represents regional powers' comparative positions in terms of the real GDP or purchasing power parity (PPP) values. During the transitional phase, geo-structural factors fluctuated when there were changes in the bi-triangular Northeast Asian system.

In the distribution of military expenditures, the U. S. and the Soviet Union/Russia ranked first and second, respectively. The Cold War military balance was maintained in the years 1987-1988. As shown in Table 5.1, military expenditures were substantially decreased in the Soviet Union/Russia, due to its disintegration. In 1990-1991, the Soviet Republics disintegrated and became the new Commonwealth of Independent States (CIS) and, later, the Russian Federation.[4] The U.S. spent $300 billion or more, except in the year 1991. China, Japan, and South Korea continued increases in military spending. South Korea spent nearly two times more than North Korea and reached a maximum of $11.6 billion, while North Korea spent $5.6 billion in 1992. Statistical data indicate that the Cold War balance-of-power mechanism collapsed in the early 1990s, since military expenditures of the U.S. and South Korea surpassed those of Russia and North Korea.

**Table 5.1. Military Expenditures of Major Powers in Northeast Asia: 1987-1992**

| Year | United States | USSR/ Russia | China | Japan | South Korea | North Korea |
|------|------|------|------|------|------|------|
| 1987 | 357 | 374 | 51.4 | 34.6 | 8.7 | 7.0 |
| 1988 | 349 | 379 | 52.0 | 36.3 | 9.3 | 6.9 |
| 1989 | 346 | 345 | 51.3 | 37.7 | 10.2 | 6.8 |
| 1990 | 334 | 318 | 54.1 | 39.1 | 11.3 | 6.5 |
| 1991 | 294 | 273 | 52.0 | 40.5 | 10.9 | 4.9 |
| 1992 | 312 | 145 | 54.9 | 41.7 | 11.6 | 5.6 |

Note: 1993 cor.stant dollars (billions). The 1991 and 1992 figures for the Russian Federation and for Russia and China are based on the U.S. ACDA's rough estimates.
Sources: U.S. Arms Control and Disarmament Agency, *World Military Expenditures and Arms Transfers* (Washington, D.C.: Government Printing Office) and Taik-young Hamm, *Arming the Two Koreas: State, Capital, and Military Power* (New York: Routledge, 1999), p. 59 and p. 93.

The level of armed forces also fluctuated during the transitional phase, as shown in Table 5.2. The number of military personnel of the U.S. and the Soviet Union/Russia steadily decreased during the years from 1988 to 1992, and China's became the greatest with 3.16 million military forces in 1992. Interestingly, North Korea's armed forces increased from .84 million in 1988 to 1.04 million in 1989. Then its armed forces grew to 1.2 million in 1990 and maintained that level, making it the world's largest army relative to its population.[5] Military personnel of the two Koreas reached about 2 million in 1991. The inverse relationship between armed forces and military expenditures of the two Koreas was sustained in the Korean peninsula. While the North had more military forces, the South increased its military expenditures to balance that military strength, and vice versa.

**Table 5.2. Armed Forces of Major Powers in Northeast Asia: 1987-1992**

| Year | United States | USSR/ Russia | China | Japan | South Korea | North Korea |
|------|------|------|------|------|------|------|
| 1987 | 2,279 | 3,900 | 3,530 | 244 | 604 | 838 |
| 1988 | 2,246 | 3,900 | 3,783 | 245 | 626 | 842 |
| 1989 | 2,241 | 3,700 | 3,903 | 247 | 547 | 1,040 |
| 1990 | 2,181 | 3,400 | 3,500 | 250 | 650 | 1,200 |
| 1991 | 2,115 | 3,000 | 3,200 | 250 | 750 | 1,200 |
| 1992 | 1,919 | 2,030 | 3,160 | 242 | 750 | 1,200 |

Note: Military personnel on active-duty (thousands) throughout the world. The 1991 and 1992 figures for the Russian Federation and figures for North Korea are based on the ACDA's rough estimates.
Sources: U.S. Arms Control and Disarmament Agency, *World Military Expenditures and Arms Transfers* (Washington, D.C.: Government Printing Office) and Taik-young Hamm, *Arming the Two Koreas: State, Capital, and Military Power* (New York: Routledge, 1999), p. 87.

Arms transfers dropped precipitously during the transitional period, particularly in 1991 when arms exports and imports reached the lowest level since 1971.[6] As shown in Table 5.3, a pattern similar to Cold War arms transfers among major powers continued in the years of 1987-1988. The Soviet Union transferred greater amounts than the U.S. until 1990; its arms trade fell significantly after 1991. Arms exports from the Soviet Union/Russia and China were reduced by more than 50% between 1988 and 1992, while U.S. exports declined only 12.8% during the same period. China imported ($1,230 million) more than it exported ($897 million) in 1992, and before 1992, about 90% of its arms transfers were exports. Arms transfers of Japan and the two Koreas also decreased. Japan exported $454 million in 1988 and $10 million in 1992, while it imported $956 million in 1988 and $666 million in 1992. Except for the year 1990, South Korea's arms exports and imports amounted to 45% of its 1988 level in 1992. North Korea also reduced its arms transfers, remaining at 5% of its 1988 level in 1992. Up until 1990, the Soviet Union was the leading arms supplier, but the U.S. has retained a unipolar position in terms of arms trade since 1991.

**Table 5.3. Arms Transfers of Major Powers in Northeast Asia: 1987-1992**

| Year | United States | USSR/ Russia | China | Japan | South Korea | North Korea |
|------|------|------|------|------|------|------|
| 1987 | 20,111 | 30,408 | 3,414 | 1,390 | 925 | 1,016 |
| 1988 | 16,617 | 28,444 | 3,945 | 1,410 | 843 | 2,002 |
| 1989 | 17,270 | 23,669 | 3,031 | 2,138 | 669 | 1,143 |
| 1990 | 16,663 | 16,880 | 1,863 | 1,392 | 1,260 | 438 |
| 1991 | 13,394 | 6,960 | 1,782 | 1,277 | 675 | 285 |
| 1992 | 11,898 | 2,358 | 2,127 | 676 | 380 | 102 |

Note: Arms transfers include exports and imports in 1993 constant dollars (millions). The 1991 and 1992 figures represent the Russian Federation.
Sources: U.S. Arms Control and Disarmament Agency, *World Military Expenditures and Arms Transfers* (Washington, D.C.: Government Printing Office).

Relative wealth distribution in a regional economic structure is measured by the purchasing power parity (PPP) values. The PPP values show the number of units of a country's currency required to buy the same quantity of goods and services in the local market as compared to what one U.S. dollar would buy in an average country.[7] The UN International Comparison Project (ICP) estimates the levels of real per capita GDP that each person in a country has earned for the year. Table 5.4 shows the relative levels of economic capabilities of regional powers estimated by per capita PPP values. The U.S. and Japan increased their per capita PPP values and maintained a bipolar economic structure in Northeast Asia. Russia and South Korea were in the medium range; the latter surpassed the former in 1991. North Korea and China were in the lower range, but China increased its values to $2,946 in 1991. In terms of total world trade, the U.S. and Japan shared 13.9% and 8.0% in 1988 and 13.4% and 7.5% in 1992, respectively.[8] Thus, the U.S. and Japan became the dominant powers in the regional economic power equilibrium.

**Table 5.4. Per Capita PPP Values of Major Powers in Northeast Asia:**
**1985-1992**

| Year | United States | USSR/ Russia | China | Japan | South Korea | North Korea |
|---|---|---|---|---|---|---|
| 1985 ~88 | 19,850 | 6,270 | 2,470 | 13,650 | 5,680 | 2,000 |
| 1987 | 17,615 | 6,000 | 2,124 | 13,135 | 4,832 | 2,000 |
| 1989 | 20,998 | 6,270 | 2,656 | 14,311 | 6,117 | 2,172 |
| 1990 | 21,449 | 7,968 | 1,990 | 17,616 | 6,733 | 2,000 |
| 1991 | 22,130 | 6,930 | 2,946 | 19,390 | 8,320 | 1,750 |
| 1992 | 22,470 | -- | -- | 20,400 | 9,500 | 1,500 |

Note: U.S. dollars; current prices and exchange rates. The 1991 figure represents the Russian Federation.
Sources: United Nations Development Program, *Human Development Report* (Oxford: Oxford University Press) and Central Intelligence Agency, *The World Factbook* (Washington, D.C.: Government Printing Office).

Despite the lack of comprehensive aggregate data, the trends of relative distribution in the regional security and economic structures show significant fluctuations during the transitional phase.[9] Militarily, the U.S. became the sole superpower in the early 1990s, and economically, the U.S. and Japan formed a bipolar economic structure. Although these structural changes had precursors (such as Gorbachev's *glasnost* [openness] and *perestroika* [restructuring], the collapse of the Soviet Union, China's open-door policy in the 1980s, and the collapse of the Berlin Wall in 1989), geo-structural factors did not cause South Korea's security policy change. The systemic constraints of regional power politics largely remained Cold War characteristics when the South initiated *nordpolitik* in 1988. In other words, the Cold War balance-of-power mechanism was sustained during the years of 1987-1988. The question is why South Korea changed its international orientation before fluctuations of systemic factors occurred. The relative distribution of military and economic capabilities does not support the view that South Korea's security policy change was the result of shifts in international power politics.

### Geo-Strategic Factors—Security Alliance Mechanisms

The Alliance mechanism or security commitment among two or more states remained consistently bilateral during the transitional period. It was bi-triangular, similar to the alliance formation during the Cold War era. The U.S.-extended deterrence provided to South Korea was implemented through annual security meetings, US-ROK military exercises, and U.S. troop commitment. The fundamental goal of the US-ROK Mutual Defense Treaty of 1953 was the same as during the Cold War: to maintain a regional balance-of-power mechanism and to deter the North's military aggression. The annual US-ROK military and security meetings were continued, and military exercises of the US-ROK Eagle (since 1961), the US-ROK Ulgi Focus (since 1976), and the US-ROK Team Spirit (since 1976), with the exception of the year 1992, were held annually. In addition, South Korea joined the biannual exercise of Rim of the Pacific Asian Countries (RIMPAC) in 1990, exercised among the U.S., Canada, Japan, Australia, and Chile since 1976. South Korea's involvement in the geo-strategic military alliance was extended toward the Asia-Pacific region. The number of U.S. forces in South Korea remained at an average of 43,000, despite the 1990 U.S. East Asian Strategy Initiative (EASI).[10] The Bush administration planned to reduce 25% of its military power in Northeast Asia.[11] But later in the 1995 U.S. EASI, the U.S. promised to retain its forces in South Korea as long as they were needed for deterrence and defense.

The U.S.-extended deterrence, consisting of a three-part strategy of stationing its forces, providing military assistance, and assuring a formal alliance system, started to change in a number of important aspects. Modification of the US-ROK alliance came about due to the changed role of the U.S. forces in South Korea, South Korea's increased financial responsibility for "burden sharing," and denuclearization of the Korean peninsula.[12] In accordance with a decline in the superpowers' global rivalry, the U.S. "was confronted with the need to formulate a new national defense strategy…countering new regional threats" (Tow, 1993b: 70). The goal was to maintain a regional power balance, and the main objective of the U.S. forces in South Korea was changed from containment to deterrence of the North's military aggression. As a means of ensuring regional balance, the U.S. also began to establish limited contacts with North Korea in the late 1980s.[13] The U.S. security commitment became regional and selective in its security engagement, shifted from global commitment.[14] Since the early 1990s, the U.S. emphasis also shifted toward those of economic liberalization and world trade, due to its trade deficits and new security commitment.

Another important issue was "burden sharing." As discussed earlier, the U.S. military aid to South Korea officially ended in 1977, and South Korea was encouraged to improve its defense capabilities during the Cold War. Thus, its Force Modernization and Improvement Plans were continued during the transitional phase. Along with the transition of the U.S. forces from a leading to a supporting role, the Cold War asymmetrical relationship began to change toward a partnership of burden sharing. The U.S. urged South Korea and Japan to strengthen their defense capabilities and to increase financial support for the U.S. forces in their countries.[15] South Korea paid $70 million in 1990 and $150 million in 1991 for support of the U.S. forces in South Korea and other maintenance costs (Ministry of National Defense, *Defense White Paper*, 1992).

Denuclearization of the Korean peninsula was also one of the most significant changes in the US-ROK alliance mechanism. After the diplomatic normalization among South Korea, Russia, and China, the strategic loss of the communist allies led North Korea to recalculate its military and security concerns and to adjust the changing regional balance-of-power system. The geo-structural change also made the two Koreas alter their inter-Korean dialogues and nuclear policies. As noted, subsequent talks between the two Koreas did not bear fruit throughout the Cold War, but a major breakthrough occurred in 1990 with the holding of high-level talks at the prime ministerial level.[16] The two sides accepted each other as legitimate partners in negotiation, and signed the Basic Agreement for Reconciliation, Non-aggression, and Exchanges and Cooperation on December 13, 1991.[17] During these talks, both Koreas agreed to conduct simultaneous nuclear inspections of facilities in the South and the North, including U.S. military bases in South Korea. Both Koreas agreed to a nuclear-free policy and signed a joint declaration on denuclearization of the Korean peninsula on December 31, 1991.[18] However, the promise of the agreement was not fulfilled, and the North's refusal to accept the International Atomic Energy Agency (IAEA) safeguards on all its nuclear facilities and its threatened withdrawal from the Nuclear Non-proliferation Treaty (NPT) caused a new security threat in the early 1990s.[19]

The bilateral US-ROK geo-strategic relations had long been durable, although a shift now occurred in a number of important issues during the transitional phase. The asymmetrical alliance system changed to a partnership of burden sharing, which accelerated the shift in geo-structural power relations and the new strategic concerns of the U.S. in the early 1990s. Prior to these shifts in geo-strategic factors, South Korea implemented *nordpolitik* and a governed interdependence policy, with the goal a peaceful process of unification. Its security policy was adjusted to promote normalization with the communist countries, mutual reconciliation with the North, and relaxation of military postures toward the North. In this respect, however, the changing geo-strategic relations did not support the international rivalry and power politics advocated by neorealists. South Korea's *nordpolitik* occurred before any regional security alliance mechanism such as the KEDO was established and the US-ROK alliance was changed. Its policy change was simultaneously accompanied by the strategic transformations of U.S. interests being shifted toward regional commitment and a partnership of burden sharing in the 1990s.

## Geo-Economic Factors—Trade and Financial Alignment Mechanisms

The transitional phase coincided with the dawning of a new era in Northeast Asia, characterized by growing international trade relations and economic interdependence. In particular, South Korea's trade with China, Russia, and

North Korea increased the importance of geo-economic factors as the primary means of maintaining regional stability and peace. Thus, the Cold War legacy of South Korea's trade relations, followed by its politico-military concerns, became nullified. With the 1986 Asian Games and 1988 Olympic Games, South Korea began its formal and informal contacts with communist countries. The link between trade and security became an obvious alternative for South Korea. Economic and diplomatic normalization aimed to increase trade relations with China and Russia that would in turn create restraints on the North's military aggression against the South. Normalization was also an attempt to have an "informal guarantee" that both China and Russia would not support the North at the expense of their economic ties.

As shown in Table 5.5, trade relations between South Korea and China, the Soviet Union/Russia, and North Korea had grown considerably since the late 1980s. South Korea's trade with China exceeded $6 billion in 1992 and with Russia $1.2 billion in 1991.[20] Including indirect trade, the South started to have commercial links with the North in 1988, and its trade reached $213.5 million in 1992.[21] Meanwhile, North Korea's bilateral trade with Russia began declining in 1990, while China remained as the North's main trading partner, representing about 30% of the North's total trade.[22] Trade with the communist countries was made in order to increase economic contacts so that increased interdependence would facilitate the North's opening its society to the outside world. However, the level of South Korea's economic interactions with the communist countries was less than 10% of its total trade volume.

**Table 5.5. South Korea's Trade with China, the Soviet Union/Russia, and North Korea: 1987-1992**

| Year | China | USSR/Russia | North Korea |
|------|-------|-------------|-------------|
| 1987 | 1,679 | 151 | -- |
| 1988 | 3,087 | 204 | 1.1 |
| 1989 | 3,140 | 599 | 22.3 |
| 1990 | 3,820 | 899 | 25.1 |
| 1991 | 4,442 | 1,202 | 192.2 |
| 1992 | 6,358 | 859 | 213.5 |

Note: Million dollars. Trade with North Korea includes indirect trade through the routes of third countries such as Hong Kong and Japan.
Sources: Hee-hyon Song, *Transport System Development Direction in Northeast Asia: With Particular Reference to Korea, USSR and China* (Seoul: Korea Maritime Institute, 1990), p. 4; Economic Planning Board, *Major Statistics of Korean Economy* (Seoul: EPB); and Korean Trade Promotion Corporation, *Statistical Yearbook* (Seoul: KOTRA).

Diversification and integration of economic relations were more salient in South Korea's trade shares with the U.S., Japan, and other European and Asian states. As shown in Table 5.6, South Korea's trade shares with Asia-Pacific economies significantly rose from 32.6% and 47.8% in 1987 to 44.8% and 50.0% in 1992, in terms of export and import shares, respectively. Trade shares, exports and imports with Europe steadily increased from 16.4% and 13.3% in 1987 to 14.1% and 14.2% in 1992. However, South Korea's export shares with the U.S. fell dramatically from 35.4% in 1988 to 23.8% in 1992, and imports shares also fell from 24.6% in 1988 to 22.5% in 1992. South Korea's trade shares with Japan developed a similar pattern, and its exports and imports decreased from 19.8% and 30.7% in 1988 to 15.2% and 23.9% in 1992. Although the U.S. and Japan remained important trading partners, South Korea's economic trade was diversified and the intensity of intra-regional trade with Asia-Pacific economies increased with the advent of APEC in 1989.[23] The product cycle and the flying geese model have also explained the economic integration of Asian regional states.[24] Compared to the years of the Cold War, South Korea's dependence on the U.S. and Japanese markets was reduced, but trade frictions among them increased in the 1990s.[25]

**Table 5.6. South Korea's Trade Shares with the U.S., Japan, Europe, and Asia: 1987-1992**

| Year | United States Ex-/Import | Japan Ex-/Import | Europe Ex-/Import | Asia Ex-/Import |
|------|--------------------------|------------------|-------------------|-----------------|
| 1987 | 38.7/21.4 | 17.8/33.3 | 16.4/13.3 | 32.6/47.8 |
| 1988 | 35.4/24.6 | 19.8/30.7 | 15.8/13.5 | 36.3/44.2 |
| 1989 | 33.2/25.9 | 21.6/28.4 | 14.0/12.4 | 38.4/42.9 |
| 1990 | 30.0/24.3 | 19.4/26.7 | 16.2/14.0 | 38.0/43.1 |
| 1991 | 26.0/23.3 | 17.2/26.0 | 15.4/14.5 | 41.9/48.8 |
| 1992 | 23.8/22.5 | 15.2/23.9 | 14.1/14.2 | 44.8/50.0 |

Note: Percentages. In figures of trades with Europe and Asia, trade with the former Soviet Union is excluded and trade shares with Asia include Japan.
Sources: Economic Planning Board, *Major Statistics of Korean Economy* (Seoul: EPB) and UN, *International Trade Statistics Yearbook* (New York: The UN Statistical Office).

In the 1990s, South Korea completed its structural transformation to become part of the knowledge-intensive industry, and Cold War asymmetrical economic interactions were reduced. South Korea moved its developmental strategy from reliance on foreign economic aid to one of international trade and foreign direct investment.[26] Foreign direct investment is a system of international financial flows that involves not only a transfer of resources but also the acquisition of control through joint ventures, ownership, and merging. As shown in Table 5.7, public and commercial loans were steadily decreased, while foreign direct investments were increased during the transitional phase. Public and commercial loans in South Korea fell from $2,667 million in 1987 to $636 million in 1992. In terms of ODA loans gross, only Japan provided $993 million during the years 1988-1992.[27] Foreign direct investment in South Korea rose from $626 million in 1987 to $1,174 million in 1991, but decreased to $803 million in 1992. South Korea's overseas investment also increased rapidly from $19.5 million in 1988, to $530 million in 1990, and to $1.3 billion in 1992.[28] Thus, foreign aid as the source of South Korea's economic growth became obsolete during the transitional period.

**Table 5.7. Shifts in Loans and FDI in South Korea: 1987-1992**

| Year | Loans | | Foreign Direct | Total |
|------|-------|--|----------------|-------|
|      | Public | Commercial | Investment | |
| 1987 | 1,109 | 1,558 | 626 | 3,293 |
| 1988 | 891 | 988 | 894 | 2,773 |
| 1989 | 475 | 860 | 812 | 2,147 |
| 1990 | 418 | 30 | 895 | 1,343 |
| 1991 | 429 | -- | 1,174 | 1,603 |
| 1992 | 486 | 150 | 803 | 1,439 |

Note: 1993 constant dollars (millions).
Sources: Ministry of Finance, *Fiscal and Financial Statistics* (Seoul: MOF); Il-Young Jung, *Review on South Korea's Half-century Diplomacy* (Seoul: Nanam, 1993), p. 391; and Bernie Bishop, *Foreign Direct Investment in Korea: The Role of the State* (Brookfield, Vermont: Ashgate, 1997), p. 90.

Economic normalization and trade linkages with the communist countries had become major factors in dissolving Cold War animosity and reducing military tensions in the region. South Korea's *nordpolitik* suggested that its security was not dependent solely upon its military strength, and that the South would de-emphasize military antagonism as a means of resolving problems with the North. South Korea's attempts to increase economic interdependence were not entirely based on politico-military motivations; both politics and economics were equally applied to the communist states. Priority was given to trade interactions and foreign direct investment, as opposed to geo-strategic military alliance and foreign economic aid. Establishing more economic links seems to support the view that states may benefit from international trade and investment.[29] Fluctuations in geo-economic factors produced the new security policy initiative of *nordpolitik*, but in the case of South Korea it was a strategic recalculation of geo-economic gains that made economic and diplomatic normalization possible, rather than economic interdependence *per se*.

## *Geo-Political Factors—Diplomacy and International Institutions*

South Korea's international relations were formatted by competitive diplomacy during the Cold War. But with the 1988 *nordpolitik*, its geo-political strategies were changed to the promotion of mutually beneficial relations with the Soviet Union/Russia, China, North Korea, and other communist countries. *Nordpolitik* was differentiated into northern policy and northern diplomacy. Whereas northern diplomacy "was a move to reach out to the former communist allies of North Korea, in terms of establishing diplomatic ties with them, northern policy was a strategic move to force [facilitate] North Korea to abandon its isolation and to open its system to outside forces" (Kihl, 1995: 127).[30]  Thus, the foremost goal of *nordpolitik* was to preserve peace and security on the Korean peninsula, while the means to reach this goal was northern diplomacy.

Modeled after West German Chancellor Willy Brant's eastern diplomacy, South Korea's northern diplomacy was an attempt to normalize inter-Korean relations via the North's allies of Russia and China. A turning point in relations with the communist states was the 1986 Asian Games and the 1988 Olympic Games held in Seoul. The year after the Olympic Games, 1989, diplomatic relations were established with Hungary, Poland, and the former Yugoslavia.[31]  Seoul also established diplomatic ties with Czechoslovakia, Bulgaria, East Germany, Mongolia, and the former Soviet Union in 1990, followed by ties with China and Vietnam in 1992. This northern diplomacy, in the end, resolved the Cold War issue of international legitimacy, in which both Koreas claimed to be the sole, legitimate government in the Korean peninsula. This resolution came about with the Basic Agreement and with both countries joining the UN simultaneously in 1991.[32]

Consequently, the Cold War competitive diplomacy and international legitimacy, which aimed to gain international recognition of South Korea's political legitimacy, were eliminated. Rather, major diplomatic concerns and inter-Korean relations were the primary factors to be considered in establishing a peaceful coexistence between the two Koreas. To facilitate a peaceful process of unification, a cross-recognition of both North and South Korea by the regional powers of the U.S., China, Japan, and Russia was suggested. It was an extension of "2+2," 2+4," and "2+6" forums, elaborated during the Cold War, which include the two Korea, the U.S., China, Japan, Russia, Canada, and Australia.[33]  However, normalization among North Korea, the

U.S., and Japan was deadlocked due to the North's nuclear ambition. South Korea alone normalized its relations with Russia and China.

After diplomatic normalization, both Russia and China encouraged the North to adopt an open-door policy toward the outside world. Although both countries retained their friendly relations with North Korea, they switched from the Cold War strategy of one Korea, with the support of North Korea, to an equi-distance policy toward the two Koreas. More specifically, Russia and China formed a politico-military relationship with the North and a diplomatic/economic relationship with the South during the transitional phase. All in all, northern diplomacy resolved the issue of political rapprochement with the communist countries and resulted in favoring the South vis-à-vis the North's geo-political alignment; the South achieved diplomatic ties with 166 countries and 18 UN institutional memberships in 1992.[34]

Generally, changes in South Korea's geo-political relations were derived from pragmatic concerns about economic interdependence. Similarly, in the case of geo-economic factors, expansion of diplomatic relations with communist countries was aimed to persuade the North to consider changing its society and opening its market. Strategic concerns of northern diplomacy were also of more importance than politico-military power politics in relations with Russia and China. In this vein, a neoliberal perspective, that is, that increased diplomatic and economic relations are conducive to regional stability and prosperity, seems to support South Korea's new alignment policy. However, northern diplomacy was also a means to implement South Korea's strategic attempts to intensify regional diplomatic and economic interdependence, rather than gain diplomatic normalization *per se*. Variations in geo-political factors were the result of South Korea's new strategic initiative, *nordpolitik*.

### Domestic Institutional Determinants

The above discussions raise an important question. Neorealism, the dominant paradigm in the international relations literature, has not offered a theoretical explanation of South Korea's security policy behaviors. Its security policy change was not the result of variations in the regional balance-of-power mechanism and regional power politics. Critical points, raised during the transitional phase, involve a theoretical failure to predict variations in states' behaviors such as the former Soviet Union, the collapse of the Cold War power structure, and domestic factors such as causal variables.[35] Advocates of domestic institutionalism argue that variations on domestic policy-making institutions do matter in explaining South Korea's security policy dynamics. Observations of South Korea's domestic political factors suggest that security policies are altered when its internal regime changes. This section specifically looks at how domestic institutional determinants affected South Korea's security policy behaviors during the transitional phase.

South Korea's domestic political character had undergone a remarkable transformation in October 1987. The democratic constitution as approved by national referendum laid out the foundation for a free and fair presidential election. Political power was not held exclusively in the executive branch, and the National Assembly became a significant contributor to policy-making and the oversight of the administration. Repressive measures of national security laws were modified or eliminated. Restrictions on the media were also lifted.[36] South Korea experienced political liberalization and democratization, institutionalized by its new constitution. Democratization involves both "political liberalization" and "economic liberalization" (Diamond, 1991; Bermeo, 1992). Political liberalization is related to the ways in which political power is diffused among different branches of government and within bureaucratic agencies, ways in which transition of power is guaranteed constitutionally, and ways in which public participation and access to the government are allowed. In a more strict sense, democratization means power sharing, power transition, and decentralization in the government. Economic liberalization includes a reduced role of the government in the market and internationalization of the domestic market toward the international standard. While shifting to a knowledge-intensive industry, government intervention in the economy was restricted, causing it to "follow," as opposed to "lead," the market.[37] The government played a more active role in intervening in and controlling market mechanisms until the mid-1980s, but high degrees of market conforming became possible in the late 1980s.[38] Figure 5.2 shows South Korea's paths to a type of market democracy during the transitional phase.[39]

**Figure 5.2. South Korea's Paths to the Market Democracy**

|  | Cold War (1954-1987) | Transitional Phase (1988-1992) | |
|---|---|---|---|
| Political Formation | Authoritarian Developmental State | Democratization ⎯⎯⎯⎯⎯⎯⎯⎯→ Political Liberalization | Democratic Government |
| Market Formation | Governed-Market System | Market Conforming ⎯⎯⎯⎯⎯⎯⎯⎯→ Economic Liberalization | Market Economy |

## Types of Government—Democratic Government

During the Noh Tae Woo administration (1988-1992), the transformation in domestic politics took place at all levels of civil-military relations, bureaucratic politics, and legal-institutional settings. Much evidence of democratic consolidation could be found in "the decline of military influence, the rise of pressure politics, and domestic constitutional arrangements and elections" (Kong and Kim, 1997: 4). The changed international context, accelerated by South Korea's rapprochement with Russia and China, no longer provided the political cause or justification for the government's claim of national security. Thus, a national security regime was not an option and the military lost its rationale to be involved in politics. Democratization also coincided with increased pressures for social and economic equality and political participation. Social and economic pressures included business lobbying, consumer demands, student demonstrations, and labor protests for democracy.[40] As a whole, all of the above, in addition to free and fair political transitions, were guaranteed by the new Constitution of 1987.

Generally, modernization theory finds economic growth, the rise of the middle class, and improvements in the quality of life as causes of regime's change to democracy.[41] As socioeconomic quality and the middle class expand, the greater the likelihood of pressure for democratization.[42] The basic tenet of modernization theory is that democratization is the result of socioeconomic development. South Korea's democratization "indicates that the introduction of factories [or economic development] means far more than…increases in personal income. It also means alterations in social and political relations" (Hart, 1993: 403). The result was the constitutional guarantee of the right to participate and the right to compete for public offices.[43] Thus, according to the Freedom House, *Annual Survey of Freedom Country Scores*, South Korea's status of political rights and civil liberties has been maintained at less than 3 since 1987-1988. The 1992-1993 status was 2 in political rights and 3 in civil liberties that are designated free.[44]

Democratization and political liberalization had important positive impacts on security matters, and accelerated the establishment of diplomatic and economic relations with the communist countries and mutual reconciliation with North Korea. President Noh Tae Woo enunciated *nordpolitik* just two weeks before the 1988 Olympiad convened in Seoul. South Korea was no longer an "anticommunist dictatorship," and mutual antagonistic policies between South Korea and the former communist countries were not a predetermined outcome. The Noh administration found that rigid anti-communism was no longer suited for the relaxation of the military tensions in the Korean peninsula. Changes away from the ideological commitment to anti-communism allowed the emergence of new policy initiatives such as *nordpolitik*, derived from a democratized legal-institutional setting and decentralized security policy-making machinery. The new democratic government also "strengthened South Korea's alliance with the U.S and Japan...[and] had shown that rapid economic development could go hand-in-hand with political reform, and it also promoted expanded dialogue with the North" (Kihl, 1995: 126).

As a whole, the Cold War goals of political legitimacy, economic development, and deterrence were shifted to those of democratic consolidation, economic liberalization, and promotion of regional interdependence for the peaceful process of unification. South Korea's new international orientation occurred prior to the end of the Cold War. The Noh administration's new initiative of *nordpolitik* was the primary security program used to reach its goals during the transitional phase. This security policy redirection occurred when South Korea underwent dramatic transformations within its political system. With democratization, regime security associated with military governments was abolished as a main security concern. As domestic institutionalists argue, South Korea's security policy change was caused by variations in its domestic political regime.

### *Legal-Institutional Setting—Legal Enactment and Party Holdings*

Political liberalization was accompanied by the lifting of security measures and the elimination of the Cold War state apparatuses. Deregulation and power sharing were the major goals of South Korea's political reform toward market democracy. Elimination of the Cold War legal-institutional setting was needed to solidify a democratic institutional structure of government. Thus, the fundamental legal apparatuses of the National Security Law, the Martial Law, and the Anti-Communist Law were modified or eliminated in 1988. Freedom of association and expression "were institutionally ensured with the abolition of the Law concerning Collective Protest and the Basic Press Law, which had served as legal instruments for controlling popular protests and the mass media, [and] other malignant legal statutes such as the Labor Law and the Social Purification Law were either amended or removed" (Moon, 1999: 8). Oppressive measures such as extraordinary laws and presidential decrees also became obsolete. Moreover, the traditional relationship between legislative and executive branches no longer had the pattern of weakening the legislative authority and strengthening executive power. The ruling party could not always control the legislature, as it did during the Cold War, and the legislature was considered as an agency independent of the executive. Rather, the transition from a military-authoritarian to a democratic government took place by the combined actions of the ruling and opposition parties.

The most rudimentary reforms were institutionalized in the new Constitution. The ninth constitutional revision of October 1987 was a dramatic departure from previous patterns in its process and meaning. The revision was achieved through government and opposition collaboration in an unrestricted atmosphere and approved in a referendum as provided in the existing Constitution. Pivotal to the new Constitution was a single-term presidency for five years, elimination of the president's rights to dissolve the National Assembly, congressional endorsement of the president's Supreme Court nominees, powers given to the National Assembly to investigate the government, a statement of the military's political neutrality, guarantees of press freedom, and the rights of *habeas corpus*.[45] As a result, the new Constitution strengthened the power of the legislature and further protected individual rights. The Constitution, which had served as an instrument to perpetuate the authoritarian government's rule during the Cold War era, now gained political legitimacy that earlier versions did not have. Thus, the legal basis for politicization of national security and the military was abolished.

Other major departures from South Korean politics were the political party system and party politics. During the Cold War, there were always a dominant ruling party and a number of weak opposition parties. However, the April 26, 1988 election ushered in a new party structure. The ruling party failed to win a parliamentary majority for the first time in South Korea's legislative history since the Korean War. The ruling Democratic Justice Party (DJP) won 125 seats (41.8%) out of 299 seats, compared with 70 seats (23.4%) for the Party for Peace and Democracy (PPD), 59 seats (19.7%) for the Reunification Democratic Party (RDP), and 32 seats (10.7%) for the New Democratic Republican Party (NDRP). Other small parties had the remaining 13 seats (4.4%).[46] After the election, the Noh government proved ineffective in the face of the National Assembly that was now dominated by the opposition parties. The new government was not free from legal and institutional restrictions and had no monolithic power for security policy-making.[47]

Under the authoritarian regimes, the Constitution, security laws, and the ruling parties were the principal institutional pillars of their political control. When the ruling government "was not willing to respect the law, law became no more than a means to justify its will. As democratic politics developed, the Constitution emerged as a basic rule for power competition, within the guidelines of the law" (Yoon, 1994: 185). Thus, with the new legal-institutional setting, the ruling parties could not enact national security laws in favor of their regime security. Rather, South Korea's wholesale redirection occurred when there were dramatic transformations in domestic institutional arrangements. An important point is that South Korea's international orientation change took place before the systemic shifts in the Northeast Asian international system, but after institutional transformations in the legal-institutional setting occurred in the years of 1987-1988.

*Policy-Making Machinery—Bureaucracies and Administrative Elites*

The Cold War policy-making machinery was dominated by the military as "an institution" which took over the state. The security policy-making system was considered to be the prerogative of the military elites. The presence of external threats and the lack of internal regime security enhanced the institutional and strategic position of the military and made military intervention in politics possible. The president's Secretary Service, the National Security Council, and the Agency for National Security Planning (ANSP, formerly the KCIA) were the top political organs of security policy-making. However, after the democratization of 1987, primary policy-making institutions were expanded to include agencies and departments in the Ministry of Foreign Affairs, the Ministry of National Defense, the National Unification Board, the Economic Planning Board, and the National Assembly. Decentralization occurred by delegating decision-making power to lower levels of the administrative apparatuses. Despite the fact that the president's Secretariat, the National Security Council, and the ANSP were still the main decision-making organs on security matters, the repressive capacity of these agencies was significantly reduced. Thus, the decentralization of bureaucratic agencies coincided with the curtailment of the power of intelligence and security agencies.[48]

Another important change during the transitional phase was the withdrawal of the military from politics. Three causes of the military's withdrawal from power include "internal pressures, international pressures, and pressures within the military" (Sundhaussen, 1984). In the South Korean case, the major reasons for the military to withdraw from political power stemmed from internal pressures and changes in the social system such as student demonstrations, political demands, the rise of the middle class, and economic growth. While the authoritarian government and the military had retained power and restricted political participation, the new democratic government retained power by the ex-military elites and expanded political participation.[49] Without social pressures "mediated by the opposition parties and often led by student radicals, political reform would probably have been postponed, or been slow in implementation, or even sabotaged by military and reactionary movements" (Bedeski, 1993: 69). In retrospect, Noh's presidency was important in ensuring the democratic settlement during the transitional phase. Since President Noh was an ex-military general, it "gave the military time to adjust to being on the political sidelines, and it gave political elites time to develop confidence that democratic elections would not empower people who would threaten their interests fundamentally" (Burton and Ryu, 1997: 13).

Political reform in the policy-making machinery was accompanied by changes in the political elite structure. The percentage of administrative elites coming from a military background significantly decreased from 24.5% in the authoritarian regime to 12.7% in the Noh administration. The percentage of academicians was 9.5%, bureaucrats 69.8%, politicians 1.6%, journalists 1.5%, lawyers 2.7%, business 1.6%, and others 0.6% (Yang, 1994: 531). The percentage of retired military officers positioned in government and public enterprises also fell significantly compared to those of the Cold War era. Cabinet ministers with military backgrounds constituted 118 (37.8%) out of 312 during the Park regime and 37 (24.5%) out of 151 during the Chun regime. During the Cold War, the average percentage of military retirees in cabinet ministries was 33.3%; this number was reduced to 14% in the Noh administration (Woo-Cumings, 1995: 155). Civilians and bureaucrats gained higher representation in the government through competitive civil service examinations and merit.[50]

The Cold War monopolistic decision-making structure was decentralized and the military withdrew from politics during the transitional phase. Political reforms created diverse communication channels and information sharing by different bureaucratic agencies. New initiatives were raised and discussed along with new security concerns. Security policy issues dealt more with normalization with the communist countries and promotion of inter-Korean dialogues than with military antagonism and regime security. Consequently, domestic institutionalists' perspectives on the pluralistic administration and decentralization support South Korea's reform in the policy-making machinery. It is also important to note that South Korea's security policy changed due to the withdrawal of the military from politics. In short, the argument that South Korea's security policy change occurred as the result of alterations in power sharing in the government is valid.

*National Capabilities—GNP and Military Expenditures*

As geo-structural and geo-economic factors determined the different political and economic systems of the two Koreas, structural differences between the economic systems of communist North Korea and capitalist South Korea led to different policies of modernization.[51] During the Cold War, with external threats and a backward economy, authoritarian governments established developmental states and a developmentalist ideology couched in terms of growth and security. However, after democratization, the twin pillars of economic growth and national security, which had often been used to provide political legitimacy for the authoritarian regimes, lost their validity. Democratization also affected the economy, both internally and externally. As mentioned, economic liberalization led to advancement in South Korea's physical quality of life, including wages and labor demands.[52]  Government intervention was minimal, and market principles were applied to negotiate labor disputes.  In addition, gradual economic liberalization occurred in the banking and financial sectors, foreign trade, and foreign investment regimes. Economic liberalization was also adopted to meet the international standards set by Asian Pacific Economic Cooperation (APEC), the International Monetary Fund, the World Bank and the General Agreement on Tariffs and Trade (GATT), which later became the World Trade Organization (WTO) in 1995.  As previously indicated, economic liberalization was also necessary to open trade with the communist countries.

South Korea's economic development in the past two decades was in transition and changed the nation from a state of underdevelopment to a newly industrializing country (NIC).  During the Noh administration, however, South Korea progressed from a developing state to an upper-middle-income country.[53]  Data in Table 5.8 show that the GNP of South Korea more than doubled from $133.4 billion in 1987, ranked as the nineteenth highest, to $305.7 billion in 1992, ranked as the fifteenth highest GNP in the world.  The per capita GNP also more than doubled from $3,218 in 1987 to $7,007 in 1992. North Korea experienced negative growth, and its per capita GNP fell to $920 in 1992, from $1,188 in 1987.  The average growth rates of the South's GNP and per capita GNP were 8.4% and 8.8% while the annual growth rates of the North's were minus 2.0% since 1990.[54]  Compared to North Korea, South Korea's lead in 1992 was 14.9:1 in GNP and 7.6:1 in per capita GNP, increasing from 5.5:1 and 2.7:1 in 1987, respectively.

**Table 5.8. GNP Comparison between the Two Koreas: 1987-1992**

| Year | South Korea | | North Korea | |
|------|------|-----------------|------|-----------------|
|      | GNP | Per Capita GNP | GNP | Per Capita GNP |
| 1987 | 133.4 | 3,218 | 24.1 | 1,188 |
| 1988 | 179.8 | 4,295 | 25.3 | 1,224 |
| 1989 | 220.4 | 5,210 | 25.8 | 1,227 |
| 1990 | 251.8 | 5,883 | 24.1 | 1,124 |
| 1991 | 292.0 | 6,757 | 22.4 | 1,029 |
| 1992 | 305.7 | 7,007 | 20.4 | 920 |

Note: Billions of dollars for GNP and dollars for per capita GNP.
Sources: Economic Planning Board, *Economic Trends* (Seoul: EPB) and Taik-young Hamm, *Arming the Two Koreas: State, Capital, and Military Power* (New York: Routledge, 1999), p. 131.

In terms of GDP distribution, on average, the agricultural sector accounted for 8.9%, the industrial sector 42.4%, and the service sector 48.7% during the transitional phase.[55] The agricultural sector's contribution to GDP was 6.9% in 1992. As a percentage of the total GDP, the manufacturing sector's contribution within the industrial sector decreased from 32.5% in 1988 to 28.2% in 1992. South Korea's manufacturing sector had undergone significant structural changes. In total manufactured exports, the share of more sophisticated items such as electrical machinery and domestic electrical equipment increased from 1.4% in 1980 to 13.6% in 1992, and similarly, the share of transport equipment such as motor vehicles and ships increased from 1.6% in 1980 to 10.3% in 1992. The restructuring of the manufacturing sector resulted in the rise of capital-intensive exports from 55.5% in 1986-1988 to about 70% in 1992.[56] After the mid-1980s, South Korea shifted its economy toward the knowledge, capital-intensive industry. As mentioned earlier, structural reforms were accompanied by the regional economic integration and regional product cycle, followed by China and ASEAN countries in the 1990s. Factors that motivated regional economic integration were economies in scale, trends of intensified international trade, and international demands for economic liberalization.

South Korea spent $9.3 billion in 1988 and $11.6 billion in 1992, while North Korea spent $6.9 billion in 1988 and $5.6 billion in 1992 in their military expenditures.[57] Compared to the North, the South's lead in military spending was 1.3:1 in 1988 and 2.1:1 in 1992. During the transitional phase, Pyongyang had 1.7:1 advantage over Seoul in the number of army artilleries, naval vessels, and combat aircraft. This rate showed the reduction of the North's advantage from 2:1. Due to the continued Force Modernization and Improvement Plans and increased research and development, the South started to manufacture submarines and jet fighters in the early 1990s. South Korean government expenditures on military research and development were $170 million in 1989 and $330 million in 1992.[58] Moreover, South Korea's government expenditures on defense decreased from 26.6% in 1985 to 23.1% in 1989 and to 19.3% in 1992 (Kim and Mo, 1999: 78). During the Cold War, the two Koreas had a heavy defense burden. However, South Korea's total defense burden, i.e., the sum of defense budget spending and military aid over GNP, was decreased since the Korean War. South Korea's burden was 5.1% in 1985, 4.2% in 1989, and 3.9% in 1992, while that of North Korea increased from 10.7-15.1% in 1985 to 15.4-17.9% in 1992 (Hamm, 1999: 129-134). Overall, the South's military capability significantly increased compared to that of the North. Antagonistic postures that generated the arms race in the Korean peninsula were no longer an option, but a mutual reconciliation policy under the *nordpolitik* framework was needed.

During the transitional phase, South Korea's increased economic capability also provided the essential underpinnings of its military capability. Statistical data show that the South had transformed its economic and military capabilities "from a dependent client power to the U.S. and Japan to a semi-independent power" (Hamm, 1999: 163). Ascent in economic terms made the South open and intensify its trade relations with the communist states. That, in turn, led to a new international orientation toward Russia, China, and North Korea via northern policy and northern diplomacy. However, the increased military capability of the South and the North's loss of its strategic allies had a negative impact, namely, the North's nuclear ambition. Nuclear weapons became a compensation for the North's relative strategic disadvantage that had occurred during the transitional phase.[59] Thus, South Korea declared a nuclear-free Korean peninsula and favored a mutual reconciliation approach toward North Korea. In summary, although the South's increased economic and military capabilities as well as its the relative advantage over the North's technological capabilities made *nordpolitik* possible, a new security threat of nuclear proliferation emerged.

**Critical Factors of Security Policy Change in the Transitional Phase**

This chapter examined the relative explanatory power of international systemic and domestic institutional factors within the context of the transitional phase (1988-1992). Interestingly, international systemic determinants did not provide an adequate explanation. Theoretical limitations of neorealism and neoliberalism were evident in attempts to explain security policy change without examining political realignments in domestic politics. Domestic institutional determinants were the principal sources of South Korea's security policy dynamics during the early years of the transitional phase, 1987-1988. South Korea's *nordpolitik*, initiated in 1988, resulted from democratization, elimination of the Cold War legal-institutional setting, and withdrawal of the military from politics that occurred before changes in international systemic factors. However, South Korea's policy dynamics were accompanied and accelerated by structural transformations in the Northeast Asian system, which occurred in the early 1990s. Actual implementation of *nordpolitik* in Northeast Asia took place following diplomatic normalization with the Soviet Union in 1990, the Basic Agreement with North Korea in 1991, and diplomatic normalization with China in 1992. The new international orientations of *nordpolitik* and governed interdependence policy were formulated by domestic institutional rearrangements, but were enhanced by international systemic fluctuations in its implementation stage.

Conditional factors have more to do with domestic political situations in the years of 1987-1988 than international systemic constraints of the bi-triangular system in Northeast Asia. As previously discussed, social and economic pressures for democracy brought out Noh's June 29, 1987 declaration for democratic reform. With political liberalization and democratization, free and fair political transitions were guaranteed by the new Constitution of 1987. The Cold War legal-controlling apparatuses of National Security Law and Anti-Communist Law were modified and eliminated. The 1988 election resulted in no majority holding by the ruling party in the National Assembly, and three different political parties merged to share power in 1990. The military withdrawal from politics and decentralization made democratic transition possible by retaining political power by ex-military elites and expanding political participation. In addition to that, the South's increased national capabilities compared to the North made the Cold War policy of mutual antagonism against North Korea obsolete. These domestic institutional constraints determined South Korea's new policy orientation of governed interdependence policy.

International systemic factors were relatively stable in the late 1980s. The balance-of-power mechanism in geo-structural power equilibrium remained the same as that in the Cold War era. Although modified in the early 1990s, the US-ROK alliance had been durable in the years of 1987-1988. For South Korea, the link between trade and security became an alternative for developing regional stability and prosperity. Trade shares with China, the Soviet Union/Russia, and North Korea increased since the mid-1980s. Although economic interactions occurred before *nordpolitik*, priority was given to strategic calculations of geo-economic benefits, rather than economic interdependence *per se*. In other words, South Korea's new international orientation did not result from increased shares of economic interactions, but from a realistic calculation of abolishing its Cold War ideological rivalry against communist countries. Geo-political factors played a similar role, since diplomatic normalization with the former communist countries would provide geo-political benefits; namely, shifts in the diplomatic alignment mechanism favorable to South Korea. Nevertheless, systemic transformations that took place in the early 1990s enhanced South Korea's new international orientation toward the former communist countries. Systemic transformations include the collapse of the Soviet Union, subsequent demise of the Cold War, and intensified regional economic interdependence with the advent of APEC. After normalization, economic interactions with Russia and China increased, and both countries declared that they would not support the North's stance on reunification of the two Koreas.

Overall, South Korea's security policy change occurred on four interrelated levels during the transitional phase: domestic political transition, economic liberalization and interdependence, structural transformation of the international context, and inter-Korean relations (Kong and Kim, 1997: 3). As shown in Figure 5.3, variations in domestic institutional factors changed South Korea's international orientation from a defensive deterrence to a governed interdependence policy.    Types of government, legal-institutional setting, policy-making machinery, and national capabilities were determining factors in its security policy goal/problem, program, and adjustment changes.  The Cold War security goals changed to promotion of regional interdependence, democratic consolidation, and economic liberalization for the peaceful process of unification, while deterrence postures against North Korea remained intact with modified U.S.-extended deterrence.   South Korea changed its security programs to those of northern policy, northern diplomacy, burden sharing and modified extended deterrence, as well as economic and diplomatic interdependence, nuclear-free policy, and mutual reconciliation with North Korea.  Its security policy was also adjusted by the mutual recognition of the two Koreas and their admission to the UN, extending alignment with the communist countries and accepting the North as a legitimate partner in negotiation.

**Figure 5.3. South Korea's Security Policy Change during the Transitional Phase**

| Security Policy During the Cold War | Security Policy During the Transitional Phase |
|---|---|
| *International Orientation Change* | |
| Defensive Deterrence ⟶ | Governed Interdependence |
| *Security Goal/Problem Change* | |
| Deterrence | Promotion of Interdependence/ Deterrence for Unification |
| Political/International Legitimacy | Democratic Consolidation |
| Economic Development | Economic Liberalization/ Regional Economic Interdependence |
| *Security Program Change* | |
| Mutual Antagonism | Northern Policy |
| Competitive Diplomacy | Northern Diplomacy |
| Extended Deterrence | Modified Extended Deterrence/ Burden Sharing |
| Economic Alignment | Economic/Diplomatic Interdependence |
| Military Modernization | Nuclear-Free Korean Peninsula/ Mutual Reconciliation |
| *Security Adjustment Change* | |
| International Diplomacy | Cross-Recognition/UN Admission |
| Alignment with Friendly Nations | Alignment with the Communist Countries |
| *De Facto* Recognition | Legitimate Partner in Negotiation |

South Korea's security policy change in the years 1987-1988 raises a number of important theoretical and analytical implications. First, theoretical neglect of domestic institutional factors left South Korea's security policy behaviors unexplained. Second, its new international orientation was not the result of variations in the regional balance-of-power mechanism and regional power politics. Third, variations in South Korea's economic interactions and trade relations resulted from its wholesale recalculation of geo-economic and geo-political interests. Fourth, as South Korea's economic and military capabilities increased, its security policy shifted to concerns for economic interdependence, rather than for the politico-military balance-of-power system. Fifth, domestic institutional factors matter in determining South Korea's new security policy orientation. In short, this chapter suggests that domestic institutional factors should be included in a security policy analysis for a better understanding of South Korea's security policy change.

The theoretical failure of international structuralism becomes more salient when the relationship between fluctuations of evaluative criteria and South Korea's security policy change is examined. Evaluative criteria of international systemic factors, the relative distribution of power, US-ROK alliance system, and formal diplomatic and trade relations do not show significant fluctuations in the years 1987-1988. Trade relations with the Soviet Union, China, and North Korea in the mid-1980s were informal and indirect through the route of Hong Kong and Japan. Increased economic interactions resulted from strategic recalculation of South Korea's geo-economic and geo-political benefits. On the contrary, changes in its political type, power sharing in the government and the National Assembly, and increased national capabilities determined South Korea's new security orientation of *nordpolitik*. Thus, the premise of domestic institutionalism remains strong pertaining to South Korea in the years 1987-1988.

In the later years of the transitional phase, domestic factors were not solely responsible for South Korea's security policy dynamics. Transformations in geo-structural, geo-strategic, geo-economic, and geo-political factors in the early 1990s contributed to diplomatic and economic normalization and promoted further economic interdependence among regional powers. Although the balance-of-power mechanism became a less important security concern, the symmetrical alliance and alignment mechanism through diplomatic ties and increased economic interactions was maintained in the Northeast Asian international system. It was the South's increased national capabilities that made economic and political rapprochement with Russia and China possible. Only North Korea was excluded from the new international geo-economic and geo-political links, due to its nuclear ambition. South Korea's new international orientation, implemented following its realistic calculation of strategic and economic interests, was derived from fluctuations in Northeast Asian systemic factors, that is, the systemic transformation from a bi-triangular to a multiple bilateral system. During the early 1990s, the dynamics of economic and security concerns were inextricably linked to South Korea's governed interdependence policy.

As shown in Figure 5.4, a comparative analysis of evaluative criteria indicates that domestic institutional determinants were intervening variables in the years of 1987-1988, and that international systemic factors were intervening variables in the early 1990s. In this vein, both neoclassical realism and neoclassical liberalism offer a better explanation of South Korea's security policy change, despite the fact that variations in domestic institutional factors occurred before those in international systemic factors. Thus, Chung-in Moon and Seok-soo Lee maintain that,

> two recent events...have precipitated the alteration of traditional conception of security: democratic transition and consolidation since 1987 and the dissolution of the bipolar Cold War system which subsequently changed the regional security environment [as well as] South Korea's international security orientation]. (1995: 99)

**Figure 5.4. Causal Determinants of South Korea's Security Policy Change during the Transitional Phase**

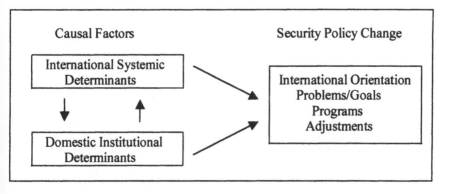

Overall, variations in both international systemic and domestic institutional factors played significant roles in South Korea's security policy change. During the transitional phase, democratic consolidation and increased economic interdependence appeared to be solutions. Internationally, shifts from a foreign aid maximization strategy to a regional economic interdependence policy increased South Korea's institutional ability to normalize diplomatic and economic relations with the former communist countries. However, despite *nordpolitik*, problems with security were not abated due to the continued military postures of North Korea. Rather, *nordpolitik* and the governed interdependence policy led the North to acquire nuclear capabilities. Internally, withdrawal of the military from political power increased its infrastructural capacity, which in turn lessened the internal insecurity dilemma. Decentralized institutional arrangements enhanced legitimacy and accountability for the new democratic government. Alterations of institutional arrangements in the legal-institutional setting and policy-making machinery also increased its institutional capacity to adopt both a responsive and a proactive security policy. In summary, democratization enabled South Korea to make changes in the international context and to enlarge the scope of its security concerns in international politics.

## Notes

[1] This declaration is known as *nordpolitik*. It was further differentiated into northern diplomacy, which aimed for normalization with the communist countries, and northern policy, which attempted to bring North Korea into the world economy. See Kim H. (1993), pp. 256-163; Park (1993), pp. 218-223; and Kihl (1995), pp. 127-128.

[2] During this transitional period, speculations mounted regarding the next stage of and in which direction the Northeast Asian system was heading. The possibility of a war or regional warfare was the most serious concern due to the uncertainty and the breakdown of the balance-of-power system. No theory or model was entirely adequate to explain what was going on in Northeast Asia. But, as Hedley Bull (1977) implied, "the absence of war" became a normal condition, rather than "the universal or permanent peace."

[3] The ideological strife between Moscow and Beijing ended with the restoration of party-to-party ties during the May 1989 Deng-Gorbachev summit. In the late 1980s, negotiations between the U.S. and the Russian federation for arms reduction were held and economic aid was given in order to support the transition of the latter to the market economy. Despite territorial disputes, Gorbachev's visit to Japan in 1990 further strengthened economic and diplomatic ties. See Menon (1997) and Spanier and Hook (1998).

[4] The Baltic states and the Republics of Kazakhstan, Uzbekistan, Belarus, Ukraine, and others became independent by December 1991. To stop the complete disintegration of the Union, these republics joined the CIS and assumed the former Soviet Union's international obligations.

[5] North Korea had 55 soldiers per thousand people in 1990. See U.S. Arms Control and Disarmament Agency, *World Military Expenditures and Arms Transfers* (Washington, D.C.: Government Printing Office, 1991).

[6] This estimation was based on 1991 constant dollars. See *ibid*, p. 8.

[7] The measures of GDP or GNP seldom reflect the relative power of a country's currency compared to others. The per capita PPP values state that currencies with high rates of inflation should devalue relative to currencies with lower rates of inflation. For example, if inflation is 5% in the U.S. and 1% in Japan, the dollar value of the Japanese yen must rise by 4% in order to equalize the dollar price of goods in the two countries. See Officer (1982), Manzur (1993), Moosa and Bhatti (1997), and Allen (1998).

[8] See International Monetary Fund, *Direction of Trade Statistics Yearbook* (Washington, D.C.: IMF).

[9] As noted in Chapter IV, published statistics on an individual country's aggregate data are notoriously unreliable. Nevertheless, the overall trends in the relative levels of distributions show a polarity in military and economic terms.

[10] The U.S. forces in South Korea were 46,000 in 1988, 44,461 in 1989, and 40,062 in the years from 1990 to 1992. See Oh, Cha, and Hwang (1990), p. 56 and U.S. Department of Commerce, *The Statistical Abstract of the United States* (Washington, D.C.: Government Printing Office).

[11] The critical policy statement setting the context for U.S. force reduction strategy is "President George Bush's Speech to the Aspen Institute Symposium," April 2, 1990, reprinted as Appendix E in *Report of the Secretary of Defense to the President and the Congress* (Washington, D.C.: Government Printing Office, 1991), pp. 131-134. See also Kim (1995), pp. 28-31.

[12] Burden sharing was imperative in order to make greater financial contributions to international and regional security for South Korea and Japan. The Gulf War was the clearest example of burden sharing. See Tow (1993), Akaha (1996), and McDougall (1997).

[13] In late 1988, the Reagan administration redefined its long standing policy toward North Korea with three different approaches: (1) permitting humanitarian trade, (2) initiating limited contacts diplomatically, and (3) liberalizing visa policies for American and North Korean citizens. See Oberdorfer (1988), p. A-28 and Tow (1993), p. 70.

[14] For the changed role of the U.S. in the global affairs, see Levin (1993), Olsen (1996), and Spanier and Hook (1998).

[15] Some critics cautioned against Japanese military buildup, for its economic power could be converted to military power. However, the Japanese government announced that it would not seek to attain the status of a military giant. Rather, it attempted to strengthen the US-Japan extended deterrence and its bilateral relations with other regional states. See Bean (1990), Morimoto (1993), and Akaha (1996).

[16] For details, see Kihl (1990).

[17] This was known as the Basic Agreement of 1991. For further discussions, see Lim (1991), pp. 213-223 and Jeong (1992), pp. 5-21.

[18] President Noh in November 8, 1991 announced that "there do not exist any nuclear weapons whatsoever, anywhere in the Republic of Korea." President Noh's Declaration of Non-nuclear Korean Peninsula Peace Initiatives was reprinted by University Press of America (1992).

[19] The result was the 1994 Korean Peninsula Energy Development Organization (KEDO), which reaffirmed the North's NPT membership. Further details will be discussed in Chapter VI.

[20] South Korea's trade with China was $1,290 million in 1985 and $1,289 million in 1986, and its trade with the Soviet Union was $102 million in 1985 and $133 million in 1986. From 1985 to 1992, the trade deficit with China was $4,105 million and with Russia $744 million. To increase trade relations, South Korea strategically imported more from China and Russia than it exported. However, trade relations during the mid-1980s were largely indirect with Japan and Hong Kong. See Economic Planning Board, *Major Statistics of Korean Economy* (Seoul: EPB).

[21] From 1988 to 1992, South Korea's trade deficit with North Korea was $366 million. See *ibid.*

[22] North Korea's trade with Russia immediately dropped from $2.7 billion in 1990 to $367 million in 1991, and the DPRK-PRC bilateral trade was $556 million in 1991. See National Unification Board, *Economic Comparison between North and South* (Seoul: NUB).

[23] The intensity of trade indices, that is, a group's share of intra-regional trade divided by that region's share of worldwide trade, was increased from 1.31 in 1985 to 1.41 in 1992 in the case of Japan, from 1.17 to 1.74 in the Asian NICs, and from 2.37 to 4.44 in the ASEAN countries. See Islam and Chowdhury (1997), pp. 13-17.

[24] For example, the light low-wage industries produced the primary exporting goods for the Asian NICs during the 1970s and 1980s, but in the 1990s, China and the ASEAN countries followed the NICs. Similar cases can be found in the heavy and high-tech industries. See Chow and Kellman (1993) and Kennedy (1993), p. 197.

[25] South Korea in the 1980s had a trade surplus with the U.S., but a trade deficit with Japan. Its trade deficit with Japan reached $7,857million in 1992 and trade surplus with the U.S. was $269 million in 1993. South Korea had a trade deficit with the U. S. in the years 1990-1992. See UN, *International Trade Statistics Yearbook* (New York: The UN Statistical Office).

[26] Since 1981, South Korea provided loans and grants to the less developed countries; e.g., $20.9 million in 1981 and $98.5 million in 1989. Its rate of official development aid (ODA) to GNP was 0.05%, compared to 0.33% of the Development Assistance Countries (DAC). This economic assistance was provided through the Economic Development Cooperation Fund (EDCF) and the Korea International Cooperation Agency (KOICA). See Seo (1992), pp. 533-534 and Jung (1993), pp. 397-399.

[27] During the same period, the U.S. provided $15 million to South Korea. See OECD, *Geographical Distribution of Financial Flows to Developing Countries* (Paris: OECD).

[28] Most South Korea FDI went to North America and Southeast Asia. See Ministry of Finance, *Trends in Foreign Direct Investment* (Seoul: MOF).

[29] Historical evidence suggests that the logic of economic interdependence is flawed because interdependence can cause conflicts and trade frictions. Economic interdependence, "at much higher levels in Europe a century ago in Pacific Asia today, did not stop European powers from going to war in 1914. High levels of economic interdependence between the U.S. and Japan in the 1930s actually contributed to the outbreak of war because the U.S. controlled vital Japanese fuel supplies" (Segal, 1997: 240).

[30] For this differentiation, see also Park (1993), pp. 218-244.

[31] President Noh's visit to Hungary was the first official visit to a communist country by a South Korean president. This diplomatic normalization opened up a new horizon for South Korea's geo-political diplomacy. See Park (1993), Sanford (1993), and Middleton (1997).

[32] The Basic Agreement and joint membership of the UN were made possible by calling for mutual inspection of military sites and Pyongyang's agreement to halt production of nuclear weapons in exchange for cancellation of the annual US-ROK Team Spirit military exercise and U.S. withdrawal of all nuclear weapons from the South. See Lim (1991), Jeong (1992), and Institute of International Affairs, *Korean Defense Yearbook* (Seoul: IIA, 1994).

[33] For regional geo-political alignment forums, see Baker (1992), Cronin (1992), and Lim (1993).

[34] South Korea became formally aligned with 136 countries in 1989 and 155 in 1991; it joined 18 UN organizations and 36 intergovernmental institutions in 1992. North Korea's diplomatic allies numbered 124 countries and it joined 13 UN organizations and 10 intergovernmental institutions in 1992. See Seo (1992), pp. 550-617 and Ministry of Foreign Affairs, *Diplomacy White Paper* (Seoul: MFA).

[35] For these critical points, see Gaddis (1992/3), Lebow and Risse-Kappen (1995), Moravcsik (1997), Rose (1998) and Wholforth (1998).

[36] The press freedom was granted by the 1987 democratic reform package. See Kim J. (1993), pp. 47-49.

[37] Amsden (1989) and Wade (1991) portray South Korea's economic policy as a "getting-the-price-wrong" strategy, and refer to its system as a governed-market system. But liberalization began in the late 1980s.

[38] The government could not handle the economy because the size of the economy was too big to control effectively. International liberalization trends and democratization also made the government lift restrictions on the market. See Scalapino (1992), Kim J. (1993), Hahm and Plein (1997), Kim and Mo (1999), and Mo (1999).

[39] Most scholars agree that democracy can grow in the Confucian soil if what is meant by democracy is the selection of leaders through free and fair elections. However, it seems that the outcome of South Korea's modernization would not correspond to "liberal democracy," as

Fukuyama (1992, 1994) proposed it as the end of history. Lee (1992), Thurow (1992), Chee (1993), and Helgesen and Xing (1996) maintain that Fukuyama's Western liberalism, which places a higher level on human rationality and freedom as the universal way of human values, may not be applicable to the Confucian notion of communitarian or collective individualism. This is so because the highest good of the individual exists in the devotion of life toward a better society rather than toward self-actualization. These scholars argue that the East Asian type of democracy corresponds to "communitarian democracy." However, no agreement has been made on its detailed meanings. Thus, it is safe to say that a market democracy emerged from an authoritarian developmental state in South Korea.

[40] Student demonstrations occurred all over the country, especially during the mid-1980s. Students demanded the elimination of authoritarian rule as well as direct popular vote, freedom of the press, and social justice. Pro-democratic pressures resulted in the June 1987 declaration of democratic reform by the president of the Democratic Justice Party, Noh Tae Woo. Workers immediately "took advantages of political liberalization to press their demands. Among the 3,617 labor disputes in 1987, approximately 3,500 of them broke out after the Noh's announcement of direct popular vote for the presidency on June 29, 1987. The number of labor unions doubled from just 4,000 in 1987 to nearly 8,000 in 1990, while union membership nearly tripled from 775,000 in 1985 to 2.1 million in 1991" (Kim J., 1993: 50-51).

[41] According to the UNDP, *Human Development Report*, South Korea's physical quality of life increased. For example, its life expectancy was 54 in 1960 but increased to 73 in 1992; the adult literacy rate increased from 86 in 1985 to 97 in 1992; its under five mortality rate declined from 120 in 1960 to 16 in 1992; and the daily calorie supply rose from 96 in 1964-66 to 130 in 1992.

[42] For studies on the causes of democratization and democratic society, see Moore (1966), Stephens (1989), Diamond (1991), Huntington (1991), and Ahn (1994).

[43] Dahl (1971) maintains that democratization is made up of at least two significant dimensions; that is, "inclusiveness"—participation and "public contestation"—political competition.

[44] The score between 1.0 and 2.5 are designated free, between 3.0 and 5.5 partly free, and between 5.5 and 7.0 not free.

[45] See Haberman (1987), pp. A1 and A4; Yoon (1990), pp. 106-106; Yang (1994), pp. 442-462; and Yoon (1994), pp. 178-186.

[46] The long-time dissidents of authoritarian governments, Kim Dae Jung and Kim Young Sam, became the party heads of the PPD and the RDP, respectively, and later became presidents. See Yonhap News Agency, *Korea Annual* (Seoul: YNA, 1988), p. 31.

[47] Despite the ongoing trend of democratization, the Noh administration also attempted to monopolize political power. Absence of a majority in the National Assembly eventually led the leading DJP to merge with the RDP and the NDRP in January 1990. The merger established the founding of the Democratic Liberal Party (DLP) which was denounced by the public as unethical. See Kim J. (1993), pp. 44-47 and Kim S. (1994), pp. 186-188.

[48] However, all political surveillance was not eliminated. In early October 1990, "an army deserter revealed that the Defense Security Command conducted illegal surveillance...on prominent opposition politicians, academics, journalists, labor activists, and student leaders characterized as potential threats to the government" (Kim J., 1993: 46).

[49] According to Samuel P. Huntington (1968), a military regime once in power may follow one of four alternatives: (1) retaining power and restricting participation, (2) retaining power and expanding participation, (3) returning power to civilians and restricting participation, and (4) returning power to civilians and expanding participation. South Korea during the transitional phase was the second case.

[50] South Korea has three national exams for government positions: judicial exam, civil service exam, and foreign service exam. In 1990, the average competition rate was 55:1. For the

changed bureaucratic arrangements and civil service exams, see Yang (1994) and Woo-Cumings (1995).

[51] The comparability of the two Koreas has many pitfalls, due to their respective methods of compiling and measuring aggregate economic variables. However, the estimated GNP in the North Korean won was converted into US dollar values by using the North's official exchange rate and trade exchange rate to make it comparable with the South's GNP in aggregate and per capita figures. Although no consensus has been made on when the South overtook the North, it is undeniable that the South surely advanced further the North during the transitional period. Scholars have argued that the South started to surpass the North in the mid-1970s. See Koh (1984) and Yang (1994).

[52] During 1987-1992, wage growth rate was 12.6% and the number of labor unions and their memberships nearly tripled. See Kim J. (1993), Mo (1999), and Moon (1999).

[53] According to the World Bank, *World Bank Atlas* and the UNDP, *Human Development Index*, South Korea moved from a medium-developed-country or middle-income-economy to a high-developed-county or upper-middle-income economy during the transitional phase.

[54] See Hamm (1999), pp. 129-132 and Yoo (1999), pp. 135-137.

[55] See UN, *Yearbook of National Accounts Statistics* (New York: The UN Statistical Office) and Bank of Korea, *Economic Statistics Yearbook* (Seoul: BOK).

[56] During the same period, the share of labor-intensive exports declined from 39% to around 24%. See Islam and Chowdhury (1997), p. 164.

[57] See U.S. Arms Control and Disarmament Agency, *World Military Expenditures and Arms Transfers* (Washington, D.C.: Government Printing Office).

[58] See Institute of International Affairs, *Korean Defense Yearbook* (Seoul: IIA) and Ministry of National Defense, *Defense White Paper* (Seoul: MND).

[59] Major incentives of North Korea's nuclear ambition lie in its intention to secure deterrence against the US-ROK military superiority. The changed alliance system, diplomatic recognition and international status, domestic economic and political factors drawn from *juche* ideology, and economic aid from the West were also major causes.

# 6. From *Nordpolitik* to Globalization/Sunshine

A "new international order" was in place in Northeast Asia, resulting from the collapse of the Berlin Wall, the disintegration of the Soviet Union, the diplomatic and economic rapprochement among regional states, and the subsequent demise of the Cold War.[1] The new Northeast Asian system included multiple alliance formations and diversified alignment mechanisms. Although not all the Cold War characteristics became obsolete, the demise of the antagonistic bi-triangular system provided new systemic constraints and opportunities for South Korea. Under these circumstances, South Korea's post-Cold War security policies shifted to globalization and sunshine policies. The major goals were to achieve regional security and prosperity as *nordpolitik*, formulated during the transitional phase.

The relatively pluralistic system in post-Cold War Northeast Asia has produced uncertainty because of the potential for power competition and the complexity of both types and sources of threats. Security threats include the North's nuclear and missile program, politico-social uncertainty, and current economic problems. Because of the North's economic decline in the 1990s, some speculate that there are as many as 100,000 refugees around the North Korea-China borders. Responding to the new security problems, South Korea's security policy changed to an economic engagement or appeasement policy that aimed to induce North Korea to voluntarily give up its isolation.[2]

South Korea's new approach also raises the question of how changes in external and internal variables affect its security policy dynamics. Specifically, this chapter will look into the relative explanatory power of international systemic and domestic institutional determinants in the post-Cold War era from 1993 to 1998. Compared to *nordpolitik*, the South's economic engagement policy is different in that it would provide economic aid to facilitate the North's entry into the world economy. I will specify the international and domestic conditions that affected South Korea's security policy dynamics. Regarding the security problem, program, and adjustment changes, I will evaluate theoretical causal claims proposed by international structuralism and domestic institutionalism. Finally, this chapter will summarize critical determinants of security policy change in the post-Cold War period and assess the institutional capacity of South Korea's security policy-making institutions.

**International Systemic Determinants**

After the systemic transition, the antagonistic bipolar system became obsolete in post-Cold War Northeast Asia.  Rather, a multiple bilateral system has prevailed among the United States, Japan, China, Russia, and South Korea, while China maintains its friendly relationship with North Korea.  Both China and Russia officially announced that they would not support any North Korean military aggression against South Korea.[3]  As a result, the North lost its security allies, while the South maintained bilateral alliance and alignment mechanisms with its allies and the former communist countries.  In addition to the multiple bilateral system, a multilateral security alliance of the Korean Peninsula Energy Organization (KEDO) was established in October 1994 to implement the US-DPRK nuclear agreement.[4]  The U.S., Japan and South Korea run the KEDO as a consensus-based consortium and implement and monitor the agreement.  Economically, the advent of the Asia-Pacific Economic Cooperation (APEC) of 1989, the 1994 agreement to open trade and investment by APEC members, and the World Trade Organization (WTO) of 1995 have intensified multilateral alignment mechanisms.  A multiple bilateral system has emerged in post-Cold War Northeast Asia, shown in Figure 6.1, and North Korea has lost its strategic allies and has become isolated.

**Figure 6.1. Multiple Bilateral System in Post-Cold War Northeast Asia**

Antagonism between the Two Koreas
Security/Economic/Diplomatic Alliances
Economic/Diplomatic Ties

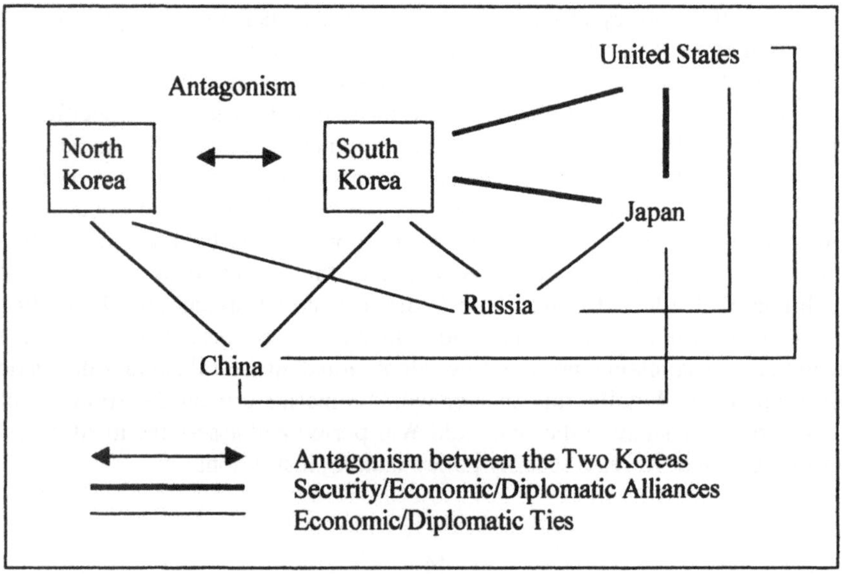

## *Geo-Structural Factors—Regional Security and Economic Structures*

The relative distribution of military powers among the U.S., Russia, China, Japan, and the two Koreas, measured by the relative levels of military expenditures, armed forces, and arms transfers, illustrates the power dispersion and concentration in the regional security structure. In the distribution of military expenditures, Russia significantly decreased its budgets, while other major powers steadily increased their expenditures compared to those of the early 1990s. Most notably, China increased its military spending to $74.9 billion while Russia decreased to $41.7 billion in 1997. China's growing military power has generated security concerns among the regional major powers and the Southeast Asian states. However, China does not seem to resort to a hegemonic status, but to rely on "economic development as national security" (Taylor, 1996). The U.S. reduced its military spending from $321 billion in 1993 to $252 billion in 1998, but remained the sole dominant military superpower. Table 6.1 illustrates the U.S. unipolarity in terms of military expenditures among the Northeast Asian major powers. China, Japan, and Russia fall into the medium range. South Korea steadily increased it expenditures to $15.0 billion in 1997 and spent the same amount in 1998. The statistical data indicate that the balance-of-power mechanism has collapsed, since South Korea surpassed North Korea in military expenditures.

**Table 6.1. Military Expenditures of Major Powers in Northeast Asia: 1993-1998**

| Year | U. S. | Russia | China | Japan | S. Korea | N. Korea |
|------|-------|--------|-------|-------|----------|----------|
| 1993 | 321 | 67.4 | 57.3 | 49.4 | 13.0 | 5.7 |
| 1994 | 305 | 65.2 | 58.0 | 49.6 | 13.6 | 5.8 |
| 1995 | 289 | 42.4 | 62.2 | 50.1 | 14.4 | 6.1 |
| 1996 | 276 | 38.3 | 67.2 | 51.2 | 15.5 | 6.2 |
| 1997 | 276 | 41.7 | 74.9 | 51.3 | 15.6 | 6.3 |
| 1998 | 252 | -- | -- | 51.3 | 15.0 | -- |

Note: 1997 constant dollars (billions); SIPRI data are used for the 1998 figures, but its data on Russia, China, and North Korea are incomplete.
Sources: U.S. Arms Control and Disarmament Agency, *World Military Expenditures and Arms Transfers* (Washington, D.C.: Government Printing Office); Stockholm International Peace Research Institute, *World Armaments and Disarmament Yearbook* (London: Taylor & Francis); and Taik-young Hamm, *Arming the Two Koreas: State, Capital, and Military Power* (New York: Routledge, 1999), p. 59 and p. 93.

The size of armed forces also fluctuated during the post-Cold War era.  As shown in Table 6.2, China still has the largest number of military personnel and this number rose to 2.8 million soldiers in 1998, although its overall numbers have decreased since 1993.  The number of military personnel of the U.S. and Russia steadily decreased in the post-Cold War era.  Japan and the two Koreas have had little fluctuation in the size of their military forces since the transitional phase.  North Korea reduced its armed forces a bit to 1.147 million in 1997 from 1.2 million in 1993, but it still has the world's largest army relative to its population, 51.6 soldiers per thousand people in 1997.[5]  The inverse relationship between armed forces and military expenditures of the two Koreas was also sustained in the post-Cold War era; i.e., while the North had more military forces, the South increased its military expenditures to balance that military strength, and vice versa.

**Table 6.2. Armed Forces of Major Powers in Northeast Asia: 1993-1998**

| Year | U. S. | Russia | China | Japan | S. Korea | N. Korea |
|------|-------|--------|-------|-------|----------|----------|
| 1993 | 1,810 | 1,500 | 3,030 | 242 | 750 | 1,200 |
| 1994 | 1,710 | 1,400 | 2,930 | 233 | 750 | 1,200 |
| 1995 | 1,620 | 1,400 | 2,930 | 240 | 750 | 1,040 |
| 1996 | 1,570 | 1,300 | 2,650 | 250 | 670 | 1,055 |
| 1997 | 1,530 | 1,300 | 2,600 | 250 | 670 | 1,147 |
| 1998 | 1,407 | 1,300 | 2,840 | 240 | 690 | 1,160 |

Note: Military personnel on active-duty throughout the world (thousands).
Sources: U.S. Arms Control and Disarmament Agency, *World Military Expenditures and Arms Transfers* (Washington, D.C.: Government Printing Office) and Taik-young Hamm, *Arming the Two Koreas: State, Capital, and Military Power* (New York: Routledge, 1999), p. 87.

The total amount of arms transfers in the region was reduced in the early 1990s; although the volume fluctuated in the mid-1990s, it declined again in 1997.  As shown in Table 6.3, the U.S. was the leading arms supplier, accounting for about 50% of world arms export.  The U.S. imported $6,530 million and exported $129,800 million from 1993 to 1997, while Russia imported $76 million and exported $14,964 million during the same period.  As previously discussed, up until 1990, Russia was the leading arms supplier, but the U.S. has retained a dominant position in terms of arms trade since the early 1990s.  China decreased its armed transfers from $1,836 million in 1993 to $1,600 million in 1997.  Japan exported $83 million and imported $11,283 million from 1993 to 1997.  Similar to Japan, South Korea exported $209 million and imported $8,446 million from 1993 to 1997.  Both Japan and South

Korea imported more than they exported, but South Korea's imports decreased to $1,100 million in 1997 from $1,836 million in 1993. The amount of North Korea's arms transfers decreased from $324 million in 1993 to $100 million in 1997. North Korea's arms imports fell from $130 million in 1993 to $30 million in 1997. The main cause of the North's decrease in arms transfers was its negative economic growth during the 1990s.

**Table 6.3. Arms Transfers of Major Powers in Northeast Asia: 1993-1997**

| Year | U. S. | Russia | China | Japan | S. Korea | N. Korea |
|------|-------|--------|-------|-------|----------|----------|
| 1993 | 28,942 | 3,779 | 1,836 | 2,063 | 1,890 | 324 |
| 1994 | 24,643 | 1,798 | 1,078 | 2,338 | 2,263 | 211 |
| 1995 | 24,745 | 3,940 | 1,527 | 1,885 | 2,019 | 168 |
| 1996 | 24,600 | 3,193 | 2,262 | 2,060 | 1,353 | 143 |
| 1997 | 33,400 | 2,330 | 1,600 | 2,620 | 1,130 | 100 |

Note: Arms transfers include exports and imports in 1997 constant dollars (millions); the 1998 data are not available.
Sources: U.S. Arms Control and Disarmament Agency, *World Military Expenditures and Arms Transfers* (Washington, D.C.: Government Printing Office).

The regional economic structure or relative wealth distribution, measured by purchasing power parity (PPP) values, shows a bipolar economic system in post-Cold War Northeast Asia. PPP values indicate that exchanges rates between countries are in equilibrium when their purchasing power is the same in each of the countries. As shown in Table 6.4, the U.S. and Japan consistently lead in their per capita PPP values, while Russia, China and North Korea lag behind. South Korea occupies the medium range. The per capita PPP for the U.S. and Japan increased from $24,750 and $21,090 in 1993 to $29,030 and $24,070 in 1997, respectively. Japanese per capita PPP decreased to $23,100 in 1998. South Korea increased its per capita PPP from $9,810 in 1993 to $13,590 in 1997, but decreased to $12,600 in 1998. Russia and North Korea steadily decreased their PPP values, while China increased their values from $2,120 in 1993 to $3,600 in 1998. In terms of total world trade, the U.S. and Japan shared 14.4% and 8.1% in 1993 and 14.7% and 6.2% in 1998, respectively, and China (including that of Hong Kong) reached its share in total world trade at 5.9% of 1998.[6] In the post-Cold War era, the U.S. and Japan have retained their dominant economic status, in terms of PPP values. In terms of world trade shares, the U.S., Japan, and China formed a tripolarity in Northeast Asia.

**Table 6.4. Per Capita PPP Values of Major Powers in Northeast Asia: 1993-1998**

| Year | U. S. | Russia | China | Japan | S. Korea | N. Korea |
|------|-------|--------|-------|-------|----------|----------|
| 1993 | 24,750 | 5,240 | 2,120 | 21,090 | 9,810 | 1,500 |
| 1994 | 26,397 | 4,828 | 2,604 | 21,858 | 10,656 | 1,500 |
| 1995 | 26,980 | 4,480 | 2,920 | 22,110 | 11,450 | -- |
| 1996 | 27,821 | -- | -- | 23,235 | 13,580 | -- |
| 1997 | 29,030 | 4,370 | 3,130 | 24,070 | 13,590 | 1,000 |
| 1998 | 31,500 | -- | 3,600 | 23,100 | 12,600 | 1,000 |

Note: U.S. dollars; current prices and exchange rates.
Sources: United Nations Development Program, *Human Development Report* (Oxford: Oxford University Press); Central Intelligence Agency, *The World Factbook* (Washington, D.C.: Government Printing Office); and World Bank, *World Bank Atlas* (Washington, D.C.: World Bank).

Compared to the early 1990s, geo-structural factors do not show any abrupt fluctuations, but the result of the transition has significant implications. The post-Cold War Northeast Asian structure reflects "unipolarity without hegemony" or "a uni-multipolar system" with one superpower and several major powers (Huntington, 1999; Wilkinson, 1999). Unipolarity without hegemony is a configuration where the preponderant capability of a single state is not matched by other states' military and economic capabilities (Wilkinson, 1999: 143). The U.S. maintains sole superpower status with preeminence in every domain of power, but requires input of other major states when deciding key international issues.[7] Thus, a U.S.-led security order (shared with Japan and South Korea in security and economic management) has emerged in post-Cold War Northeast Asia.

This regional order appears to be characterized by U.S.-led unipolarity militarily and by a tripolarity in terms of total world trade, consisting of the U.S., Japan, and China. Russia declined as a military superpower, while China militarily and economically increased its capabilities. These changed regional security and economic structures led North Korea to find a strategic equalizer, namely its nuclear and missile programs. Since the Cold War balance-of-power structure disappeared after the collapse of the Soviet Union, North Korea attempted to utilize "the nuclear card" as a countervailing deterrent against the US-ROK military superiority.[8] Pyongyang's nuclear and missile programs changed Seoul's policy from *nordpolitik* to one of economic engagement or appeasement. Thus, the systemic constraints of geo-structural factors have had a decisive impact on South Korea's security policy dynamics.

*Geo-Strategic Factors—Security Alliance Mechanisms*

The security alliance mechanism, similar to the transitional phase, was predominantly bilateral in the post-Cold War Northeast Asia. Despite the fact that systemic transformations called for a new rationale for the US-ROK alliance, the U.S.-extended deterrence has continuously been guaranteed through annual security meetings, US-ROK military exercises, and U.S. troop commitment. The annual US-ROK military and security meetings were continued, and military exercises of the US-ROK Eagle (since 1961) and the US-ROK Ulgi Focus (since 1976) were held annually. However, the US-ROK Team Spirit (since 1976) exercise was indefinitely postponed, because the 1994 US-DPRK agreement required its cancellation in exchange for the North's confirmation to the Nuclear Non-proliferation Treaty (NPT) and International Atomic Energy Agency (IAEA) regimes. The biannual exercises of Rim of the Pacific Asian Countries (RIMPAC—since 1990) were held with the U.S., Canada, Japan, Australia, and Chile. South Korea exercised the annual Reception, Staging, Onward Movement & Integration (RSOI), led by the US-ROK Combined Forces Corps (CFCs), to enhance military procurement since 1994. The 1995 U.S. EASI and South Korea's *Defense White Paper* state that the U.S. forces in South Korea are necessary to preserve deterrence and defense as well as U.S. leadership in the region. Thus, the number of U.S. forces in South Korea remained at an average of 39,000 from 1993 to 1998. It was 35,950 in 1998.

As previously discussed, the US-ROK bilateral relationship shifted from an asymmetrical alliance to a partnership of burden sharing. Under the agreement on burden sharing, South Korea contributed $330 million in 1997 and $175 million in 1998.[9] Along with the framework of the trilateral security regime, KEDO, international financing for two modern light-water nuclear reactors (LWRs) was promised at an estimated cost of $4 billion by the target date of 2003. The 1994 US-DPRK agreement preceded KEDO. It was negotiated by the former Assistant Secretary of State Robert Gallucci and Vice Foreign Minister of North Korea Kang Suk-Ju in Geneva. In exchange for the North's reentry to the NPT regime, the U.S. agreed to provide economic aid, two light water reactors, and diplomatic recognition.[10] South Korea agreed to pay for more than $2 billion of the cost, with Japan contributing more than a billion, and the remainder coming from a consortium of the U.S., Germany, and Russia.

The partnership of burden sharing and the trilateral commitment, KEDO, created a consensus-based consortium operated by the U.S., Japan, and South Korea. However, the strengthening of military ties among these nations is necessary, not simply an ad hoc alliance for KEDO implementation. A new trilateral security alliance system has been proposed as one step toward the establishment of a multilateral security regime in Northeast Asia and the peaceful process of reunification of the two Koreas. In other words, a bilateral alliance formed to prevent communist expansionism and to deter the North's military aggression "needs to be reformulated toward a regional multilateral alliance and a comprehensive partnership for security, unification, interdependence, and democracy" (Ahn, 1996: 18).

Another factor that changed the basic characteristics of regional alliance formation was the change of the U.S.-extended deterrence provided to South Korea. During the Korean War, South Korea's military-operational-control was transferred to the UN Forces and later in 1978 to the US-ROK CFCs. South Korea was scheduled to take over peacetime-operational-control of its forces in December 1994.[11] The operational-control-at-war is currently in the US-ROK CFCs. This means that in wartime, the chairperson of the joint chiefs of staffs of the CFCs will control operations of the U.S. and South Korean forces. The combined defense setup was meant to assure regional security in the most effective and prudent way. Consequently, South Korea called for a leading role in its own defense and a greater burden in defense expenditures, according to the partnership framework of burden sharing.

Close bilateral alliance with the U.S. for the last 50 years has provided security and stability in Northeast Asia. Although the glue of the Cold War alliance, anti-communism, is gone, the changing structure of regional order generates new security concerns for regional security and prosperity. New concerns include the maintenance of nuclear and missile non-proliferation, stable market economies, and democratic regimes. South Korea has been proactive in support of Washington's policy toward North Korea nuclear non-proliferation. An economic engagement policy has also been maintained in regard to North Korea. Rather than anticipating the collapse of the North, the South attempts to control the process of economic/political/social integration with North Korea. Despite the changing regional structure, Seoul-Washington relations will continue to be an important factor in South Korea's future international relations.

*Geo-Economic Factors—Trade and Financial Alignment Mechanisms*

In the post-Cold War world, global and regional economic integration has been explored as an alternative to the danger of nationalism and mercantile protectionism. Globally, the Uruguay Round was completed in December 1993 and the WTO, the former GATT, was established in January 1995. Regionally, the European Union (EU) and APEC have promoted regional economic and trade integration. Although the economic crisis of 1997 has slowed the process, "open regionalism" in the Asia-Pacific region in particular has intensified open trade and investment. APEC set the timetable in 1994 for achieving the goals for developed countries by 2010 and for developing countries by 2020.[12] With the intensified trends of geo-economic alignment, South Korea's "globalization" and economic engagement policies involved the liberalization of its market and economic integration among regional powers, including North Korea.[13]

One of South Korea's key post-Cold War policy adjustments has been the elevation of economic interests in its overall security agenda. As shown Table 6.5, trade relations between South Korea and China, Russia, and North Korea have continuously grown, except in the years of 1997 and 1998. South Korea's trade with China exceeded $20 billion and with Russia $3.6 billion in 1996.[14] The economic crises of South Korea and Russia in 1997 and 1998 reduced trade volumes, but the 1999 figure shows a steady increase in South Korea's bilateral trades. China emerged as South Korea's major trading partner, accounting for 11.9% of its total trade in 1997 and 7.2% in 1998.[15] The South's direct and indirect trade with the North reached $221.9 million in 1998. South Korea viewed North Korea as an economic partner in hopes of achieving regional integration.[16] North Korea had a trade surplus with South Korea throughout the 1990s, with this surplus reaching $40.4 million in the years of 1997 and 1998. On the contrary, the North's bilateral trade with China decreased from $931 million in 1993 to $699 million in 1997 and with Russia from $234 million in 1993 to $96 million in 1997.[17] Despite the uncertainty that was created by Russia and North Korea shifting their economic systems to market economies, economic trade with them created conditions conducive to peaceful reunification.

**Table 6.5.  South Korea's Trade with China, Russia, and North Korea: 1993-1998**

| Year | China | Russia | North Korea |
|------|-------|--------|-------------|
| 1993 | 9,080 | 1,576 | 186.6 |
| 1994 | 11,666 | 2,192 | 194.6 |
| 1995 | 16,587 | 3,318 | 287.3 |
| 1996 | 20,019 | 3,682 | 252.0 |
| 1997 | 23,577 | 3,275 | 308.3 |
| 1998 | 18,428 | 2,113 | 221.9 |

Note: Millions of dollars. Trade with North Korea includes indirect trade through the routes of the third countries such as Hong Kong and Japan.
Sources: International Monetary Fund, *Direction of Trade Statistics Yearbook* (Washington, D.C.: IMF); Economic Planning Board, *Major Statistics of Korean Economy* (Seoul: EPB); and Ministry of Unification, *Inter-Korean Trade Volume* (Seoul: MOU).

What is salient in regional economic integration "is the rapid growth of intra-Asian trade and investment reaching as high as some 40% of the total among Asian countries" (Ahn, 1996: 10).  As statistics indicate, the Asia-Pacific region has emerged as one of the world's top trading regions, with its share of world trade increasing from about 15% in the 1980s to about 25% in the 1990s. Economic growth has been the major force in this trend toward regional economic integration.  The Asia-Pacific countries' share of world economic output has soared from about 4% in the 1960s to about 30% in the 1990s.[18] South Korea's export shares with Asia-Pacific economies, as shown in Table 6.6, continuously increased to 50.0% in 1996 and its import shares reached 40.7% in 1994.  However, due to the economic crisis of 1997, the 1998 shares decreased to 43.4% and 38.3% in terms of export and import shares, respectively.  Similar to the time of the transitional phase, South Korea's trade shares with the U.S., Japan, and the EU have decreased or remained relatively flat, but export shares among them increased during the years of 1997 and 1998, owing to currency depreciation.

**Table 6.6. South Korea's Trade Shares with the U.S., Japan, Europe, and Asia: 1993-1998**

| Year | United States Ex-/Import | Japan Ex-/Import | Europe Ex-/Import | Asia Ex-/Import |
|------|------------|------------|------------|------------|
| 1993 | 22.2/21.4 | 14.1/23.9 | 12.1/13.3 | 45.9/40.6 |
| 1994 | 21.6/21.1 | 14.1/24.8 | 11.7/14.2 | 46.3/40.7 |
| 1995 | 19.5/22.5 | 13.6/24.1 | 13.0/13.5 | 48.7/40.1 |
| 1996 | 16.9/22.2 | 12.2/20.9 | 11.9/14.1 | 50.0/37.6 |
| 1997 | 15.9/20.7 | 10.9/19.3 | 11.1/13.0 | 49.6/37.4 |
| 1998 | 17.4/21.9 | 9.1/18.1 | 18.0/13.7 | 43.3/38.3 |

Note: Percentages; trade shares with Asia include Japan.
Sources: Economic Planning Board, *Major Statistics of Korean Economy* (Seoul: EPB); International Monetary Fund, *Direction of Trade Statistics Yearbook* (Washington, D.C.: IMF); and UN, *International Trade Statistics Yearbook* (New York: The UN Printing Office).

South Korea's economic and financial liberalization was accelerated with the drive toward economic integration in the Asia-Pacific economies.  However, the Kim Young Sam administration's "globalization" policy (1993-1997) turned out to be "a magic flute that led the nation into a foreign exchange crisis...[and] a wholesale deregulation of the financial sector paved the way to a financial crisis, while the government's negligence in overseeing corporate investment served to encourage Korea's large *chaebol* conglomerates to continue their reckless business expansion" (Ahn, 1999: 70-71).[19] Eventually, the failed management of currency and loans led to a full-blown financial crisis. The crisis, which started in Thailand in July and Indonesia in November 1997, forced Seoul to place its economy under IMF oversight in December 1997 with a $57 billion bailout package.[20]

Substantial amounts of foreign funds that flowed into emerging economies in 1994 and 1995 ended up in unproductive investments, contributing to economic "bubbles."[21] By the mid-1990s, emerging economies were absorbing 40% of global foreign direct investments compared to15% in 1990 and received 30% of global portfolio equity flows versus only 2% at the beginning of the decade.[22] In the case of South Korea, FDI inflows increased from $1,044 million in 1993 to $8,852 million in 1998. FDI inflows during the financial crisis remained remarkably stable or actually increased. However, through the 1990s, FDI outflows were in fact greater than FDI inflows, as the *chaebol* expanded international markets. South Korea's overseas investment, FDI outflows, increased from $1,261 million in 1993 to $3,864 million in 1998. In addition, between 1992 and 1996, international lending to South Korea "surged by 58%, and loans accounted for 66% of all lending by international banks, while 28% went to the non-banking private sector and 6% went to the public sector" (Smith, 1998: 72). Moreover, portfolio investments decreased from $14,295 million in 1997 to minus $1,995 million in 1998. Except for Taiwan, South Korea by mid-1997 had the highest amount of short-term debt among borrowers in Asia, and its short-term debt was more than three times the size of its reserves.[23] Its foreign debt increased from $5,051 million in 1996 to $24,425 million in 1998. Table 6.7 shows the fluctuations of South Korea's loans, foreign direct investments, and foreign debt.

**Table 6.7. Loans, Investments, and Debts: 1993-1998**

| Year | Foreign Loans Asset | Foreign Loans Liability | Total Portfolio Investment | FDI Inflow | FDI Outflow | Foreign Debt |
|------|-------|-----------|----------|--------|---------|-------|
| 1993 | -538 | 10,552 | 10,014 | 1,044 | 1,261 | 5,494 |
| 1994 | -2,029 | 8,149 | 6,120 | 1,317 | 2,290 | 5,666 |
| 1995 | -2,284 | 13,875 | 11,591 | 1,941 | 3,070 | 5,241 |
| 1996 | -5,998 | 21,183 | 15,185 | 3,203 | 4,237 | 5,051 |
| 1997 | 2,008 | 12,287 | 14,295 | 6,970 | 3,221 | 15,321 |
| 1998 | -1,655 | -340 | -1,995 | 8,852 | 3,865 | 24,425 |

Note: 1998 constant dollars (millions).
Sources: Ministry of Finance and Economy, *Fiscal and Financial Statistics* (Seoul: MOFE); Bank of Korea, *Economic Statistics Yearbook* (Seoul: BOK); and International Monetary Fund, *International Financial Statistics Yearbook* (Washington, D.C.: IMF).

Increased trade and economic interactions were influential in dissolving Cold War animosity against the former communist countries. But regional economic integration and globalization led to the financial and economic crisis of 1997. South Korea has opened the domestic equity market and eased regulation for FDI and commercial loans, since the economic and financial liberalization of the late 1980s. South Korea's foreign debt increased as the government encouraged commercial banks and *chaebol* to borrow heavily abroad to finance international expansion. Thus, it was the private sector's borrowing that caused financial crisis, not the public sector's borrowing. In theory, economic liberalization and financial integration can result in economy-wide benefits for advanced and emerging economies alike. However, financial recipients face an increased vulnerability to reversed capital flows; this led to the financial crisis of 1997 in East Asia. Eventually, the crisis led to financial reforms and large-scale economic reforms set by the IMF. Fortunately, the economic crisis did not cause any dramatic changes in South Korea's economic engagement policy with North Korea and the formerly communist countries, although their trade volumes were reduced.

### Geo-Political Factors—Diplomacy and International Institutions

At the time of *Nordpolitik* during the transitional phase, South Korea successfully established diplomatic ties with the former communist countries, and in turn encouraged them to persuade North Korea to open its society. As an extension of northern diplomacy, South Korea's geopolitical relations focused on this kind of economic diplomacy in the post-Cold War era. Open economic diplomacy has developed gradually, according to a pre-announced schedule of globalization in the areas of merchandise, services, foreign exchange and finance. For South Korea, the reason for establishing economic diplomacy "is to expand trades and economic interactions with its principal trading partners, the U.S., Japan, and the EU, on the one hand, while on the other hand, seeking to increase multi-faceted commerce and economic collaboration with developing countries, including North Korea" (Seung, 1993: 20). South Korea advocated economic normalization among the U.S., Japan and North Korea with the condition of nuclear and missile non-proliferation.

Kim Young Sam administration's "globalization" or "open and global diplomacy" and Kim Dae Jung administration's "sunshine" policy (1998-present) have articulated three fundamentals for the new diplomacy.[24] These include globalism and regional cooperation, diversification and multi-dimentionalism, and engagement with North Korea. With the emergence of the new world order, South Korea's international relations are characterized by increased interdependence and globalization in the fields of information, communication and technology, and trade and capital movement. As previously discussed, South Korea's membership in APEC in 1989, WTO in 1995, and OECD in 1996 have been the catalysts in its efforts to achieve multilateral economic diplomacy. As of December 1998, South Korea had established diplomatic ties with 183 countries and was received into 21 UN institutional memberships.[25]

A greater emphasis was given to diversification and multi-dimensionalism in South Korea's geopolitical relations. Along with free trade and globalization, it was at the "Rio Summit" that the world was introduced to the idea of the preservation of the global environment. A wide range of international regulations was designed to protect the global environment in the areas of industrial production, trade and economic development. For its part, South Korea as a member of the Council of the Committee on Sustained Development (CSD) has fulfilled its UN-centered environmental obligations. The scope of its activities was also expanded to include the UN-centered peacekeeping activities, such as participating in UNOSOM II of Somalia. South Korea's global involvement included promoting the issues of human rights, disarmament, and non-proliferation of weapons of massive destruction, after its election to a two-year term (1996-1997) as a non-permanent member of the UN Security Council. In addition, South Korea started to take an active stance in international development assistance. During the 1993-1998 period, South Korea's economic aid expanded 65% and bilateral aid increased 14%; e.g., its aid through Official Development Assistance (ODA) was $111.6 million in 1993 and increased to $185.6 million in 1997. But due to the economic crisis, the 1998 assistance decreased somewhat to $182 million.[26]

South Korea has consistently sought an engagement policy with North Korea to improve inter-Korean relations by promoting peace, reconciliation, and cooperation as framed by the 1991 Basic Agreement. The Kim Dae Jung administration has stressed that national reunification should be achieved through promotion of the following three principles: first, no armed provocation by North Korea will be tolerated; second, a takeover or absorption of North Korea will not be attempted; and third, reconciliation and cooperation with the North will be encouraged.[27] Under this "sunshine" engagement policy, South Korea promoted both a "strategy to keep peace" (deterrence) and a "strategy to make peace" (economic appeasement), as opposed to the posturing of a mutual hostile stance against North Korea.

International attempts have been made to resolve the problems of nuclear and missile programs through the effective implementation of the NPT regime and the Missile Technology Control Regime (MTCR). The North's March 1993 withdrawal from the NPT until its reaffirmation in October 1994 caused serious international threats of nuclear proliferation. Nuclear and missile proliferation was not acceptable due to the potential snowball effect on the region. Threats were twofold: "first, a nuclear-armed North Korea may instigate a military attempt to reunify Korea under communist control. Second, due to its economic decline, it may attempt to sell weapons related materials and delivery systems to other prominent proliferators" (Kil, 1995: 78). Clandestine nuclear sites in Youngbyun were targeted for preemptive military strikes.[28] However, economic rewards and diplomatic recognition, unilateral initiatives, and the establishment of multilateral security mechanism were all suggested as solutions.    Following negotiations, the 1994 US-DPRK agreement, as previously discussed, resulted and established the KEDO as a means to effectively implement the NPT and IAEA regimes.    However, speculation remains as to whether North Korea possesses nuclear weapons and has the technical capability to produce ICBMs. Recently, North Korea test-fired the Nodong-1 (with a range of 1,000 km), Nodong-2 (1,300 km), Daepodong-1 (2,000 km) and Daepodong-2 (4,000-6,000 km). Negotiations between Washington and Pyongyang are still in progress. The key to success is to gradually build confidence and set up security measures through diplomacy and market forces, rather than perpetuating military posturing.

Another serious issue is the North Korean refugee problem. Estimates of the number of refugees who have fled North Korea and taken refuge in China and Russia "range from as few as 1,000 to as many as 100,000" (Son, 1999:1). The Red Cross, the Korean Red Cross, the UN Food and Agriculture Organization, and other private organizations have provided humanitarian aid to the North Korean government.    Separating economics from politics, the South-North Cooperation Fund also raised $586.3 million and provided $300.8 million from 1993 to 1998.[29] In addition, Seoul has pursued direct support and contacts with Pyongyang that it considers more effective than its indirect contacts through international organizations. As a result, more than 10,000 Koreans visited North Korea in the 1990s and there was an increase in the number of dispersed families who were able to confirm the whereabouts of their families or were actually reunited.[30] Moreover, the government has tried to accommodate all North Korean defectors and has focused on helping them to get settled and support themselves in South Korea. From 1993 to 1998, there were 313 defectors; more than 80% of them reside in South Korea.[31] The government provides a special monthly allowance, settlement subsidies, and occupational training to North Korean defectors who have fled to the South.

Variations in geopolitical factors have had a significant impact on South Korea's security policy change. New security threats of nuclear and missile proliferation posed a serious challenge to the US-ROK security alliance mechanism. The North Korean refugee problem also caused Seoul to establish humanitarian aid funds and formulate an economic appeasement policy. Thus, South Korea's "peace-making" or economic engagement policies marked a major positive shift toward Pyongyang. Its sunshine policy operated in tandem with Washington's goals of nuclear non-proliferation and easing tensions through inter-Korean contacts and dialogue rather than through isolation and containment of North Korea.

## Domestic Institutional Determinants

The discussions above clearly demonstrate that international systemic factors have been critical determinants of South Korea's security policy change. However, advocates of domestic institutionalism point out that alterations in domestic institutional factors also lead to changes in South Korea's security policy behaviors.[32] Democratic governments, realignments in institutional arrangements and policy-making machinery, and national capabilities are suggested as causal variables. This section examines the extent to which variations of domestic institutional determinants affected South Korea's security policy change during the post-Cold War era. Specifically, it looks into domestic institutional conditions that have been conducive to democratic reform and in turn directed South Korea's security policy dynamics.

South Korea's transition to democracy was consolidated through its direct presidential elections held in 1987, 1992, and 1997. This is regarded as one of the best examples of countries making the transition from authoritarianism to democracy during "the third-wave democratization" (Huntington, 1991). The 1987 election was a landmark free and fair election and the 1992 election was held for the first civilian president. The 1997 election has been characterized as the first transfer of power to the opposition through a popular election in the 50 years of its constitutional government. The democratic government was "the only legitimate and viable alternative to the authoritarianism" (Huntington, 1991: 58; Doh, 1994: 4). South Korea has instituted democratic reform, but it is not yet fully democratized. Undemocratic characteristics are ubiquitous in party politics, election campaign funding, and government-business relations that this section will discuss in detail.

The government, as previously discussed, reduced its role in the market and the domestic market has become liberalized in the direction of the international standard set by APEC, WTO, OECD, and IMF. Consolidating democracy requires sustained economic growth that is advanced through financial reform and fiscal policy reform of market forces; however, the traditional government-business symbiotic relationship is not fully eliminated. This implies that democracy cannot survive without economic growth and long lasting prosperity cannot be sustained without democracy. South Korea's economic system requires a long-term structural reform to remedy the "high cost, low efficiency" factor in government-business relations. Currently, South Korea's political form resembles a so-called "communitarian type of democracy" or "market democracy" (Lee, 1992; Thurow, 1992; Chee, 1993; Helgesen and Xing, 1996). South Korea finds itself in the midst of two momentous worldwide transformations, democratization and economic liberalization.

### Types of Government—Democratic Government, But Not Fully Consolidated

A decade has passed since democratic fundamentals were guaranteed under the 1987 Constitution, and democratic reforms have been implemented in almost all spheres of society. As a result, according to the Freedom House, *Annual Survey of Freedom Country Scores*, South Korea's status of political rights and civil liberties has been given a score of 2 on a scale of 7 during the period of 1993-1994 to 1998-1999, that is, designated free. Democratic consolidation, economic liberalization, and promotion of regional interdependence for the peaceful process of unification were the on-going goals of South Korea's first civilian government. The Kim Young Sam administration initiated political reform in order to "break with the authoritarian past" or "rectify" history.[33] The former President Chun Do Whan was indicted on master-minding the military mutiny of 1979 and instigating the suppression of the 1980 Kwangju pro-democratic uprising. President Chun was indicted on December 21, 1995 along with his military co-conspirator, the former President Noh Tae Woo.[34] Through its efforts to "break with the past," South Korea finally dismantled its old military authoritarianism.

However, South Korea has not yet succeeded in stabilizing and deepening its democratic system. The growing skepticism about democratic principles and the inefficiency of the political system has brought strong demands for overall reforms. Political reforms have been geared to improving the method of selecting political leaders and reducing election campaign funds. Traditionally, the candidates were nominated by the national party convention comprised of no more than 5,000 delegates. The New Korea Party (NKP) amended the provision governing the number of delegates at the party's national committee convention on May 1997, increasing the number to 12,430. The National Congress for New Politics (NCNP) also changed the presidential candidate vote to 4,300 delegates.[35] Political reforms, however, still had limitations because increasing the number of party delegates did not necessarily guarantee the public's participation in the candidate nomination process. In an attempt to increase the number of candidates' policy debates, explore the policy positions of political parties, and check candidates' abilities to carry out public policies, mass media-centered elections were implemented during the 1997 election. What was lacking, however, was a wide range of participants with diverse policy perspectives.

Criticisms have also been mounted regarding the ways that campaign funds are raised and spent. Traditionally, large businesses had to make political donations to curry favor with political leaders. Politicians "needed funds for political uses, and to procure these funds they pressured bureaucrats to award contracts for public projects to certain businesses, which in turn made political contributions" (Soh, 1997: 60). This symbiotic relationship between politicians and businesspersons led to the problem of high political cost with low economic efficiency. The government-led and bureaucrat-controlled economy or "governed-market" system of the past forced the private sector to rely on the government, leading to the widespread problems of "moral hazard;" that is, reckless and excessive over-investment and business failures. Disclosure of political fund raising and funding sources is not yet fully established. What is required is strengthening the power of election management committees so that they can prosecute election political funding violations independent of political influence.

Another serious pitfall in South Korean politics is political regionalism. Voting patterns often show distinctive patterns in which people support only one's own regional candidates. For example, people from Kyongsang province support candidates from Kyongsang province and people from Cholla province vote solely for Cholla candidates. Regional divisions have contributed to obscuring genuine policy debates and visions. Regionalism also led top party leaders to circumvent institutional changes in the candidate nominating process and the process of solving major political problems. Thus, no country "can be regarded as truly democratic if its president not only controls domestic, foreign and defense policies, but also controls the nomination of his party's candidates for the legislature based on regional bases and directs how legislators will vote" (Kim T., 1997: 131).

Due to these shortcomings, a "clean break with the past" has not yet been fully executed, and the Kim Young Sam administration's "rectification of history" lost its political and moral integrity. President Kim himself was the party (New Korea Party) leader under the Noh Tae Woo government; later, he brought charges of mutiny and subversion against the former presidents. President Kim and other presidential candidates were charged with spending campaign funds in excess of the limit set by law. As judged by critics, the presidents Kim Young Sam and Kim Dae Jung are "the products of South Korea's regional party politics, and thus, they cannot claim the right to judge their fellow politicians" (Kim and Suh, 1997: 25). According to Weber's typology (1947), South Korea may be in the process of moving from traditional (authoritarianism) to charismatic (democracy under presidents Kim Young Sam and Kim Dae Jung) and thence to rational-legal democracy. What has been shown in this transitional stage of democratization is the absence of predictable "rules of the game" and political uncertainty due to a mixture of an old authoritarian regime and a new democratic government.[36]

One result of democratic reforms was that the Cold War antagonistic postures were no longer an influence upon political utility and regime security. Although North Korea uses nuclear and missile programs to maximize its regime's survival and economic interests, South Korea consistently attempts a reconciliation with North Korea. South Korea's economic engagement policy is clearly different from the former policy of mutual antagonism. However, a dilemma for the architects of the economic engagement policy is that the North may be just buying time in order to recover its balance of military and economic capabilities. A still open question is how economic engagement will bring about real changes in North Korean society. The 1991 Basic agreement has not been implemented in full. Another question is how long South Koreans will remain mere bystanders to nuclear and missile deals while the 1994 US-DPRK agreement forced South Korea to bear most of the expenses for the KEDO project.

### *Legal-Institutional Setting—Legal Enactment and Party Holdings*

The fundamental legal apparatus of the National Security Law was modified, and the legal basis for politicization of national security and the military was fully eradicated. But political initiatives of legal-institutional reforms were largely implemented through the top-down method. Political reforms were to abolish the collusive links between politics and business and the military's involvement in politics. These reforms include the registration of personal assets of administrative elites, disbanding of secret cliques within the military, legislation of the Integrated Election Law, and implementation of a real-name financial transaction system.[37]   Nonetheless, the traditional politics of authoritarian regimes that were above the law still remained. It was not the Constitution and national security laws that controlled the political process, but political authority, usually the president ruling through executive orders, that implemented political and economic reforms without much deliberation or debate.[38]   Meanwhile, some deplored the fact that democracy "was degenerating into civilian authoritarianism, while others demanded a turn to a pluralistic form of government" (Kim and Suh, 1997: 24). As radical reforms were not followed by adequate democratic institutionalization, President Kim's approval ratings dropped from 88.3% in 1993 to 13.9% in 1997.[39]

Party politics and the party system were not exempted. Presidents Kim Young Sam and Kim Dae Jung had to find ways to effectively implement reforms and coalesce old political elites and new reformers in the National Assembly. However, the oligarchical and authoritarian tendencies of the parties' inner organizations made reform more difficult than revolution.

Instead, there have been continuous patterns of renaming political parties and merging parties, following partisan interests and not the public's interests. For example, the Democratic Justice Party (DJP) was disbanded in 1990 when it merged with two opposition parties—the Reunification Democratic Party (RDP) and the New Democratic Republican Party (NRDP)—to create the Democratic Liberal Party (DLP). The DLP renamed itself to the New Korea Party (NKP) and changed its name again in 1997 to the Grand National Party (GNP). The National Congress for New Politics (NCNP) was established from the Democratic Party (DP). The NRDP separated from the DLP and renamed itself the United Liberal Democrats (ULD). In 1997, the NCNP and the ULP merged to create a joint government, but currently its coalition is in a stalemate.

The failure of the ruling party to win a parliamentary majority caused these frequent coalitions and separations. In the March 24, 1992 election, the ruling DLP won 149 seats (49.8%) out of 299 seats, compared with 97 seats (32.4%) for the DP, 31 seats (10.4%) for the United People's Party (UPP), and 22 seats (7.4%) for other small parties and independents.[40] In the April 11, 1996 election, the ruling NKP won 139 seats (46.5%) out of 299 seats, compared with 79 seats (26.4%) for the NCNP, 50 seats (16.7%) for the ULD, and 31 seats (10.4%) for the DP and independents.[41] Certainly, political power was shared and no monolithic power was guaranteed in the National Assembly. However, political parties with intra-party disputes and frequent coalitions and separations have tended to incapacitate the policy-making function of the Assembly and undermine its representation function.

Since the Cold War institutional pillars of political controlling, security laws and the ruling parties' monopoly in the National Assembly were abolished, an antagonistic hostile policy was not an alternative. Rather, the new economic engagement policy was formulated in order to achieve national goals of regional security and prosperity for the peaceful process of reunification. However, the security policy change did not result from the institutionalization of new democratic values and the democratic consolidation of party politics. This was to develop the international trends of globalization and open regionalism. Power sharing in the National Assembly only contributed to the elimination of the ruling party's monolithic power over security policy-making, and not to the reorientation of South Korea's security policy.

*Policy-Making Machinery—Bureaucracies and Administrative Elites*

The institutional and strategic positions of the military have become obsolete in the post-Cold War era. In the transitional phase, the president's Secretariat, National Security Council, Agency for National Security Planning (ANSP or the former KCIA), National Unification Board, and Ministry of Foreign Affairs were the top political organs of security policy-making. Decentralization continued by the delegation of decision-making power to lower levels of the administrative apparatuses. The political surveillance duties of the intelligence and security agencies were eliminated and their functions were changed to that of gathering information on North Korea military activities and international economic trends. Reorganization of and reinventing the government also aimed to increase governmental effectiveness and cut collusive relationships between the bureaucracy and the industry. But reorganization was also implemented through the top-down method, without extensive debate or deliberation.

Along with political reforms, President Kim Young Sam initiated a drastic reorganization of the administrative branch in December, 1994. The Economic Planning Board merged with the Ministry of Finance and became the Ministry of Finance and Economy. The integration of the Trade-Industry-Energy Ministry into the Ministry of Trade and Industry, later changed to the Ministry of Foreign Affairs and Trade, was done to reinforce deregulation of the industry and to foster economic liberalization. The Ministry of Communication was revamped into the Ministry of Information and Communication, absorbing relevant functions from Trade-Industry-Energy, Science-Technology and Information Ministries. The restructuring of the administrative branch eliminated two ministerial and three vice minister's posts, 23 directors and bureau chiefs, and 700 lower-level officials.[42]

As previously noted, another important change was the Kim Young Sam administration's reform in order to "break with the past" or "rectify" history. Former presidents Chun Do Whan and Noh Tae Woo and their aides were on trial and most of them were indicted for military mutiny and conspiracy that occurred during the period of 1979-1980. The Kim administration reformed the political system to return power to civilians and to restrict military involvement in politics.[43] The prosecution of former presidents Chun and Noh "was an effort to bring a final judgment on violators of human rights and civil liberties and to establish a legal precedent to punish coup leaders" (Kim and Suh, 1997: 25). However, the clear "break with the past" was only partially successful, for the Kim administration's efforts simply did not eliminate the deeper-rooted authoritarian tradition of Korean politics.

Elimination of the military in the policy-making machinery was accompanied by changes in the political elite structure. The three past presidents Park Chung Hee, Chun Do Whan, and Noh Tae Woo had been in the military, which also provided 41% of the National Assembly standing committee chairpersons, 33% of the cabinet ministers and 39% of the vice minister-level administrators (Kim K., 1994: 8). Reforms have been enacted within the military and access to public office for the military elite has been limited. The percentage from a military background was 3.9% in the administrative branch. The percentage of academicians was 10.1%, bureaucrats 60.3%, politicians 11.8%, journalists 2.2%, lawyers 3.9%, business 7.3%, and others 0.5% during the Kim Young Sam administration. In the current Kim Dae Jung administration, the percentage from a military background is 5.5%, academicians 5.5%, bureaucrats 54.2%, politicians 19.4%, journalists 2.8%, lawyers 2.8%, business 4.2%, and other 5.6%.[44] The average percentage of military retirees in cabinet ministries is 9.5% in the post-Cold War era, reduced from 14% in the transitional phase.

Political reforms aimed to decentralize administrative branches and limit military involvement in politics. The Kim Young Sam administration attempted to prohibit military authoritarianism. Bureaucratic restructuring, however, was not democratic. Although the percentage of the military among administrative elites was reduced, the president's Secretariat, National Security Council, and ANSP, which became the National Intelligence Service in January 1999, were still the primary decision-making organs regarding security matters. Thus, South Korea's security policy change was not the result of transformations in the policy-making machinery. Rather, South Korea's globalization and sunshine policies aimed to foster the international trends of economic liberalization and to encourage North Korea to open its economy to the outside world. Its economic engagement approach toward the North is meant to encourage the non-proliferation of weapons of massive destruction in Northeast Asia.

*National Capabilities—GNP and Military Expenditures*

After democratization, the Cold War pillars of economic growth and national security became obsolete. Economic liberalization was implemented to meet the international standards set by APEC, WTO, OECD, and IMF in the areas of trade, finance, and investment. With the 1996 OECD entry, South Korea "opened the champagne bottle," celebrating its membership in one of the chief organizations of the world's wealthiest countries. However, critics soon argued that it celebrated too early and failed to reform its economic infrastructure. In the end, the IMF bailout of 1997 with $57 billion saved South Korea from the road to a national moratorium.

The causes of South Korea's financial and economic crisis are largely fourfold. First, as noted, there was the problem of reversed capital flows. Up to the mid-1990s, capital and technology flowed from North America and Western Europe to the Asia Pacific, but capital flows were reversed after the "bubble" economy developed with high currency depreciation. Secondly, financial regulations of the banking system have been systemically ineffective. Due to semi-monopolistic relationships between banks and firms, banks and financial intermediates financed business by way of foreign capital inflows that increased external debt, especially short-term loans.[45]   Thirdly, fierce external competition in the international market was another factor. External pressures from China and Southeast Asian states intensified the problem of South Korea's export-oriented strategies, and thus, profitability fell dramatically in the 1990s. In addition, the costs of land, labor, and capital were higher than in other competing countries. Fourthly, as discussed, a symbiotic relationship between government and business caused "high cost and low efficiency" in its political economy. Consequently, South Korea and IMF reached an agreement on December 3, 1997, in which South Korea "should narrow the external current account deficit to below 1% of GDP in 1998 and 1999, contain inflation at or below 5%, and limit the deceleration in real GDP growth to about 3% in 1998.[46] The agreed IMF program also included tightened fiscal and monetary policy, financial sector restructuring, trade liberalization, capital sector liberalization and labor market reform.

Except for the year 1998, South Korea's average GNP growth rate was 6.8% in the post-Cold War era. Its 1998 growth rate was minus 5.5%. As shown in Table 6.8, South Korea's GNP and per capita GNP were $476.6 billion and $10,307 in 1997, ranked as the eleventh highest in the world, but these figures decreased to $321.3 billion and $6,823 respectively in 1998. North Korea experienced continuous negative growth in the 1990s, and its GNP was $21.7 billion in 1998. Economic decline, reduced trade, and natural disasters caused an economic and social crisis in North Korea. Estimated North Korean grain shortfalls increased from 2.31 million tons in 1993 to 3.28 million tons in 1996. With international food aid, this shortage was reduced to 2.2-2.7 million tons in 1999.[47] Compared to North Korea, South Korea's lead in 1997 was 21.8: 1 in GNP and 9.7:1 in per capita GNP, but this decreased to 14.8:1 and 6.8:1 in 1998, respectively.

**Table 6.8. GNP Comparison between the Two Koreas: 1993-1998**

| Year | South Korea | | North Korea | |
|------|------|------|------|------|
| | GNP | Per Capita GNP | GNP | Per Capita GNP |
| 1993 | 330.8 | 7,513 | 23.0 | 1,090 |
| 1994 | 378.0 | 8,508 | 22.5 | 1,050 |
| 1995 | 452.6 | 10,076 | 21.7 | 1,010 |
| 1996 | 480.2 | 10,543 | 21.8 | 1,020 |
| 1997 | 476.6 | 10,307 | 21.8 | 1,020 |
| 1998 | 321.3 | 6,823 | 21.7 | 1,010 |

Note: Billions of dollars for GNP and dollars for per capita GNP; 1997 constant dollars.
Sources: Economic Planning Board, *Economic Trends* (Seoul: EPB); U.S. Arms Control and Disarmament Agency, *World Military Expenditures and Arms Transfers* (Washington, D.C.: Government Printing Office); and Taik-young Hamm, *Arming the Two Koreas: State, Capital, and Military Power* (New York: Routledge, 1999), p. 131.

In terms of GDP distribution, on average, the agricultural sector accounted for 6.7%, the industrial sector 41.4%, and the service sector 51.9%.[48] As a percentage of total GDP, the manufacturing sector's contribution within the industrial sector increased from 28.9% in 1993 to 30.1% in 1998. In a process similar to that of the transitional phase, South Korea's manufacturing sector had undergone significant restructuring. The GDP share of textiles and leather industries decreased from 7.6% in 1993 to 3.5% in 1998. The share of fabricated metal products, machinery and equipment increased to 48% in 1998 from 40% in 1993. South Korea's economy was continuously changing it industries into high-tech, capital-intensive ones. But due to the economic crisis of 1997, the unemployment rate increased to 7.8% in 1998 from 2.4% in the 1990s. Wages in manufacturing decreased about 9% and industrial production index decreased about 7.5%.[49] Although recent statistical indicators show a remarkable recovery from the economic crisis, large-scale fundamental reforms in the financial market, capital sector, and labor market are still necessary.

South Korea's 1997 military expenditure was $15 billion, while that of North Korea was $6 billion.[50] The South's lead in military spending was 2.5:1 in 1997, increasing from 2.1:1 in 1993. In the post-Cold War era, North Korea has a numerical advantage over South Korea in most aspects of conventional weapons: man power (1.68:1), tanks (1.73:1), artillery (2.47:1), naval vessels (4.8:1), and aircraft (1.3:1).[51] But South Korea's technological advantages offset the North's numerical superiority. With the continued Force Modernization and Improvement Plans or *Yulgok* Project, almost a third of its military spending has been allocated to military procurement and research and development. South Korea ranked fifth among recipients of major conventional weapons from 1993 to 1998.[52] South Korea's total defense burden, i.e., the sum of defense budget spending and military aid over GNP, also decreased from 3.64% in 1992 to 3.39% in 1997, while that of North Korea maintained around 16.0-20.0% in the 1990s (Hamm, 1999: 129-134).

Certainly, South Korea, coupled with the US-ROK alliance, has less of a defense burden and more technological advantages over North Korea. However, South Korea is highly vulnerable to North Korea's reinforced capabilities, special operation forces, and unconventional weapons that include chemical, biological, and probable nuclear weapons with delivery capabilities.[53] North Korea has deployed large quantities of Scud-Bs and Scud-Cs, and recently test-fired Nodong-1 and 2, Daepodong-1 and 2 which have ranges that include all of the Korean peninsula and Japan. If North Korea initiates a limited war or mistakenly launches missiles at South Korea, South Korea's defense at the initial stage will be ineffective. The North's current economic problems and the uncertainty of its social and political situations also add to speculation as to the possibility of the initiation of limited war and the North's abrupt systemic collapse.[54] Although the sunshine policy aims to neutralize the threat of the North's nuclear and missile programs, it needs to "traverse many minefields, given Pyongyang's apparent need to maintain a degree of tension for its own survival" (Kim, 1999: 500).

## Critical Factors of Security Policy Change during the Post-Cold War

This chapter examined the relative explanatory power of international systemic and domestic institutional factors within the context of the post-Cold War era (1993-1998). As in the case of the Cold War era, the principal source of South Korea's security policy change was the configuration of international systemic determinants. Changed geo-structural factors led North Korea to implement a nuclear and missile program as a security deterrent to equalize the US-ROK military superiority. The North's nuclear threats created a need for negotiations, which resulted in the 1994 US-DPRK agreement that formed the trilateral security alliance regime, KEDO. Economic liberalization and "globalization" were instituted in order to meet international trends and standards set by APEC, WTO, OECD, and IMF. However, reversed capital flows and ineffective economic reforms caused an economic crisis in South Korea in 1997. South Korea's "open global policy" and "sunshine" policy were responsible for dissolving Cold War antagonism and intensifying economic interdependence. In order to induce the North to open its society and remove its coat of geo-political isolationism, South Korea implemented an economic appeasement policy, providing financial and humanitarian aid.

Domestic institutional factors were not primary determinants. Although South Korea transformed its political system to one of the market democracy, its democracy is not fully consolidated. For the most part, political reforms were top-down and thus many aspects of political and economic restructuring were implemented without extensive debate and deliberation. Despite its efforts to "rectify" history, only a break with the military, not with the authoritarian past, was accomplished. One factor that affected South Korea's security policy change was the size of its GNP and military spending. The South had military and economic superiority over the North, but new security threats of nuclear and missile proliferation made the South vulnerable to the North's "diplomatic brinkmanship" that aimed to increase economic aid from the West. North Korea also attempted to use its nuclear programs as a strategic equalizer in respect to the US-ROK military superiority.

To a larger extent, South Korea's security policy change occurred when there were variations in international systemic factors. First of all, the balance-of-power mechanism collapsed in the post-Cold War era. International systemic transformation from a bi-triangular antagonistic system to a multiple bilateral system was the major cause of South Korea's economic engagement policy that was implemented to halt the North's nuclear ambition. The new US-ROK alliance system formed for the partnership of burden sharing and KEDO had a decisive effect upon the South's nuclear non-proliferation policy. Increased intra-regional trade relations and economic interactions with the former communist countries were conducive to dissolving Cold War antagonism. The South's membership in APEC in 1989, WTO in 1995, and OECD in 1996 have been catalysts in its efforts to achieve multilateral economic diplomacy and diplomatic diversification. As the South has fewer defense burdens and more technological advantages over the North, it has implemented a mutual reconciliation policy toward the North. Conditional factors that determined South Korea's security policy change were the multiple bilateral system and increased national capabilities.

Similar to the time of transitional phase, South Korea's security policy change occurred on four inter-related levels: democratic political reforms, economic liberalization and globalization, international systemic transformation, and inter-Korean relations. During the post-Cold War, its security goals were the same as those in the transitional phase; these include democratic consolidation, economic liberalization, economic interdependence, and deterrence for reunification. However, as shown in Figure 6.2, despite lessened military threats, major security problems now included those of nuclear and missile proliferation as well as North Korea's political and economic instability. South Korea's security programs were shifted to globalization and sunshine, economic engagement and appeasement, partnership of burden sharing and modified extended deterrence, economic regionalism including North Korea, nuclear and missile non-proliferation, and peaceful coexistence. Its security programs were also adjusted to those of UN-centered diplomacy and economic diplomacy, direct economic contacts through inter-Korean dialogues and negotiations, and economic partnership for regional integration.

**Figure 6.2. South Korea's Security Policy Change during the Post-Cold War**

| Security Policy During the Transitional Phase | Security Policy During the Post-Cold War |
|---|---|
| **Security Problem Change** | |
| North Korea's Military Aggression Communists' Expansionism ⟶ | Nuclear and Missile Proliferation Political and Economic Instability Lessened Military Threats |
| **Security Program Change** | |
| Northern Policy Northern Diplomacy Modified Extended Deterrence/ Burden Sharing Economic/Diplomatic Interdependence ⟶ Nuclear-Free Korean Peninsula/ Mutual Reconciliation | Globalization and Sunshine Economic Engagement Partnership of Burden Sharing/ Modified Extended Deterrence Economic Regionalism including North Korea Nuclear/Missile Non-proliferation/ Peaceful Coexistence |
| **Security Adjustment Change** | |
| Cross-Recognition/ UN Admission Alignment with the ⟶ Communist Countries Legitimate Partner in Negotiation | UN-Centered Diplomacy/ Economic Diplomacy Direct Economic Contacts through Inter-Korean Dialogues Economic Partner for Regional Integration |

Major criteria that are used to identify the relative importance of critical factors are variations in the distribution of power, the US-ROK alliance system, formal diplomatic and trade relations, types of government, power sharing in the government and the National Assembly, and national military and economic capabilities. The principal source of the South's security problems was changes in the international security alliance and alignment mechanisms. The strategic loss of the North's allies shifted the balance-of-power system in Northeast Asia and in the Korean peninsula. North Korea attempted to ensure national survival, while playing the nuclear card and obtaining economic aid from the West. This occurred because North Korea had both an economic decline and a food shortage in the 1990s. Thus, South Korea's economic engagement policy was utilized to prevent the North's sudden collapse and to delay the reunification process between the two Koreas. Upon implementation of the US-DPRK nuclear agreement, the US-ROK bilateral alliance shifted to a partnership of burden sharing. Increased economic and trade relations were conducive to an economic regionalism that intended to include North Korea. However, domestic institutional factors have retained relatively similar characteristics compared to the transitional phase. No significant institutional restructuring was implemented. Political reforms contributed only to the elimination of the ruling regime's monolithic power in the National Assembly and the "break with the military." Its increased national capabilities contributed to South Korea's "globalization" and "sunshine" policies.

Although international structuralism failed to explain the causes of South Korea's security policy change in the early transitional period, both neorealism and neoliberalism remain as valid theoretical premises regarding post-Cold War South Korea. Changes in regional power politics and balance-of-power system have had decisive effects on South Korea's overall alliance and alignment politics. Neoliberal views on economic interdependence were also applied to South Korea's security policy of reconciliation with the former communist countries and North Korea. On the contrary, domestic institutionalism has lost theoretical ground in explaining South Korea's security policy change in the post-Cold War era. Except for national capabilities, variations in South Korea's domestic politics did not determine its security policy dynamics. As its economic and military capabilities increased, its security priority shifted to concerns for intensifying economic interdependence, rather than for a balance-of-power mechanism. Overall, South Korea's security policy change suggests that international factors have more explanatory power than domestic factors in post-Cold War Northeast Asia. South Korea's security policy now fuses neorealist and neoliberal visions of the international system drawn from multiple bilateralism. As shown in Figure 6.3, international systemic factors became intervening variables that determined South Korea's security policy change and shifts in domestic institutional factors.

**Figure 6.3. Causal Determinants of South Korea's Security Policy Change during the Post-Cold War**

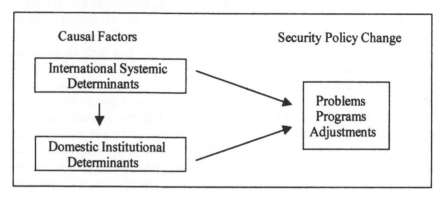

Despite the South's efforts to extend and diversify its international activities through UN-centered diplomacy, it was not able to persuade the North to open its society to the outside world. In addition to the Cold War security dilemma that stemmed from the North's military aggression, the South has to deal with the North's nuclear and missile programs. South Korea also faces new security threats following the North's social and economic crisis, caused by subsequent economic decline and natural disasters in the 1990s. Internally, only a break with the military, not the rectification of history, was accomplished. Ineffective political and economic reforms led to a financial and economic crisis in 1997. In the post-Cold War era, South Korea does not possess an institutional capacity capable of adapting to internal and external changes. International systemic factors have had decisive effects on South Korea's security policy change, but domestic institutional factors have inhibited it from achieving the goal of regional stability and prosperity. South Korea is still in a stage of democratic transition, with both old authoritarian and new democratic characteristics incorporated in its government.

**Notes**

[1] Many claim different time frames for the end of the Cold War in Northeast Asia. In terms of geo-structural perspectives, a systemic transformation in Northeast Asia was completed with the formal alignment between South Korea and China in 1992. Thus, the Cold War system of bi-triangular antagonism disappeared and the post-Cold War era emerged in 1992. For discussions

on the demise of the Cold War, see Harris and Cotton (1991), Hogan (1992), Dobbes-Higginson (1994), Schroeden (1994), and Wanandi (1996).

[2] I use terms of economic engagement and appeasement interchangeably. This policy aims to facilitate economic integration in the region, including North Korea. See Ministry of National Defense, *Defense White Paper* (Seoul: MND, 1998).

[3] The Russia-DPRK Defense Treaty was formally abrogated in 1996, and China also confirmed its objection to any military action in the Korean peninsula. *Ibid.*

[4] South Korea and Japan formed the KEDO alliance to prevent nuclear proliferation in Northeast Asia. But this alliance is not the same politico-military alliance as the mutual defense treaty.

[5] See U.S. Arms Control and Disarmament Agency, *World Military Expenditures and Arms Transfers* (Washington, D.C.: Government Printing Office, 1998).

[6] See International Monetary Fund, *Direction of Trade Statistics Yearbook* (Washington, D.C.: IMF).

[7] The establishment of KEDO by the U.S., Japan, and South Korea is a good example.

[8] From Pyongyang's perspective, nuclear weapons "would provide a countervailing deterrent against U.S. nuclear threats...[that] still exist in the form of the nuclear umbrella held over South Korea—nuclear umbrella simply being a polite way of saying that, under certain circumstances, the United States would use nuclear weapons against North Korea" (Mack, 1994: 27). See also Lee J. S. (1995).

[9] See Ministry of National Defense, *Defense White Paper* (Seoul: MND, 1998) and Lee (1999), pp. 8-9.

[10] For further details on the US-DPRK agreement, see Koh (1994), Lehman (1994), and Mazarr (1995).

[11] The transfer took effect as scheduled for which Foreign Minister Sung-Joo Han and U.S. Ambassador James Laney signed an agreement on November 1993. See Ministry of National Defense, *Defense White Paper* (Seoul, MND, 1995).

[12] APEC leaders agreed to open trade, investment, tourism, and other links between the economies in Bogor, Indonesia. It was known as the 1994 Bogor declaration for "open regionalism." See Koh (1998), pp. 288-290.

[13] Globalization is pursued as a means of economic integration for national reunification. South Korea planned a gradual process of economic and social integration with North Korea by 2010 and a unified Korea by 2020. See Department of Public Information, *Globalization Blueprint: 1995-2020* (Seoul: DPI, 1995) and Yoon (1995), pp. 13-28.

[14] From 1993 to 1998, trade surplus with China was $15,797 million and trade deficit with Russia was $696 million. See Economic Planning Board, *Major Statistics of Korean Economy* (Seoul: EPB).

[15] See International Monetary Fund, *Direction of Trade Statistics Yearbook* (Washington, D.C.: IMF).

[16] South Korea was North Korea's major trading partner. In 1995, the South's percentage share of the North's total exports was 21%, 4% in its total imports. Japan ranked the first with 28% in total exports and China shared 33% in total imports. See Central Intelligence Agency, *The World Factbook* (Washington, D.C.: Government Printing Office).

[17] From 1993 to 1998, North Korea's trade deficit was $1,979 million and with Russia $543 million. North Korea's importation of Russian crude oil fell from 410,000 tons in 1990 to a mere 40,000 tons in 1997. It is also reported that its bilateral trade has declined by 70% since 1994. See International Monetary Fund, *Direction of Trade Statistics Yearbook* (Washington, D.C.: IMF).

[18] See World Bank, *World Development Report* (Washington, D.C.: World Bank).

[19] It is difficult to explain the Asian financial and economic crisis from any single factor or perspective. Instead, the crisis should be viewed as resulting from a combination of domestic

and international causes. This section only addresses international factors, and in the later part of this chapter, I will discuss domestic causes of economic crises.

[20] In July 1997, when Thailand ended the peg of the baht to the U.S. dollar, a chain reaction occurred in the currencies of neighboring countries. By October 1997, the baht had fallen 60%, the Indonesian rupiah 47%, the Malaysian ringgit by 35%, and the Philippines peso by 34%. By November 1997, South Korean won had fallen by 46%. See World Bank, *World Bank Indicators* (Washington, D.C.: World Bank).

[21] The classic "bubble" economy is one in which "real estate prices continue to rise well beyond the levels justified by the productivity of the assets, but as long as the prices continue to rise, existing investors are rewarded and collateral is created for new loans to finance further investment, and so on—until the inevitable crash" (Warr, 1998: 60). In the Asian case, with capital inflows and foreign loans, the currency and stock markets were overvalued beyond the levels justified by the productivity of the industries; eventually, reversed capital flows led to a financial crisis.

[22] See World Bank, *Private Capital Flows to Developing Countries: The Road to Financial Integration* (London: Oxford University Press, 1997).

[23] In June 1997, foreign bank debt "was 24% of GDP, while total short-term debt was equal to around 350% of foreign exchange reserves, [and] the biggest 30 *chaebol* had average debt-equity ratio around 400%, compared with an average of 70% for large U.S. firms" (Laurence, 1999: 363). See also International Monetary Fund, *International Financial Statistics Yearbook* (Washington, D.C.: IMF) and Smith (1998), p. 67.

[24] The sunshine policy is aimed to improve inter-Korean relations in line with peaceful coexistence, reconciliation and cooperation. The sunshine, as opposed to strong wind, also attempts to remove the North's coat of isolation. See Ministry of National Defense, *Defense White Paper* (Seoul: MND, 1999).

[25] See Ministry of Foreign Affairs and Trade, *Diplomacy White Paper* (Seoul: MFAT).

[26] About 55% to 65% of its aid was bilateral, and only about 30% was transferred through multilateral agencies. Its ODA/GNP rate was 0.06% in 1998. Major recipients were China and Southeast Asian States. See Ministry of Finance and Economy, *Korea's Economic Assistance for Developing Countries* (Seoul: MOFE).

[27] See Ministry of National Defense, *Defense White Paper* (Seoul: MND, 1999).

[28] Secretary of Defense William Perry in an interview on NBC on May 23, 1995, said that the U.S. is considering military action or international economic sanctions if the North were to re-rod its nuclear reactors in Youngbyun.

[29] See Ministry of Unification, *Status of South-North Cooperation Fund* (Seoul: MOU, 2000).

[30] Following to the Korean War, there are still about 10 million separated families.

[31] As of the end of January 1999, a total of 965 North Koreans have defected to the South. See Ministry of Unification, *Status of Arrivals in the South by North Korean Defectors* (Seoul: MOU, 2000).

[32] Domestic insitutionalists include Park, Ko, and Kim (1994), Yang (1994), and Kong and Kim (1997).

[33] President Kim was elected with 42% of the vote in November 1992. As the first civilian president, he initiated large-scale political and economic reforms that he called a "rectification of history." See Election Management Committee, *History of Elections in Korea* (Seoul: EMC).

[34] They were released under President Kim Young Sam's programs of amnesty in 1997.

[35] Kim Dae Jung, the president of NCNP, won the 1997 presidential election with 40.3% of the vote, while Lee Hoi Chang, the presidential candidate of NKP, had 38.7% of the vote. *Ibid.*

[36] South Korea is still in the transitional phase of democratization, if democratization is understood as a complex process with several analytically distinct but empirically overlapping

stages: "decline of authoritarian rule, transition, consolidation, and maturity of democracy." See Schmitter and O'Donnell (1986) and Huntington (1991).

[37] Many well-to-do and middle-class citizens complained about the real-name financial system. Many criticized that the financial reform aimed to punish political adversaries by "a selective political house-cleaning." See Hahm (1996), pp. 5-7.

[38] President Kim Young Sam was portrayed as "rule of man," rather than "rule of law." See Kim Y. (1994) and Hahm and Rhyu (1997).

[39] The approval rate was lower than 5% in December 1997. Interestingly, President Kim's approval rates were collapsing as South Korea's economy was deteriorating. See Hahm and Rhyu (1997), pp. 45-46.

[40] See Election Management Committee, *History of Elections in Korea* (Seoul: EMC).

[41] *Ibid.*

[42] See Yonhap News Agency, *Korea Annual* (Seoul: YNA).

[43] See Huntington (1968), passim.

[44] See Ministry of Public Information, *The Governmental Elites of the Republic of Korea* (Seoul: MPI, 1999).

[45] For further details on South Korea's financial crisis, see Amsden and Hikino (1998), Garnaut (1998), Greenspan (1998), and Krugman (1998).

[46] See Ministry of Finance and Economy, *IMF Program for Korea* (Seoul: MOFE, 2000).

[47] See National Unification Board, *Humanitarian Aid to North Korea* (Seoul: NUB) and Reese (1998), pp. 28-32.

[48] See OECD, *OECD Economic Outlook* (Paris: OECD) and Bank of Korea, *Economic Statistics Yearbook* (Seoul: BOK).

[49] *Ibid.*

[50] Despite the economic crisis of 1997, the 1998 defense budget was fixed at approximately 1997 levels. See U.S. Arms Control and Disarmament Agency, *World Military Expenditures and Arms Transfers* (Washington, D.C.: Government Printing Office).

[51] See Ministry of National Defense, *Defense White Paper* (Seoul: MND).

[52] See Stockholm International Peace Research Institute, *World Armaments and Disarmament Yearbook* (London: Taylor & Francis).

[53] In 1993, the former Secretary of Defense, Les Aspin, stated that the North possibly had one or two nuclear warheads. See Engleberg and Gordon (1993), p.1.

[54] After the death of Kim Il-Sung in July 1994, speculation about the North's systemic collapse mounted. His son Kim Jung-Il succeeded him in power, but his leadership has been criticized because of his lack of charisma and experience in military affairs. How he is rated as a leader will depend upon his ability to handle the nuclear and missile issue and improve the sluggish economy. Kim Jung-Il, the dear leader, formally became the General Secretary of the North Korean Workers Party in October 1997.

# 7. Conclusion: Critical Factors of Security Policy Change

In the preceding chapters, I discussed contextual determinants of South Korea's security policy change within the context of the Cold War era (1954-1987), transitional phase (1988-1992), and post-Cold War era (1993-1998). Each chapter examines the relative explanatory power of international structuralism and domestic institutionalism. It also identifies specific conditional factors that affected South Korea's security policy behavior. Its institutional capacity in adapting to internal and external changes is also spelled out. This chapter will recapitulate the principal themes and discuss the theoretical implications. Finally, I will elaborate on future aspects of South Korea's international relations with regional major powers and possible reunification scenarios.

## Overall Patterns of Security Policy Change

South Korea's security policy change illustrates both incremental and dramatic characteristics in its overall trends of change, contents of change, and scope and levels of involvement. The goals of South Korean security policies have been evolutionary, changing from strengthening military and economic capabilities to helping to establish regional economic interdependence. Its security policy change was also dramatic, shifting its international security orientation toward the communist countries from one of ideological antagonism to diplomatic/economic rapprochement. Thus, both incremental and dramatic changes show shifts in South Korea's priority concerns from a deterrence aspect of regional balance-of-power to the creation of international interdependence through the extended security alliance and alignment mechanism.

During the Cold War era, the external structure of military confrontation and the bi-triangular system led South Korea to retain international structuralists' prescriptions. These prescriptions include strengthening military capabilities, economic development, competitive diplomacy, and effective formation of extended deterrence. Through these security programs, South Korea aimed to maintain the balance-of-power mechanism in the Korean peninsula and Northeast Asia. However, South Korea's security policy during the transitional phase and post-Cold War era showed a dramatic change in its international interactions and levels/scope of involvement. Democratization in the years of 1987-1988 was conducive to eliminating traditional concerns of regime security and political legitimacy, thereby abolishing the Cold War ideological rivalry against the communist countries. With *nordpolitik*, domestic institutional rearrangements instituted a dramatic policy restructuring with a change to governed interdependence from one of a defensive deterrence policy. But the variations in international systemic factors with the goal of transformation to the multiple bilateral system have had decisive effects on South Korea's security programs of regional economic interdependence, economic engagement, partnership of burden sharing, and nuclear non-proliferation in the 1990s. New international determinants that include the North's nuclear ambition and increased economic interdependence have imposed systemic constraints as well as opportunities upon South Korea. The governed interdependence policy aims to intensify regional economic interactions including those with North Korea and to encourage that nation to open its autarchic system.

There have been three major changes in South Korea's security policy: (1) from absolute anti-communism to mutual antagonism, (2) from defensive deterrence to governed interdependence, and (3) from *nordpolitik* to globalization and sunshine policy. First, the shift from anti-communism to mutual antagonism involved South Korea's security policy goal, program, and adjustment changes. The scope and levels of the Syngman Rhee regime's (1948-1960) international involvement were limited within the spheres of its Western allies, while those of the Park Chung Hee (1961-1979) and Chun Do Whan (1980-1987) regimes were extended toward Japan and non-aligned developing countries. The latter regimes' goals were shifted to deterrence, economic development, and political/international legitimacy. Lacking regime security and political legitimacy, authoritarian regimes institutionalized economic development, while strengthening the US-ROK alliance mechanism. To reach these goals, they implemented security programs of mutual antagonism, competitive diplomacy, extended deterrence, and economic/military modernization. The South's policy toward the North was adjusted from the no two Koreas policy to de facto recognition of North Korea. To a great extent, South Korea attempted to sustain the regional balance-of-power mechanism through a defensive deterrence policy during the Cold War.

Second, the Noh Tae Woo administration (1988-1992) restructured its international security orientation by easing its Cold War ideological antagonistic postures; this led to changes in South Korea's security goal/problem, program, and adjustment. Unexpectedly, its scope and levels of international involvement expanded to the former communist countries. Democratization eliminated the Cold War authoritarian military regime, and its security goals changed to promotion of regional interdependence, democratic consolidation, and economic liberalization. To reach these goals, South Korea implemented new security programs of *nordpolitik*, economic/diplomatic interdependence, and modified extended deterrence/burden sharing. South Korea also adjusted its policy from de facto recognition of North Korea to seeking mutual recognition of the two Koreas by the regional major powers. However, in the early 1990s, a new security problem of nuclear proliferation emerged due to a shift in international alliance and alignment mechanisms. Thus, South Korea's governed interdependence policy aims to achieve regional stability and prosperity through economic interdependence and mutual reconciliation with North Korea.

Third, the Kim Young Sam administration's (1993-1997) globalization and the Kim Dae Jung administration's (1998-present) sunshine policies have been implemented to achieve a peaceful coexistence between the two Koreas and eventual unification. South Korea's security problem, program, and adjustment changes took place during the 1990s. The shift resulted from new security problems, such as the North's nuclear and missile programs as well as its social/economic crisis. To meet the new security problem, the US-ROK extended deterrence was modified and the partnership of burden sharing was expanded to KEDO for nuclear non-proliferation. The purpose of the South's economic regionalism and engagement policy was to pressure the North into taking off its coat of isolationism. The South adjusted its policy to induce the North to open its society to the outside world and treated North Korea as an economic partner for regional economic integration. South Korea in the post-Cold War era finds itself in the midst of two momentous worldwide transformations, democratization and economic liberalization, and endeavors to promote the peaceful process of national reunification through governed interdependence policy. Figure 7.1 shows the overall trends of South Korea's security policy change, and security policy goals are largely defined as defensive deterrence during the Cold War era and governed interdependence during the post-Cold War era.

**Figure 7.1. Overall Trends of South Korea's Security Policy Change**

Trends of Security Policy Change

| Cold War | Transitional Phase | Post-Cold War |
|---|---|---|
| (1954-1987) | (1988-1992) | (1993-1998) |

Defensive Deterrence · · · · · · · · · · Governed Interdependence

| Anti-Communism | Mutual Antagonism | *Nordpolitik* | Globalization/Sunshine |
|---|---|---|---|
| Non-Alignment | Competitive Diplomacy | Economic/Diplomatic Interdependence | Economic Diplomacy/ Engagement |
| Alliance with the West | ⇒ Extended Deterrence | ⇒ Modified Extended Deterrence | ⇒ Partnership of Burden Sharing |
| No Two Koreas ▲ | *De Facto* Recognition ▲ | Mutual Recognition ▲ | Peaceful Coexistence/ No Nuclear Policy |

Contents of
Change

| Adjustment | International Orientation | Adjustment |
|---|---|---|
| Program | Adjustment | Program |
| Goal | Program | Problem |
| | Problem/Goal | |

| 1961/1980 | 1987-1988 | 1993/1998 |
|---|---|---|

Scope and Levels of Involvement

| Western Allies | Western Allies and Developing Countries | International and Communist States | International and North Korea |
|---|---|---|---|

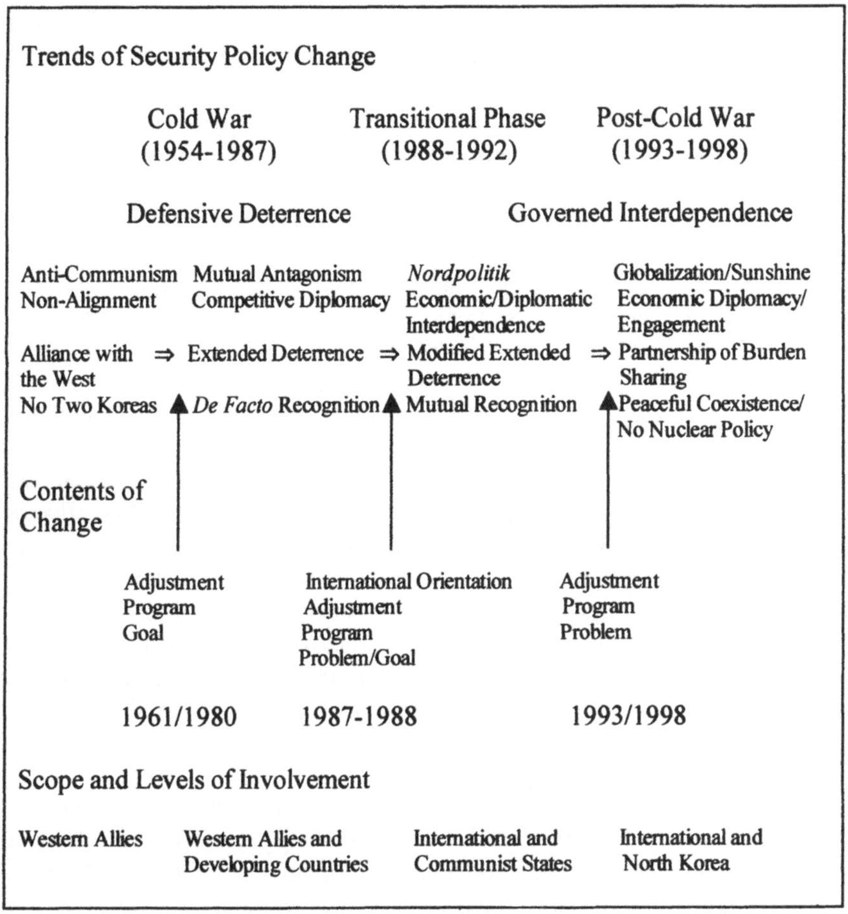

## Critical Determinants of South Korea's Security Policy Change

In this study of South Korea's security policy behaviors, a number of questions are raised. First and foremost, under what conditions does a policy change occur? Second, which determinants are most influential in the security policy change? Third, are security policy-making institutions capable of adapting to internal and external changes? This study's primary question is: Under what conditions do domestic politics take precedent over international politics, or vice versa? To answer these questions, a historical-comparative approach has been applied to South Korea's policy restructuring in the international security orientation, integrating system- and state-level analyses. This approach explores the historically continuous and discontinuous patterns of South Korea's policy change as influenced by international systemic and domestic institutional factors.

The dependent variable is South Korea's security policy change; security policies are defined as the government's official security policies as declared and stated in the Ministry of National Defense, *Defense White Paper* and the Ministry of Foreign Affairs, *Diplomacy White Paper*. The independent variables include international and domestic determinants. International factors are classified into these categories: geo-structural factors of regional security and economic structures, geo-strategic factors of alliance formations, geo-economic factors of economic interdependence and financial alignment mechanisms, and geo-political factors of diplomacy and international institutions. Domestic factors include types of government, legal-institutional setting, policy-making machinery, and national capabilities. In order to determine the relative importance of these international and domestic factors, evaluative criteria such as the relative distribution of power, US-ROK alliance system, formal diplomatic and trade relations, types of government, power sharing in the government and the National Assembly, and national military and economic capabilities are employed. These evaluative criteria are used to test theoretical causal claims and the relative explanatory power of international structuralism and domestic institutionalism. While these criteria do not cover all aspects of South Korea's security policy change, they indicate the major direction of causal relations between international systemic and domestic institutional factors.

To a great extent, South Korea's security policy change resulted from fluctuations in both international systemic and domestic institutional conditions. Both bi-triangular system/authoritarian regimes during the Cold War era and multiple bilateral system/market democracy during the post-Cold War era resulted in important systemic constraints on and opportunities for South Korea's security policy behaviors. In certain situations, it followed systemic constraints and opportunities, while under other conditions it implemented a new security orientation. If South Korea did not respond to external fluctuations, then conditional factors were usually found in internal political factors. If external factors imposed significant systemic constraints and opportunities, then South Korea either actively responded to the strategic imperatives of the international system or passively became a mere bystander in regional power politics. I will now review the critical factors that determined South Korea's security policy change throughout the Cold War era, transitional phase, and post-Cold War era.

During the Cold War era, conditional factors that determined South Korea's security policy change were both the bi-triangular antagonistic system and the nation's authoritarian military regime. This policy change followed international systemic constraints derived from the bipolar hegemonic security blocs structured by the U.S. and the Soviet Union as well as the bi-triangular antagonistic system formed by the U.S., Japan, and South Korea on the capitalist side and the Soviet Union, China, and North Korea on the communist side. International systemic factors caused the emergence of a military security regime that imposed constraints on South Korea's security policy behaviors. Preoccupied with the concerns of regime security and political legitimacy, this authoritarian military regime established mutual antagonism involving the formerly communist countries. South Korea chose not to become actively involved in the changing regional alignment mechanism formulated by the U.S., China, and Japan during the détente of the 1970s.

The principal source of South Korea's security policy change was the configuration of international systemic determinants during the Cold War era. Regional structures were militarily bipolar (structured by the U.S. and the Soviet Union) and economically unipolar, dominated by the U.S. South Korea allied itself with the U.S. in order to deter the North's military aggression and communist expansionism. There were phased reductions in the U.S. forces stationed in South Korea and the U.S. economic/military aid after the late 1950s. This change led the South to strengthen its US-ROK alliance and modernize its military forces. A high degree of economic dependence upon the U.S. and Japan necessitated diversification of its diplomatic and economic relations with non-aligned developing countries. Economic development also required foreign capital and therefore South Korea normalized its relationship with Japan. Internally, the authoritarian military regime monopolized political power in the government and the National Assembly, and initiated "total defense" through a mutually hostile policy toward North Korea. External threats were often utilized to ensure regime survival, and mutual antagonism was necessary in order to justify the authoritarian rule. The ideological rivalry against the former communist countries prevented South Korea from improving relations with China and North Korea. South Korea's national capabilities were not strong enough to maintain a balance-of-power mechanism in Northeast Asia. South Korea could not survive without the U.S. extended deterrence because it could not defend itself by its own means.

During the transitional phase, both domestic institutional and international systemic factors played major roles in South Korea's security policy change. Conditional factors had more to do with domestic institutional factors in the years of 1987-1988 than did international systemic factors. Pro-democratic movements in the mid-1980s resulted in the issuing of the June 29, 1987 declaration for democratic reform. Democratization had an important, positive impact on security matters. The new democratic government realized that rigid anti-communism was no longer necessary to sustain regional stability and prosperity. Abandoning the ideological commitment to anti-communism allowed the emergence of the new policy initiative of *nordpolitik*. Thus, South Korea in the years of 1987-1988 implemented a new security orientation that was not derived from changes in external systemic factors. South Korea's security policy reorientation preceded major shifts in international systemic factors.

In the years of 1987-1988, the balance-of-power mechanism in the geo-structural power equilibrium remained the same as in the Cold War era. The US-ROK alliance retained its Cold War characteristics of deterrence against North Korea and containment against communist expansionism. Formal diplomatic and economic relations were intensified after the mid-1980s, but these interactions were largely informal and resulted from a realistic calculation to gain geo-economic and geo-political benefits. Internally, South Korea changed to a market democracy, which guaranteed a free and fair election via the new Constitution of 1987. Democratization was accompanied by the lifting of security measures and the elimination of the Cold War state apparatuses. The military was forced to withdraw its role in the government, and the ruling party could no longer hold a majority in the National Assembly. The South's increased economic and military capabilities as compared to those of the North provided the essential underpinnings for the new security orientation of a governed interdependence policy. As a result, the configuration of domestic institutional factors became a critical determinant in the years of 1987-1988.

Contrarily, the role of international conditional factors became reversed in the early 1990s. Conditional factors included shifting patterns of the international system that eliminated the Cold War antagonistic postures and promoted South Korea's increased national capabilities. Transformations in international systemic factors had decisive effects upon South Korea's international security reorientation toward regional economic interdependence. The bi-triangular system was shifting to the multiple bilateral system as the result of diplomatic and economic normalization among South Korea, Russia, and China. Diplomatic and economic rapprochement also occurred among the U.S., Russia, China, and Japan. The South's increased national capabilities made the approach of economic interdependence possible. In the early 1990s, South Korea followed external systemic constraints and opportunities and actively responded to the strategic imperatives of the international system.

Transformations in geo-structural, geo-strategic, geo-economic, and geo-political factors contributed to further economic interdependence and the end to military and strategic antagonism among regional major powers in the early 1990s. The Soviet Union/Russia began to decrease its military spending, while the U.S. became the sole military superpower. The U.S. and Japan retained their economic status in the regional economic power equilibrium. The US-ROK alliance system shifted to a partnership of burden sharing and its extended deterrence formula was changed to one of nuclear non-proliferation. New diplomatic ties and increased economic interactions made the South implement *nordpolitik* that aimed to pressure the North to open its autarchic system. Domestic factors included the ongoing processes of democratization and political liberalization. Power sharing in the government and the National Assembly remained similar to the patterns in the years of 1987-1988. Only increased national capabilities were conducive to intensifying regional economic interdependence. Thus, critical determinants in the early 1990s were the configuration of international systemic factors.

During the post-Cold War era, conditional factors were international systemic factors of the multiple bilateral system and national capabilities. South Korea completed its economic and diplomatic normalization with the former communist countries, but North Korea was excluded from these new geo-economic and geo-political links. The new Northeast Asian system incorporated multiple alliance formations and diversified alignment mechanisms among the U.S., Japan, China, Russia, and South Korea. This new multiple bilateral system caused a new security problem: the nuclear proliferation of the North. South Korea has attempted to induce North Korea to take off its coat of isolationism by implementing globalization and sunshine policies. While maintaining economic and military advantages over the North, the South has provided financial and humanitarian aid in order to foster the process of national reunification and to prevent the North's sudden collapse. During the post-Cold War era, South Korea has taken advantages of systemic constraints and opportunities and has actively searched for the means to make peace and stop nuclear/missile proliferation in Northeast Asia.

To a large extent, critical determinants can be found in international systemic factors during the post-Cold War era. The U.S. retains sole superpower status with its preeminence in every domain of power, but it relies upon other major states to manage its security and economic tasks. Economically, the U.S. and Japan formed a bipolar structure, while China increased its military and economic capabilities. The US-ROK bilateral relationship shifted from an asymmetrical alliance to a partnership of burden sharing. A trilateral commitment, KEDO, operated by the U.S., Japan, and South Korea, was established to implement the 1994 US-DPRK nuclear agreement. South Korea's open economic diplomacy aimed to meet international trends of economic liberalization set by APEC, WTO, and OECD. Increased trade relations were conducive to dissolving Cold War animosity, but led to the financial and economic crisis of 1997. Internally, democratic reforms only contributed to the elimination of the ruling regime's monolithic power in the National Assembly and the break with the military in the government. No significant institutional restructuring was implemented. Only increased national capabilities were of importance in the South's "peace-making" or economic engagement policy to the North that aimed to relax military antagonism through inter-Korean contacts and dialogues rather than through isolation and containment.

South Korea's security policy change was influenced by international systemic factors as the bi-triangular system shifted to a multiple bilateral system. The governmental system, a transitional democracy shifting toward a market democracy that evolved from developmental authoritarianism, has profound security implications. In authoritarian regimes, economic growth supported by massive military and economic aid from the U.S. and Japan appeared to be a solution. But the authoritarian regimes' lack of political legitimacy and regime security undercut the institutional capacity to respond to external changes. South Korea faced both an internal insecurity dilemma and an external security dilemma. But democratization enabled South Korea to make changes before shifts occurred in international systemic factors and increased its institutional capacity to respond to domestic pro-democratic demands. The democratic government reduced internal insecurity but faced a new security threat, that of nuclear proliferation. In the post-Cold War order, security threats resulted from the North's nuclear and missile programs and its social/economic crisis. Internally, political and economic reforms were in progress but ineffective economic reforms led to the financial and economic crisis of 1997. South Korea does not possess an institutional capacity that can adapt to internal and external changes, and its democracy is not yet fully consolidated. As shown in Table 7.1, South Korea's security policy behaviors can best be described in terms of policy patterns, conditional factors, and critical determinants as well as institutional capacity in dealing with contextual changes.

**Table 7.1.  Analytic Framework of Critical Determinants in South Korea's Security Policy Change**

| Time Frame | Policy Patterns | Conditional Factors | Critical Determinants | Institutional Capacity |
|---|---|---|---|---|
| Cold War Era (1954-1987) | Mutual Antagonism. Competitive Diplomacy. Extended Deterrence. *De Facto* Recognition. | Bi-triangular Antagonistic System and Authoritarian Military Regime. | Relative Distribution of Power. US-ROK Alliance System. Formal Diplomatic and Economic Relations. Authoritarianism. | Lack of Political Legitimacy and Regime Security. External Insecurity Dilemma. |
| Transitional Phase (1988-1992) | *Nordpolitik.* Economic/ Diplomatic Interdependence. Modified Extended Deterrence. Mutual Recognition. | Democratization and National Capabilities in the Years of 1987-1988. | Democratic Government. Power Sharing in the Government and the National Assembly. National Capabilities. | Lessened Internal Insecurity Dilemma. New Security Problem of Nuclear Proliferation. |
|  |  | Multiple Bilateralism and National Capabilities in the Early 1990s. | Relative Distribution of Power. US-ROK Alliance System. Formal Diplomatic and Economic Relations. National Capabilities. |  |
| Post-Cold War Era (1993-1998) | Globalization/ Sunshine. Economic Engagement. Partnership of Burden Sharing. Peaceful Coexistence/ Nuclear Non-proliferation. | Multiple Bilateralism and National Capabilities. | Relative Distribution of Power. US-ROK Alliance. Formal Diplomatic and Economic Relations. National Capabilities. | Ineffective Political and Economic Reforms. New Security Dilemma of the North's Nuclear/Missile Programs. |

## Theoretical Implications

This study explores the concept of "restructuring" or "policy reorientation," one behavior of a state that has been largely neglected in the field of security policy analysis. Theoretical questions raised in this study involve the linkages between international systemic/domestic institutional factors and South Korea's security policy change. Questions include how South Korea defines its security goals, why it chooses certain policies and rejects others, and how it responds to external and internal changes. This study analyzes contextual conditions that provide systemic constraints on and/or opportunities in South Korea's security policy-making. Profound theoretical insights are gained from the examination of changes in South Korean security policies throughout the Cold War era, transitional phase, and post-Cold War era. These finding and themes stemmed from international systemic factors, domestic institutional factors, and contextual factors, all of which determined South Korea's security policy change.

South Korea's security policy change is reflective of changes in international systemic factors. That is, its security policy resulted either from externally imposed constraints or from the loosening of constraints. For the most part, South Korea's security policy behaviors were derived from external systemic pressures generated in the international context of the bi-triangular antagonistic and multiple bilateral system. For example, the North's military aggression and communist expansionism forced the South to formulate mutually antagonistic policies against the communist countries. As previously pointed out, South Korea's policy variations were determined by the prevailing balance-of-power mechanism within the bi-triangular antagonistic framework. The distribution of capabilities in the Northeast Asian system—that is, the bipolar structure of power—influenced both North and South Korean security policies. This supports hypothesis (1) employed in Chapter 3. Changes in the U.S. security policy also significantly affected South Korea's security alternatives, but variations in regional power politics did not alter the latter's alliance and alignment politics. An example is the South Korea's relations toward China during the détente of the 1970s. Thus, hypothesis (2) was not applied to South Korea during the Cold War era.

South Korea's economic engagement policy was a shift that resulted from the new security problem of nuclear proliferation and the lessened antagonism in post-Cold War Northeast Asia. Transformations in the balance-of-power mechanism during the early 1990s made economic interdependence possible. Russia lost its status as a superpower and the U.S. remained as sole superpower, dominating every realm of power. Changes in economic interactions and trade relations also had decisive effects on South Korea's international security orientation. Every state in the Northeast Asian region became formally aligned and their economic relations intensified after the early 1990s. South Korea's increased national capabilities made it to shift its security priority to concerns for economic interactions. Only North Korea was excluded from the new international geo-economic and geo-political links.

Shifts in regional power politics determined South Korea's alliance and alignment politics. Discussions above, therefore, support hypotheses (1), (2), (3), (5), and (6), except (4), during the early 1990s and the post-Cold War era.

In the case of South Korea, international systemic factors provide security means or programs to achieve its security goals. Alliances, economic trades, and diplomacy generate avenues through which South Korea can react to any external security dilemma. External factors also influence the process and timing of alliance and alignment mechanisms, as seen in the Cold War bi-triangular and the post-Cold War multiple bilateral system. To a large extent, international factors generated systemic constraints that restricted other alternatives except containment and deterrence against communism, while allowing systemic opportunities for market access as provided by the U.S. and Japan during the Cold War era. Systemic constrains resulted from the North's nuclear/missile programs, while systemic opportunities expanded following the intensifying of economic interdependence during the post-Cold War era. Consequently, external structural conditions channeled South Korea's security policy orientation, goal/problem, program, and adjustment changes. In this respect, the neorealist premise retained its theoretical validity throughout the years of 1954-1998, except during the years of 1987-1988. Neoliberal views on economic interdependence may also be equally applied to South Korea's security policy change toward the communist countries in the 1990s.

Shifts in South Korea's institutional arrangements have had a significant impact on its security policy decisions. For example, democratization and elimination of the military in politics allowed South Korea to implement a new international security orientation that aimed to maintain regional stability and prosperity. This new security policy orientation was possible after the Cold War antagonism postures toward the former communist countries ceased. Increased national capabilities enabled the South to propose diplomatic/economic normalization with the former communist countries and to advocate mutual reconciliation with the North in order to implement the peaceful process of national reunification. As South Korea's national capabilities increase, its security policy shifts from concerns of politico-military balance-of-power to those of economic interactions. In this vein, hypotheses (4) and (5) are supported in the years of 1987-1988.

South Korea's security policy change resulted from domestic institutional factors that generated institutional constraints and opportunities to adopt certain security policies and eliminate others. The authoritarian military regime discouraged any alternative other than mutual antagonism. In the years 1987-1988, shifts in institutional arrangements led to a change in South Korea's perception of security problems, programs, and goals. The legal-institutional setting and policy-making machinery now provided specific guidance for South Korea's security policy behaviors. With the abolishment of the Cold War ideological antagonism and the elimination of the military, new patterns of power sharing made possible a new security orientation including *nordpolitik*, economic interdependence, and mutual reconciliation. A major change in South Korea's domestic institutional factors includes the increased institutional capacity to implement different courses of action and formulate alternative security goals. In the years 1987-1988, a security policy change occurred prior to the shift in international systemic factors. This does not support hypothesis (6) and the theoretical premise of domestic institutionalism remains valid during the democratic transitional phase.

The discussions above suggest that South Korea's security policy change resulted from both internally and externally imposed opportunities and/or constraints. Institutional arrangements of domestic politics and structural factors of international politics have had interactive impacts on South Korea's security policy change. As previously discussed, both bi-triangular antagonistic system/authoritarian military regime and multiple bilateral system/market democracy imposed both systemic and institutional constraints on and opportunities in South Korea's security policy. Thus, neoclassical realism and neoclassical liberalism that include domestic political factors in their systemic analyses provide a better understanding of South Korea's security policy change. Policy variations are consequences of complex dynamic processes in which both external and internal factors causally condition each other over time. South Korea's change in international security orientation, programs, and goals/problems resulted from fluctuations in contextual determinants of domestic and international politics. During the transitional phase, a dramatic policy change resulted from domestic institutional rearrangements, and was enhanced by international systemic fluctuations in the implementation stage.

However, given South Korea's unique geo-strategic situations, international systemic factors have a greater explanatory power than do domestic institutional factors. As pointed out, evaluative criteria of South Korea's security policy change prove that international determinants have greater systemic impacts than domestic determinants. This supports hypothesis (6). Both external and internal factors condition South Korea's security policy behavior, but critical determinants are largely found in international systemic factors except for the years 1987-1988. For example, the primary motive of South Korea's economic development and political legitimacy was to sustain national survival during the Cold War. Its defensive deterrence policy aimed to maintain the balance-of-power mechanism structured by the bi-triangular antagonistic system. Since the transitional phase, South Korea's primary security concerns are intensifying economic interdependence and relaxing military confrontation with North Korea. Its governed interdependence policy aims to establish a system of sustained regional stability and prosperity that can be portrayed as "mature anarchy." To establish a mature anarchy, South Korea combines both strategies of deterrence against the North's military and nuclear threats and economic interdependence that includes North Korea. This strategy is referred to as a "stick and carrot" approach. Thus, in the post-Cold War era, South Korea appears to be a fusion of neorealist and neoliberal visions of the international system.

This study tests theoretical causal claims of existing theories. It points out limitations in terms of the theories' analytical perspectives and methodologies, emphasis on continuity, linkage politics, and critical determinants in explaining South Korea's security policy change. As illustrated in explaining conditional factors, an integrated approach of system-level and state-level analyses is suggested as an alternative. The South Korean case clearly illustrates that an integrated explanation is necessary to establish a comprehensive understanding of its security policy change. In order to examine the relative importance of conditional factors, evaluative criteria are employed, since South Korea constantly changed its policies in response to perceived changes in international and domestic contexts. By comparing these evaluative criteria over different time frames, a comparative-historical approach underscores the relative importance of critical determinants. Comparative analysis of evaluative criteria over the Cold War era, transitional phase, and post-Cold War era indicates that there are interactive effects of international systemic and domestic institutional factors. However, changes in South Korea's international systemic postures have had a greater impact on its security policy change than those in domestic institutional arrangements.

What does the above explanation, that South Korea's security policy change resulted from variations in external and internal contexts, imply? The theoretical contributions of this study are fivefold. First, this study helps to understand the changing nature and character of security contexts that generate the state's distinctive security policies. It maps the overall direction of South Korea's security policy change, conditional factors, and critical determinants over time. Second, it broadens theoretical and analytical perspectives by including institutional dynamics of domestic politics in the security studies. The South Korean case clearly demonstrates that fuller explanations of security policy behaviors require an integrated level and multi-variable explanatory framework. In this vein, further research is required incorporating political culture-level and individual-level analyses. Third, this study clarifies the relative importance of contextual factors that determine the state's security policy change. Through a comparative-historical analysis, this study demonstrates conditional factors and critical determinants that determined South Korea's security policy dynamics. Fourth, it enriches policy formulation and implementation for policy-makers by illustrating how states perceive external threats and define their goals, choose programs, and adjust their international security orientation.   By showing conditional constraints and opportunities generated over time, this study evaluates different governments' institutional capacities.   Fifth, it explains why states act as they do toward one another in the area of international politics.   It demonstrates why, how, and under what conditions South Korea changes its security policy, responding to external and internal changes.   Since the demise of the Cold War, and through the present, there is little agreement on what alternative approaches are most promising in explaining the state's behavior in world politics.   As Kenneth N. Waltz maintains, an understanding of the third image of international politics alone does not make it possible to understand the state's behavior without comprehending the second image of domestic politics.   This study proposes an integrated comparative-historical approach in security policy analysis.

## Future Aspects of International Politics in Northeast Asia

South Korea's security environment in the post-Cold War has become more complex in terms of the type and source of threats.   Issues such as the North's nuclear and missile programs, social/economic crisis, and refugee problems in the DPRK-PRC borders require the South to expand its regional security policy beyond the traditional peninsula-focused military dimension.   In addition to those problems, the Cold War antagonism still remains in the Korean peninsula.   About 70% of two million armed forces in the two Koreas point their guns toward each other in the de-militarized zone (DMZ).   Throughout Northeast Asia, much of the structure of international politics has been shaped by how the regional major powers, the U.S., the Soviet Union/Russia, China, and Japan, have defined their interests and identified their strategic allies and adversaries.   The U.S. and the Soviet Union/Russia have exercised profound influences in shaping the structure of international politics as well as the security policies of the two Koreas.   As regional powers, China and Japan have continued in their roles and have reacted to regional politics.   Thus, South Korea's deterrence and interdependence policies depend upon the future relations between the two Koreas and among the regional major powers.   This leads us to examine historical and future relations between South Korea and other major powers that are associated with changes in the Northeast Asian security system.

The primary security policy objective of the U.S. has been the maintenance of regional stability through a balance-of-power approach in Northeast Asia.   The U.S. has supported South Korea in order to maintain a military balance through extended deterrence that includes the presence of its forces, arms transfers, and a nuclear umbrella.   It has maintained a three-part strategy that includes maintenance of military forces, economic and political assistance, and a formal alliance system. Currently, the U.S. goal is to maintain its Asian/Pacific hegemony and nuclear non-proliferation in Northeast Asia. The underlying framework is the U.S.-Japan and US-ROK Mutual Defense Treaties as well as KEDO. The U.S. also supports reunification of the two Koreas on South Korean terms. The future emphasis of the U.S. security policy toward the Korean peninsula will be based on the containment of North Korea. Containment refers to the policy that attempts to prevent the expansion of one's adversaries beyond prescribed limits by employing extended deterrence and strengthening alliance networks. Its containment policy evolved from the containment of communist expansionism and the North's military aggression during the Cold War era as well as the containment of the North's nuclear/missile ambition during the post-Cold War era. Future emphasis also includes the promotion of trade relations, intensification of economic interdependence, and the spread of market democracies in Northeast Asia.

Until 1996, the Soviet Union and Russia provided extended deterrence to North Korea as a counterpart of the US-ROK security alliance. The Soviet Union favored the maintenance of balance-of-power mechanism and status quo in Northeast Asia. After *perestroika* and *glasnost*, Gorbachev's visit to South Korea in 1990 caused a dramatic shift in the traditional Soviet policy to a more "charming diplomacy" in favor of jointly building new relations in Northeast Asia. Currently, Russia advocates a "two plus four" security forum, which includes the U.S., Japan, China, Russia, and the two Koreas. In this multilateral security forum, Russia may attempt to regain its declining influence in the region. Russia opposes any nuclear proliferation in Northeast Asia. Russia withdrew its unconditional support for the North's stance on national reunification of the two Koreas and also abolished the Russia-DPRK Basic Friendship Treaty in September 1996. Russia has encouraged North Korea to move toward economic openness and societal reform, but recent serious political and economic difficulties have further diminished Russia's role in Northeast Asia.

Along with the Soviet Union, China supported North Korea and attempted to induce North Korea to move closer to China through military/economic assistance and by maintaining a friendly relationship. Although China maintains a friendly relationship with North Korea, it switched its Cold War strategy to an equi-distance policy that includes both a politico-military relationship with North Korea and an economic and trade relationship with South Korea. China recently announced that it does not wish to support either the North's belligerent behavior or its nuclear/missile programs. Shifting to a pragmatic economic policy, China prefers the maintenance of the status quo and stability in Northeast Asia. It supports the principles of self-determination and peaceful reunification of the two Koreas. China continuously supports regional economic interdependence and has encouraged the North to open its doors to the outside world. China, with a greater economic and military capability, will play an important role in the peaceful resolution of the Korean peninsula situation, since China alone remains as an ally to North Korea.

Japan's security policy has been formulated and implemented via the 1953 bilateral security relationship with the U.S. It has consistently supported the status quo and the reduction of tensions in the Korean peninsula. Although Japan has recently attempted to move toward opening relations with North Korea, it opposes the North's ambition to acquire nuclear weapons. For the sake of its own interests, Japan will not normalize relations with North Korea until satisfactory guarantees of non-proliferation are given concerning the North's nuclear and missile programs. Japan has contributed financial support for the trilateral consortium, KEDO. It supports a "two plus four" formula for the peaceful unification process of the two Koreas. Japan does not favor communist control over a unified Korea, as this would hold major threats to its own security and economic interests. The future of Japan's role in Northeast Asia will be based on a commitment to the spread of market democracies shared with the U.S. and South Korea.

After reviewing policy adjustments made by regional major powers in Northeast Asia, it can be concluded that all four powers prefer to maintain stability and the peaceful process of reunification in the Korean peninsula. This means that regional stability and prosperity can be enhanced by improving inter-Korean relations and intensifying economic interdependence. To this end, I propose a multilateral security community based on hexagonal or "two plus four" consortium. This will provide a *de facto* security alignment and alliance among the U.S., Russia, China, Japan, and the two Koreas. This multilateral initiative needs to build commonalities based on economic factors through diplomatic normalization. Diplomatic/economic normalization includes US-DPRK and Japan-DPRK normalization. Within this security formula of a hexagonal consortium, the reductions of military forces, strict limits on arms sales and transfers, and nuclear/missile non-proliferation could be negotiated without resort to imperial dictate, new imbalances of power or war. Based on the principle of common security and respect for national sovereignty, such an alternative formula could facilitate both economic interdependence and the relaxation of military tensions. This system not only creates a ground for the manageable Korean reunification, but also helps to implement a strategic instrument that would restrict Japanese military reemergence and Chinese hegemonic ambition. However, regional powers need to overcome obstacles that stem from the lack of experience in multilateralism, lack of common perceptions of external threats, and asymmetrical military strategies among nations in order to establish this formula. The most difficult task will be the incorporation of the North into the multilateral security framework. The future of regional stability and prosperity depends upon how North Korea handles its "structural entrapment" that put it in a position of gridlock, offering no positive alternatives. The North has put forth tentative gestures such as opening some coastal cities as free trade zones, but as yet has not had economic interactions to any great extent. Recently, it followed a Chinese model, opening some free trade zones in the Golden Triangle of Rajin and Sonbong located in the northeast areas of the DPRK and the Tumen Delta, but a lack of experience in capitalism diminished the amount of economic activity. More importantly, North Korean leaders would not allow any systemic breakdown after they recognized the experiences of Russia and East European countries. Other serious barriers include North Korea's *juche* ideology of self-reliance, autarchic economic system, and poor economic infrastructure. Thus, after the demise of the Cold War North Korea chose the policy of strategic isolationism, using the nuclear card to assure its survival.

North Korea, as of yet, has not initiated any systemic reforms within its society due to the problem of "structural entrapment." Conditions including food shortages, malnutrition, refugee problems, and human rights violations have received wide international attention. As a result, those who predict the North's collapse point out its economic stagnation and its food/energy crisis as signs of a systemic breakdown. They argue that a crisis involving either collapse or aggressive action is only a matter of time. However, the conditions that define a collapsed system are not yet clear. Thus far, three foreseeable scenarios of unification have been specified: war or limited warfare, economic absorption, and gradual reunification.

There are reasons to speculate that North Korea could initiate a military attack or limited warfare. North Korea's socio-political crisis, in addition to its economic decline, brings this nation to the brink of collapse and also raises concerns that Kim Jong-Il or his military followers could initiate war against the South in desperation. War is also possible if a military coup d'etat occurs. According to Lee Chull-Soo, who defected with a MIG-19 in May 1996, and Hwang Jang-yop, the former Secretary for International Affairs of North Korea's Workers Party, many members of the Korean Peoples' Army want to fight against the South, despite the possibility of losing the war. Those who foresee a collapse of the North believe that war is a probable choice for Pyongyang's leadership. Yet, war is the worst alternative of the unification scenarios. With about two million combat forces positioned along the 38th parallel, a war would not guarantee the survival of either side. The eruption of military conflict will result in countless human casualties as well as refugees. Furthermore, another Korean war would jeopardize trade and investment relations that have been established throughout the Asia-Pacific region. Therefore, South Korea should make every effort to prevent military conflict on the Korean peninsula.

Another possible scenario is one of economic absorption. If North Korea collapses, South Korea will have no choice but to absorb North Korea in order to avoid protracted economic, social and political turbulence in the North. However, such a German-style solution is improbable due to the cost involved in reunification. Some analysts predict that unification could cost $60 billion to $300 billion and that the South would need at least 40 years to recover its economic strength. Moreover, Korean domestic political and economic conditions are not similar to those of Germany in 1990. Thus, economic absorption is beyond the scope of South Korean resources. This leads to an anther possibility: the U.S. and Japan's assisting South Korea in the absorption of North Korea. This view is not realistic, because neither the U.S. nor Japan could afford such an expensive unification project. However, the remaining question is whether the U.S. and Japan as well as China and Russia can afford not to incur such costs, given their interests in regional stability if the North collapses.

Peaceful gradual reunification is the most desirable scenario but there is no guarantee that this can be achieved according to the South's designs. The North may implode before gradual economic and political reforms take hold. The continuation of external pressures on the North is also not desirable. The best-case scenario is to support North Korea's economy through economic and diplomatic channels rather than to perpetuate the continuation of military confrontation which forces North Korea to view South Korea as a mortal enemy instead of a source for the Pyongyang's survival and recovery. At this time, the South needs to patiently and persistently continue its efforts to convince the North that South Korea's policy does not amount to a zero-sum game of sovereignty where only one of the two Koreas can gain control of the peninsula. The question of how unity can be achieved remains unresolved, but the ball is now in North Korea's court. Despite the fact that nearly 47 years have passed since the signing of the Armistice in 1953, several million Koreans are still separated from their families. They are unable to exchange communications or even a single e-mail with their friends and families who happen to be on the other side of the DMZ. Koreans hope that the summit meeting between the two Koreas, scheduled in June 12-14, 2000, would resolve above problems. Korea still awaits the promise of the 1943 Cairo meeting—"Korea shall be free and independent at the earliest possible moment."

# Bibliography

Achen, Christopher and Duncan Snidal. 1989. "Rational Deterrence Theory and Comparative Case Studies." *World Politics* 41: 43-69.

Adler, Emanuel. 1992. "Conclusion: Epistemic Communities, World Order, and the Creation of a Reflective Research Program." *International Organization* 46: 367-90.

Ahn, Byung-joon. 1996. "Regionalism in the Asia-Pacific: Asian or Pacific Community?" *Korea Focus* 4: 5-19.

Ahn, Byung-joon. 1999. "Beware the Trap of Neoliberalism." *Korea Focus* 7: 66-76.

Ahn, Chung-Si. 1994. "Democratization and Political Reform in Korea: Development, Culture, Leadership and Institutional Change." In *Korea in the Global Wave of Democratization*, eds., Doh Chull Shin, Myeong-Han Zoh, and Myung Choy. Seoul: Seoul National University Press.

Akaha, Tsuneo. 1996. "Japanese Security in Post-Cold War Asia." In *The Major Powers of Northeast Asia: Seeking Peace and Security*, eds., Tae-Hwan Kwak and Edward A. Olsen. Boulder, Colorado: Lynne Rienner.

Allen, John L. 1998. *Student Atlas of World Politics*. Guilford, Connecticut: Dushkin/McGraw-Hill.

Allison, Graham T. 1961. *Essence of Decision: Explaining the Cuban Missile Crisis*. Boston, Massachusetts: Little, Brown.

Allison, Graham T. and Morton H. Halperin. 1972. "Bureaucratic Politics: A Paradigm and Some Policy Implications." *World Politics* 24: 40-79.

Almond, Gabriel and G. Bingham Powell. 1966. *Comparative Politics: A Development Approach*. Boston, Massachusetts: Little, Brown.

Amsden, Alice H. 1989. *Asia's Next Giant: South Korea and Late Industrialization*. New York: Oxford University Press.

Amsden, Alice H. and Takashi Hikino. 1998. "East Asia's Financial Crisis: What Can an Activist Government Do?" *World Policy Journal* 15: 43-6.

Anderson, Charles W. 1978. "The Logic of Public Problems: Evaluation in Comparative Policy Research." In *Comparing Public Policies: New Concepts and Methods*, ed., Douglas E. Ashford. Beverly Hills, California: Sage.

Art, Robert and Robert Jervis. 1986. *International Politics*. Boston: Little, Brown.

Axelord, Robert. 1984. *The Evolution of Cooperation*. New York: Basic Books.

Axelord, Robert and Robert O. Keohane. 1993. "Achieving Cooperation Under Anarchy: Strategies and Institutions." In *Neorealism and Neoliberalism: The Contemporary Debate*, ed., David A. Baldwin. New York: Columbia University Press.

Ayoob, Mohammed. 1984. "Security in the Third World: The Worm about to Turn?" *International Affairs* 60: 41-51.

Ayoob, Mohammed. 1995. *The Third World Security Predicament: State Making, Regional Conflict, and the International System*. Boulder, Colorado: Lynne Rienner.

Azar, Edward E. and Chung-In Moon. 1988. "Legitimacy, Integration and Policy Capacity: The Software Side of Third World National Security." In *National Security in the Third World: The Management of Internal and External Threats*, eds., Edward E. Azar and Chung-In Moon. College Park, Maryland: Center for International Development and Conflict Management.

Baek, Jong-Chun. 1985. *Thesis on National Defense (Han-Kuk-Bang-Wi-Ron)*. Seoul: Parkyoungsa.

Baker, James. 1992. "America in Asian Emerging Architecture for a Pacific Community." *Foreign Affairs* 71: 1-18.

Baker, Richard W. and Charles E. Morrison. eds. 2000. *Asia-Pacific Security Outlook*. Washington, D.C.: Brookings Institute.

Balassa, Bela A. 1981. *Newly Industrializing Countries in the World Economy*. Elmsford, New York: Pergamon.

Baldwin, David A. 1971. "Money and Power." *Journal of Politics* 33: 578-614.

Baldwin, David A. 1993. "Neoliberalism, Neorealism, and World Politics." In *Neorealism and Neoliberalism: The Contemporary Debate*, ed., David Baldwin. New York: Columbia University Press.

Barash, David P. 1999. *Approaches to Peace: A Reader in Peace Studies*. Oxford: Oxford University Press.

Barnds, William J. 1976. "Old Issues in a New Context." In *The Two Korea in East Asian Affairs*, ed., William J. Barnds. New York: New York University Press.

Baumgartner, Frank R. and Bryan D. Jones. 1993. *Agendas and Instability in American Politics*. Chicago, Illinois: University of Chicago Press.

Bean, R. Mark. 1990. *Cooperative Security in Northeast Asia: A China-Japan-South Korea Coalition Approach*. Washington, D.C.: National Defense University Press.

Bedeski, Robert E. 1993. "State Reform and Democracy in South Korea." In *Korea Under Roh Tae-Woo: Democratization, Northen Policy, and Inter-Korean Relations*, ed., James Cotton. Canberra: Allen & Unwin.

Bermeo, Nancy. ed. 1992. *Liberalization and Democratization*. Baltimore, Maryland: The Johns Hopkins University Press.

Berry, William. 1990. "Alliance Commitments and Strategies: Asia." In *American Defense Policy*, eds., Schuyler Foerster and Edward Wright. Baltimore, Maryland: The Johns Hopkins University Press.

Betts, Richard. 1995. "Wealth, Power, and Conflict: East Asia after the Cold War." In *East Asia in Transition*, ed., Robert Ross. New York: M. E. Sharpe.

Bishop, Bernie. 1997. *Foreign Direct Investment in Korea: The Role of the State*. Brookfield, Vermont: Ashgate.

Black, Joseph E. and Kenneth W. Thompson. eds. 1963. *Foreign Policies in a World of Change*. New York: Harper & Row.

Blackwill, Robert D. and Paul Dibbs. eds. 2000. *America's Asian Alliances.* Cambridge, Massachusetts: The MIT Press.

Blainey, Geoffrey. 1988. *The Causes of War.* New York: The Free Press.

Blomqvist, Hans. C. 1997. *Economic Interdependence and Development in East Asia.* Westport, Connecticut: Praeger.

Bobrow, Davis. B. 1999. "Prospecting the Future." *International Studies Review*, Special Issue 1: 1-10.

Boyd, Gavin and Gerald W. Happle. eds. 1987. *Political Change and Foreign Policies.* London: Frances Pinter.

Bracken, Paul. 1993. "Nuclear Weapons and State Survival in North Korea." *Survival* 35: 137-53.

Brams, Steven J. 1985. *Superpower Games: Applying Game Theory to Superpower Conflict.* New Haven, Connecticut: Yale University Press.

Brennan, Donald. ed. 1961. *Arms Control, Disarmament and National Security.* New York: George Braziller.

Brown, Archie. 1996. *The Gorbachev Factor.* New York: Oxford University Press.

Brzoska, Michael. 1982. "Arms Transfer Date Sources." *Journal of Conflict Resolution* 26: 77-108.

Brzoska, Michael and Thomas Ohlson. eds. 1986. *Arms Production in the Third World.* New York: Taylor and Francis.

Buck, James H. 1975. *The Modern Japanese Military System.* Beverly Hills, California: Sage.

Bull, Hedley. 1961. *The Control of Arms Race.* London: Weidenfeld and Nicolson.

Bull, Hedley. 1977. *The Anarchic Society: A Study of Order in World Politics.* New York: Columbia University Press.

Burton, Michael G. and Jai P. Ryu. 1997. "South Korea's Elite Settlement and Democratic Consolidation." *Journal of Political and Military Sociology* 25: 1-24.

Buzan, Barry. 1991. *People, States, and Fear*. Boulder, Colorado: Lynne Rienner.

Buzan, Barry and R. J. Barry Jones. eds. 1981. *Change and the Study of International Relations: The Faded Dimension*. New York: St. Martin's Press.

Buzan, Barry and Richard Little. 1996. "Reconceptualizing Anarchy: Structural Realism Meets World History." *European Journal of International Relations* 2: 403-38.

Campbell, Donald T. and Julian C. Stanley. 1963. *Experimental and Quasi-Experimental Designs for Research*. Dallas, Texas: Houghton Mifflin.

Cardoso, Fernando. 1973. "Associated-Dependent Development: Theoretical and Practical Implications." In *Authoritarian Brazil*, ed., A. Stephen. New Haven, Connecticut: Yale University Press.

Cassidy, Kevin J. 1993. "Introduction and Overview." In *Real Security: Converting the Defense Economy and Building Peace*, eds., Kevin J. Cassidy and Gregory Bischak. Albany, New York: State University of New York Press.

Castley, Robert. 1997. *Korea's Economic Miracle: The Crucial Role of Japan*. New York: St. Martin's Press.

Cha, Victor D. 1996. "Bridging the Gap: The Strategic Context of the 1965 Korea-Japan Normalization Treaty." *Korean Studies* 20: 123-60.

Chee, Chan Heng. 1993. "Democracy: Evolution and Implementation: An Asian Perspective." In *Democracy and Capitalism*, ed., Robert Bartley. Singapore: Institute of Southeast Asian Studies.

Chen, Jian. 1994. *China's Road to the Korean War: The Making of the Sino-American Confrontation*. New York: Columbia University Press.

Chow, Peter C. Y. and Mitchell H. Kellman. 1993. *Trade: The Engine of Growth in East Asia*. New York: Oxford University Press.

Christensen, Thomas J. 1996. *Useful Adversaries: Grand Strategy, Domestic Mobilization, and Sino-American Conflict, 1947-1958*. Princeton, New Jersey: Princeton University Press.

Christensen, Thomas J. and Jack Snyder. 1990. "Chain Gangs and Passed Bucks: Predicting Alliance Patterns in Multipolarity." *International Organization* 44: 137-68.

Clad, James. 1992. "The Half-Empty Basin." *Wilson Quarterly* 16: 76-86.

Claude, Inis. 1962. *Power and International Relations*. New York: Random House.

Clifton, Morgen T. and Sally H. Campbell. 1991. "Domestic Structure, Decisional Constraints, and War: So Why Kant Democracies Fight?" *Journal of Conflict Resolution* 35: 187-211.

Cohen, Eliot A. 1988. "Toward Better Net Assessment: Rethinking the European Conventional Balance." *International Security* 13: 50-89.

Collins, John M. 1997. *The Insecurity Dilemma and the End of the Cold War*. New York: St. Martin's Press.

Cossa, Ralph A. and Jane Khanna. 1997. "East Asia: Economic Interdependence and Regional Security." *International Affairs* 73: 219-34.

Cotton, James. 1995. "Korea in Comparative Perspective." In *Politics and Policy in the New Korean State*, ed., James Cotton. New York: St. Martin's Press.

Cowhey, Peter F. and Matthew D. McCubbins. 1995. *Structure and Policy in Japan and the United States*. Cambridge, Massachusetts: Cambridge University Press.

Crawford, Sue and Elinor Ostrom. 1995. "A Grammar of Institutions." *American Political Science Review* 89: 582-600.

Cronin, Patrick. 1992. "Pacific Rim Security: Beyond Bilateralism?" *The Pacific Review* 5: 209-20.

Cumings, Bruce. 1981. *The Origins of the Korean War*. Princeton, New Jersey: Princeton University Press.

Cumings, Bruce. 1984. "The Origins and Development of the Northeast Asian Political Economy." *International Organization* 38: 1-40.

Cumings, Bruce. 1997. *Korea's Place in the Sun: A Modern History.* New York: Norton.

Czempiel, Ernst-Otto and James N. Rosenau. 1989. "Governance and Democratization." In *Governance without Government: Order and Change in World Politics*, eds., James N. Rosenau and Ernst-Otto Czempiel. Cambridge, Massachusetts: Cambridge University Press.

Czempiel, Ernst-Otto and James N. Rosenau. eds. 1992. *Global Changes and Theoretical Challenges: Approches to World Politics for the 1990s*, Lexington, Massachusetts: Lexington Books.

Dahl, Robert A. 1971. *Poliarchy: Participation and Opposition.* New Haven, Connecticut: Yale University Press.

Davis, Winston. 1995. "Religion and Development: Weber and the East Asian Experience." In *Understanding Political Development*, eds., Myron Weiner and Samuel P. Huntington. Prospect Heights, Illinois: Waveland.

Deng, Yong. 1997. *Promoting Asian-Pacific Economic Cooperation: Perspectives from East Asia.* New York: St. Martin's Press.

Desch, Michael. 1998. "Culture Clash: Assessing the Importance of Ideas in Security Studies." *International Security* 23: 141-70.

Dessler, David. 1989. "What's at Stake in the Agent-Structure Debate?" *International Organization* 43: 441-73.

Diamond, Larry. 1991. *Political Culture and Democracy in Developing Countries.* Boulder, Colorado: Lynne Rienner.

DiMaggio, Paul J. 1988. "Interest and Agency in Institutional Theory." In *Institutional Patterns and Organizations: Culture and Environment*, ed., Lynne.G. Zucker. Cambridge, Massachusetts: Ballinger.

Dixon, William J. and Stephen M. Gaarder. 1994. "Explaining Foreign Policy Continuity and Change: U.S. Dyadic Relations with the Soviet Union, 1948-1988." In *Foreign Policy Restructuring: How Governments Respond to Global*

*Change*, eds., Jerel A. Rosati, Joe D. Hagan, and Martin W. Sampson. Columbia, South Carolina: University of South Carolina Press.

Dobbs-Higginson, Michael S. 1994. *Asia Pacific: A View on Its Role in the New World Order*. London: Heinemann.

Doh, Chull Shin. 1994. "Recent Theory and Research on Democratic Transitions and Consolidations: A Synthesis." In *Korea in the Global Wave of Democratization*, eds., Chull Shin Doh, Myeong-Han Zoh, and Myung Chey. Seoul: Seoul National University Press.

Doran, Charles F. 1999. "Why Forecasts Fail: The Limits and Potential of Forecasting in International Relations and Economics." *International Studies Review*, Special Issue 1: 11-41.

Dougherty, James E. and Robert I. Pfaltzgraff. 2000. *Contending Theories of International Relations*. New York: Longman.

Doyle, Michael. 1996. "Kant, Liberal Legacies, and Foreign Affairs." In *Debating the Democratic Peace*, eds., Michael E. Brown, Sean Lynn-Jones, and Steven Miller. Cambridge, Massachusetts: The MIT Press.

Dunn, David J. 1981. "The Emergence of Change as a Theoretical Concern in International Relations." In *Change and the Study of International Relations: The Evaded Dimension*, eds., Barry Buzan and J. Barry Jones. New York: St. Martin's Press.

Dupont, Alan. 1997. "New Directions of Security." In *The New Security Agenda in the Asia-Pacific Region*, ed., Denny Roy. New York: St. Martin's Press.

Dutta, Manoranjan. 1999. *Economic Regionalization in the Asia-Pacific: Challenges to Economic Cooperation*. North Hampton, Massachusetts: Edward Elgar.

Eckert, Carter J., Ki-Baik Lee, Young Ick Lew, Michael Robinson, and Edward W. Wagner. 1990. *Korea Old and New A History*. Seoul: Ilchokak.

Eisner, M. Allen. 1993. *Regulatory Politics in Transition*. Baltimore, Maryland: The Johns Hopkins University Press.

Engleberg, Steven and Michael Gordon. 1993. "Intelligence Study Says North Korea Has Nuclear Bombs." *New York Times*, December 26, p. 1.

Ethington, J. Philip and Eileen L. McDonagh. 1995. "The Common Space of Social Science Inquiry." *Polity* 28: 85-90.

Evangelista, Matthew. 1997. "Domestic Structures and International Change." In *New Thinking in International Relations Theory*, eds., Michael W. Doyle and G. John Ikenberry. Boulder, Colorado: Westview.

Evans, Peter B. 1979. *Dependent Development: The Alliance of Multinational, State, and Local Capital in Brazil.* Princeton, New Jersey: Princeton University Press.

Evans, Peter B. 1995. *Embedded Autonomy: States and Industrial Transformation.* Princeton, New Jersey: Princeton University Press.

Ferris, Elizabeth G. and Jennie K. Lincoln. ed., 1981. *Latin American Foreign Policies: Global and Regional Dimensions.* Boulder, Colorado: Westview.

Finnemore, Martha. 1996. "Constructing Norms of Humanitarian Intervention." In *The Culture of National Security: Norms and Identity in World Politics*, ed., Peter Katzenstein. New York: Columbia University Press.

Fischer, R. L. 1976. "Defending the Central Front: The Balance of Forces." *Adelphi Paper* No. 127. London: International Institute for Strategic Studies.

Forester, Schuyler and Edward N. Wright. eds. 1965. *American Defense Policy.* Baltimore, Maryland: The Johns Hopkins University Press.

Frankel, Benjamin. 1996. "Restating the Realist Case: An Introduction." *Security Studies* 5: ix-xx.

Friedland, Roger and Robert Alford. 1991. "Bringing Society Back In: Symbols, Practices, and Institutional Contradictions." In *The New Institutionalism in Organizational Analysis*, eds., Walter W. Powell and Paul J. DiMaggio. Chicago, Illinois: University of Chicago Press.

Fukuyama, Francis. 1992. *The End of History and the Last Man.* New York: The Free Press.

Fukuyama, Francis. 1994. "Reflections on the End of History, Five Years Later." In *After History?: Francis Fukuyama and His Critics*, ed., Timothy Burns. Lanham, Maryland: Rowman and Littlefield.

Gaddis, John L. 1987. *The Long Peace: Inquiries into the History of the Cold War*. New York: Oxford University Press.

Gaddis, John L. 1992/3. "International Relations Theory and the End of the Cold War." *International Security* 17: 5-58.

Gargan, John. 1997. "Reinventing Government and Reformulating Public Administration." *International Journal of Public Administration* 20: 221-47.

Garnaut, Ross. 1998. "The East Asian Crisis." In *East Asia in Crisis: From Being a Miracle to Needing One?*" eds., Ross H. McLeod and Ross Garnaut. New York: Routledge.

George, Alexander L. and Timothy J. McKeown. 1985. "Case Studies and Theories of Organizational Decision Making." In *Advances in Information Processing in Organizations*, eds., Richard F. Coulam and Robert A. Smith. Greenwich, Connecticut: JAI Press.

George, Alexander L. and Richard Smoke. 1974. *Deterrence in American Foreign Policy*. New York: Columbia University Press.

Gereffi, Gary and Christopher Ellison. 1991. "Explaining Strategies and Patterns of Industrial Development." In *Manufacturing Miracle: Paths of Industrialization in Latin America and East Asia*, eds., G. Gereffi and D. Wyman. Princeton, New Jersey: Princeton University Press.

Gerner, Deborah J. 1995. "The Evolution of the Study of Foreign Policy." In *Foreign Policy Analysis: Continuity and Change in Its Second Generation*, eds., Laura Neack, Jeanne Hey, and Patrick J. Haney. Englewood Cliffs, New Jersey: Prentice Hall.

Gershenkron, Alexander. 1962. *Economic Backwardness in Historical Perspective*. Cambridge, Massachusetts: Harvard University Press.

Gibney, Frank. 1992. "The Promise of the Pacific." *Wilson Quarterly* 16: 64-75.

Gilbert, Stephen P. 1988. "The Northeast Asian Arena." In *Security in Northeast Asia: Approaching the Pacific Century*, ed., Stephen P. Gilbert. Boulder, Colorado: Westview.

Gilks, Anne and Gerald Segal. 1985. *China and the Arms Trade*. New York: St. Martin's Press.

Gilpin, Robert. 1975. *U.S. Power and the Multinational Corporation*. New York: Basic Books.

Gilpin, Robert. 1981. *War and Change in World Politics*. New York: Cambridge University Press.

Gilpin, Robert. 1987. *The Political Economy of International Relations*. Princeton, New Jersey: Princeton University Press.

Goldman, Kjell. 1988. *Change and Stability in Foreign Policy: The Problems and Possibilities of Détente*. Princeton, New Jersey: Princeton University Press.

Gong, Gerrit and Chi Leng. 1995. "US-Chinese-Japanese Relations in a Period of Structural Adjustment." *The Journal of East Asian Affairs* 9: 132-56.

Gourevitch, Peter. 1978. "The Second Image Reversed: The International Sources of Domestic Politics." *International Organization* 32: 881-911.

Grabendorff, Wolf 1984. "The Role of Regional Powers in Central America: Mexico, Venezuela, Cuba and Colombia." In *Latin American Nations in World Politics*, eds., Heraldo Munoz and Joseph S. Tulchin. Boulder, Colorado: Westview.

Greenspan, Alan. 1998. "Statements to the Congress—January 30, 1998." *Federal Reserve Bulletin* 84: 186-90.

Greffenius, Steven F. 1994. "Foreign Policy Stabilization and the Camp David Accords: Opportunities and Obstacles to the Institutionalization of Peace." In *Foreign Policy Restructuring: How Governments Respond to Global Change*, eds., Jerel A. Rosati, Joe D. Hagan, and Martin W. Sampson. Columbia, South Carolina: University of South Carolina Press.

Grieco, Joseph M. 1988. "Anarchy and the Limits of Cooperation: A Realist Critique of the Newest Liberal Institutionalism." *International Organization* 42: 485-507.

Grieco, Joseph M. 1993. "Understanding the Problem of International Cooperation: The Limits of Neoliberal Institutionalism and the Future of Realist Theory." In *Neorealism and Neoliberalism: The Contemporary Debate*, ed., David A. Baldwin. New York: Columbia University Press.

Griffith, William E. ed. 1975. *The World and the Great-Power Triangles*. Cambridge, Massachusetts: The MIT Press.

Grimmett, Richard F. 1994. *Conventional Arms Transfers to the Third World, 1986-1993*. Washington, D. C.: Congressional Research Service.

Ha, Young-Sun. 1984. "American-Korean Military Relations: Continuity and Change." In *Korea and the US: A Century of Cooperation*, eds., Young-Nok Koo and Dae-Sook Suh. Honolulu, Hawaii: University of Hawaii Press.

Ha, Young-Sun. 1990. *A New Approach on the Korean War (Han-Kuk-Jun-Jang-E-Dae-Han-Sae-Ro-Un-Jeop-Geun-Bang-Bup)*. Seoul: Nanam.

Haberman, Clyde. 1987. "Seoul Government and Opposition Reach Agreement on Constitution." *New York Times*, September 1, pp. A1 and A4.

Haftendorn, Helga. 1991. "The Security Puzzle: Theory-Building and Discipline-Building in International Security." *International Security Quarterly* 35: 3-17.

Hagan, Joe D. 1987. "Regimes, Political Oppositions and the Comparative Analysis of Foreign Policy." In *New Directions in the Study of Foreign Policy*, eds., Charles F. Hermann, Charles W. Kegley, Jr., and James N. Rosenau. Winchester, Massachusetts: Unwin Hyman.

Hagan, Joe D. 1995. "Domestic Political Explanations in the Analysis of Foreign Policy." In *Foreign Policy Analysis: Continuity and Change in Its Second Generation*, eds., Laura Neack, Jeane A. K. Hey, and Patrick J. Haney. Englewood Cliffs, New Jersey: Prentice Hall.

Hagan, Joe D. and Jerel A. Rosati. 1994. "Emerging Issues in Research on Foreign Policy Restructuring." In *Foreign Policy Restructuring: How Governments Respond to Global Changes*, eds., Jerel A. Rosati, Joe D. Hagan, and Martin W. Sampson. Columbia, South Carolina: University of South Carolina Press.

Hahm, Chai-bong. 1996. "Future of Korean Political Drive." *Korea Focus* 4: 5-11.

Hahm, Chai-bong and Sang-young Rhyu. 1997. "Democratic Reform in Korea: Promise For Democracy." *Korea Focus* 5: 38-49.

Hahm, Sung Seuk and L. Christopher Plein. 1997. *After Development: The Transformation of the Korean Presidency and Bureaucracy*. Washington, D.C.: Georgetown University Press.

Hall, Peter. 1986. *Governing the Economy*. New York: Oxford University Press.

Hall, Peter. 1992. "The Movement from Keynesianism to Modernism: Institutional Analysis and British Economic Policy in the 1970s." In *Structuring Politics: Historical Institutionalism in Comparative Analysis*, eds., Sven Steinmo, Kathleen Thelen, and Frank Longstreth. Cambridge, Massachusetts: Cambridge University Press.

Hamm, Taik-young. 1992. *Arms Race and Arms Control between North and South Korea*. Seoul: The Center of Northeast Asian Affairs.

Hamm, Taik-young. 1999. *Arming the Two Koreas: State, Capital and Military Power*. New York: Routledge.

Han, Sung-joo. 1985. "Policy Toward the United States." In *The Foreign Policy of the Republic of Korea*, eds., Youngnok Koo and Sung-joo Han. New York: Columbia University Press.

Han, Yong-Sup. 1997. "Korea's Security Strategy for 21st Century: Cooperation and Conflict." *Korea Focus* 5: 63-79.

Han, Yong-Won. 1993. *Military Politics in Korea (Han-Kuk-E-Seo-Eui-Gun-Sa-Jung-Chi)*. Seoul: Daewangsa.

Harf, James E., David G. Hoovler, and Thomas E. James. 1974. "Systemic and External Attributes in Foreign Policy Analysis." In *Comparing Foreign Policies: Theories, Findings, and Methods*, ed., James Rosenau. New York: John Wiley and Sons.

Harris, Stuart. 1995. "The Economic Aspects of Security in Asia/Pacific Region." *Journal of Strategic Studies* 18: 32-51.

Harris, Stuart and James Cotton. 1991. *The End of the Cold War in Northeast Asia*. Boulder, Colorado: Lynne Rienner.

Hart, Dennis M. 1993. "Political Stability in an Industrializing Culture: Shifting Forms of State Legitimacy in South Korea." *Contemporary Southeast Asia* 14: 396-404.

Hart, Dennis M. 1999. "Creating the National Order: Opposing Images of Nationalism in South and North Korean Education." *Korean Studies* 23: 68-93.

Hauss, Charles. 1999. *Comparative Politics: Domestic Response to Global Challenges*. New York: Wadsworth.

Hayter, Theresa. 1985. *Aid: Rhetoric and Reality*. London: Pluto.

Helgesen, Geir and Li Xing. 1996. "Democracy or *Minzhu*: The Challenge of Western vs. East Asian Notions of Good Government." *Asian Perspective* 20: 95-124.

Hermann, Charles F. 1990. "Changing Course: When Governments Choose to Redirect Foreign Policy." *International Studies Quarterly* 34: 3-21.

Hermann, Charles F. 1995. "Epilogue: Reflections on Foreign Policy Theory Building." In *Foreign Policy Analysis: Continuity and Change in Its Second Generation*, eds., Laura Neack, Jeanne A. K. Hey, and Patrick J. Haney. Englewood Cliffs, New Jersey: Prentice-Hall.

Hermann, Charles F., Charles Kegley, and James N. Rosenau. eds. 1987. *New Directions in the Study of Foreign Policy*. Boston, Massachusetts: Allen & Unwin.

Hermann, Richard. 1985. *Perceptions and Behavior in Soviet Foreign Policy*. Pittsburgh, Pennsylvania: University of Pittsburgh Press.

Higley, John and Michael G. Burton. 1989. "The Elite Variable in Democratic Transitions and Breakdowns." *American Sociological Review* 54: 17-32.

Hill, Christopher. 1996. "Introduction: The Falkland War and European Foreign Policy." In *Domestic Sources of Foreign Policy: Western European Reactions to the Falklands Conflict*, eds., Stelios Stavridis and Christopher Hill. Washington, D.C.: Berg.

Hilsman, Roger. 1967. *To Move a Nation*. New York: Doubleday.

Hirschman, Albert O. 1969. *National Power and the Structure of Foreign Trade*. Berkeley, California: University of California Press.

Hoag, Malcom W. 1961. "On Stability in Deterrent Races." *World Politics* 13: 505-27.

Hofheinz, Roy and Kent Calder. 1982. *The Eastasia Edge*. New York: Basic Books.

Hogan, Michael. ed. 1992. *The End of the Cold War: Its Meaning and Implications*. New York: Cambridge University Press.

Hollis, Martin and Steve Smith. 1991. "Beware of Gurus: Structure and Action in International Relations." *Review of International Studies* 17: 393-410.

Holsti, Kal J. 1970. "National Role Conceptions in the Study of Foreign Policy." *International Studies Quarterly* 14: 233-309.

Holsti, Kal J. 1982. "Restructuring Foreign Policy: A Neglected Phenomenon in Foreign Policy." In *Why Nations Realign: Foreign Policy Restructuring in the Postwar World*, ed., K. J. Holsti. London: Allen and Unwin.

Holsti, Ole R. 1982. "Operational Code Approach: Problems and Some Solutions." In *Cognitive Dynamics and International Politics*, ed., Christer Jansson. New York: St. Martin's Press.

Holsti, Ole R. 1989. "Crisis Decision Making." In *Behavior, Society, and Nuclear War*, eds., Philip E. Tetlock, Charles Tilly, Robert Jervis, Jo L. Husbands, and Paul C. Stern. New York: Oxford University Press.

Hook, Steven W. 1995. *National Interest and Foreign Aid*. Boulder, Colorado: Lynne Rienner.

Hook, Steven W. 1996. "Introduction: Foreign Aid in a Transformed World." In *Foreign Aid toward the Millennium,* ed., Steven W. Hook.   Boulder, Colorado: Lynne Rienner.

Howlett, Michael. 1994. "Policy Paradigms and Policy Change: Lessons from the Old and New Canadian Policies toward Aboriginal Peoples."   *Policy Studies Journal* 22: 631-49.

Hudson, Valerie M. and Christopher S. Vore. 1995. "Foreign Policy Analysis Yesterday, Today, and Tomorrow." *Mershon International Studies Review* 39: 209-38.

Hughes, Barry. 1997. *Continuity and Change in World Politics.* Upper Saddle River, New Jersey: Prentice Hall.

Huh, Tae-Hoi. 1997. "Economic Interdependence and International Conflicts in the Asia-Pacific." *Asian Perspective* 21: 233-58.

Humana, Charles. 1986. *World Human Rights Guide.* New York: Facts on File Publications.

Huntington, Samuel. 1968. *Political Order in Changing Societies.* New Haven, Connecticut: Yale University Press.

Huntington, Samuel. 1991. *The Third Wave Democratization in the Late Twentieth Century.* Norman, Oklahoma: University Oklahoma Press.

Huntington, Samuel. 1996. *The Clash of Civilizations and the Remaking of World Order.* New York: Simon and Schuster.

Huntington, Samuel. 1999. "The Lonely Superpower." *Foreign Affairs* 78: 35-49.

Huth, Paul. 1988. "Extended Deterrence and the Outbreak of War." *American Political Science Review* 82: 423-43.

Huth, Paul. 1993. "Extended Deterrence to Protect Allies." *American Political Science Review* 87: 61-72.

Hwang, Jong-Sung. 1997. "Analysis of the Structure of the Korean Political Elites." *Korea Journal* 37: 98-117.

Ikenberry, G. John. ed. 1996. *American Foreign Policy: Theoretical Essays*. New York: Harper Collins.

Islam, Iyanatul and Anis Chowdhury. 1997. *Asia-Pacific Economies*. New York: Routledge.

Jackson, John H. and Carl G. Rosberg. 1982. "Why Africa's Weak State Persists: The Empirical and the Juridical in Statehood." *World Politics* 35: 1-24.

James, Patrick and John R. Oneal. 1991. "The Influence of Domestic and International Politics on the President's Use of Force." *Journal of Conflict Resolution* 35: 301-32.

Jannis, Irving L. 1982. *Groupthink: Psychological Studies of Policy Decisions and Fiascoes*. Boston, Massachusetts: Houghton Mifflin.

Jeong, Se-hyun. 1992. "Legal Status and Political Meaning of the Basic Agreement Between the South and the North." *Korea and World Affairs* 17: 5-21.

Jervis, Robert. 1978. "Cooperation Under the Security Dilemma." *World Politics* 30: 167-214.

Jervis, Robert. 1979. "Deterrence Theory Revisited." *World Politics* 31: 289-324.

Job, Brian. 1992. *The Insecurity Dilemma: National Security of Third World States*. Boulder, Colorado: Lynne Rienner.

Johnson, Charlmers. 1982. *MITI and the Japanese Miracle*. Stanford, California: Stanford University Press.

Johnston, Alastair. 1995. "Thinking about the Strategic Culture." *International Security* 19: 32-64.

Jordan, Amos A., William J. Taylor, Jr., and Lawrence J. Korb. 1993. *American National Security: Policy and Process*. Baltimore, Maryland: The Johns Hopkins University.

Jung, Chang-Yeul. 1984. *The Annual Encyclopedia of World History* (*Sae-Gye-Neuk-Sa-Yeun-Bo*). Seoul: Yeukmin.

Jung, Il-Young. 1993.   *Review on South Korea's Half-Century Diplomacy* (Han-Kuk-Wei-Gyo-E-Dae-Han-Ban-Sae-Gi-Eui-Sung-Chal). Seoul: Nanam.

Kang, Young Hoon. 1985. "Security Policy." In *The Foreign Policy of the Republic of Korea*, eds., Youngnok Koo and Sung-Joo Han. New York: Columbia University Press.

Katzenstein, Peter J. 1976. "International Relations and Domestic Structures: Foreign Economic Policies of Advanced Industrial States." *International Organization* 30: 1-45.

Katzenstein, Peter J. 1989. "International Relations Theory and the Analysis of Change." In *Global Changes and Theoretical Challenges: Approaches to World Politics for the 1990s*, eds., Ernst-Otto Czempiel and James N. Rosenau. Lexington, Massachusetts: Lexington Books.

Katzenstein, Peter J. 1996.   *The Culture of National Security: Norms and Identity in World Politics*. New York: Columbia University Press.

Kaufman, Robert G. 1956.   *Military Policy and National Security*.   Princeton, New Jersey: Princeton University Press.

Kaufman, Robert G. 1994.   "A Two-Level Interaction: Structure, Stable Liberal Democracy, and U.S. Grand Strategy." *Security Studies* 3: 678-717.

Kegley, Charles Jr. 1993. "The Neoidealist Moment in International Studies? Realist Myths and the New International Realities." *International Studies Quarterly* 37: 131-46.

Kegley, Charles Jr. and Eugene R. Wittkopf. 1993. *World Politics: Trend and Transformation*. New York: St. Martin's Press.

Kennedy, Paul. 1989. *The Rise and the Fall of the Great Powers*. New York: Vintage Books.

Kennedy, Paul. 1993. *Preparing for the Twenty-First Century*. New York: Vintage Books.

Keohane, Robert O. 1982. "Hegemonic Leadership and U.S. Foreign Economic Policy in the 'Long Decade' of the 1950s." In *America in a Changing World Political Economy*, eds., William P. Avery and David P. Rapkin. New York: Longman.

Keohane, Robert O. 1988. "International Institutions: Two Approaches." *International Studies Quarterly* 32: 379-96.

Keohane, Robert O. 1989. *International Institutions and State Power.* Boulder, Colorado: Westview.

Keohane, Robert O. and Helen V. Milner. 1996. *Internationalization and Domestic Politics.* Cambridge, Massachusetts: Cambridge University Press.

Keohane, Robert O. and Joseph Nye. 1973. "World Politics and the International Economic System." In *The Future of the International Economic Order: An Agenda for Research*, ed., C. Fred Bergsten. Lexington, Massachusetts: Lexington Books.

Keohane, Robert O. and Joseph Nye. 1974. "Transgovernmental Relations and International Organizations." *World Politics* 27: 39-62.

Keohane, Robert O. and Joseph Nye. 1989. *Power and Interdependence: World Politics in Transition.* Boston, Massachusetts: Little Brown.

Kihl, Young Whan. 1984. *Politics and Policies in Divided Korea: Regimes in Contest.* Boulder, Colorado: Westview.

Kihl, Young Whan. 1990. *The 1990 Prime Ministers' Meetings Between North and South Korea: An Analysis.* New York: The Asia Society.

Kihl, Young Whan. 1995. "Democratization and Foreign Policy." In *Politics and Policy in the New Korean State*, ed., James Cotton. New York: St. Martin's Press.

Kil, Byung-ok. 1995. *Nuclear Proliferation Problem on the Korean Peninsula* (*Han-Ban-Do-E-Seo-Eui-Hak-Hwak-San-Mun-Je-Wa-Jang-Gi-Juk-Dae-Eung-Bang-An*). Seoul: Hong-Mun-Kwan.

Kim, Byung-Ki. 1993. "North Korea's Nuclear Policy in the Year 2000: Sources, Strategies, and Implications for the Korean Peninsula." *The Journal of East Asian Affairs* 7: 32-57.

Kim, Byung-kook and Suh Jin-young. 1997. "Politics of Reform in Confucian Korea." *Korea Focus* 5: 8-32.

Kim, C. I. Eugene and Han Kyo Kim. 1967. *Korea and the Politics of Imperialism: 1876-1910*. Berkeley, California: University of California Press.

Kim, Dal-Jung. 1998. "Theory and Reality of South Korean Foreign Policy." In *South Korea's Foreign Policy (Han-Kuk-Eui-Wei-Gyo-Jung-Chaek)*, ed., Dal-Jung Kim. Seoul: Orm.

Kim, Eun Mee. 1993. "Contradictions and Limits of a Developmental State: With Illustrations from the South Korean Case." *Social Problems* 40: 228-49.

Kim, Hak-Joon. 1993. "The Republic of Korea's Northern Policy: Origin, Development, and Prospects." In *Korea Under Roh Tae-Woo: Democratization, Northern Policy, and Inter-Korean Relations*, ed., James Cotton. Canberra: Allen & Unwin.

Kim, Jae-Youl. 1993. "Democratization in South Korea." In *Korea Under Roh Tae-Woo: Democratization, Northern Policy, and Inter-Korean Relations*, ed., James Cotton. Canberra: Allen & Unwin.

Kim, Jun-Il and Jongryn Mo. 1999. "Democratization and Macroeconomic Policy." In *Democracy and the Korean Economy*, eds., Jongryn Mo and Chung-in Moon. Stanford, California: Hoover Institution.

Kim, Ki Hoon. 1990. "The Role of the United States in the Economic Development of Korea." In *Forty Years of Korea-U.S. Relations, 1948-1988 (Han-Mi-Kwan-Gye-Eui-Sa-Sip-Neun-Sa, 1948-1988)*, eds., Tae-Hwan Kwak and Seong Hyong Lee. Seoul: Kyung Hee University Press.

Kim, Kwang-woong. 1994. "Who Runs Korea?: An Analysis of Power Groups." *Korea Focus* 2: 5-11.

Kim, Kyung-Won. 1979. "Korea and Security in Northeast Asia." In *Strategy and Security in Northeast Asia*, eds., Richard B. Foster, James E. Dornan, and William M. Carpenter. New York: Crane, Russak & Co.

Kim, Min-Seok. 1995. "The U.S. Northeast Asian Security Strategy." *The Unified Korea* 143: 28-31.

Kim, Sang-Joon. 1994. "Characteristic Features of Korean Democratization." *Asian Perspective* 18: 181-96.

Kim, Seung-Hwan. 1988. "Prospects for Korean Security." In *Security in Northeast Asia*, ed., Stephen Gilbert. Boulder, Colorado: Westview Press.

Kim, Taewoo. 1999. "South Korea's Missile Dilemmas." *Asian Survey* 39: 486-503.

Kim, Tschol-su. 1997. "What Created a Civilian Autocracy?" *Korea Focus* 5: 129-31.

Kim, Woo-Sang. 1997. "Power Transition and Strategic Stability in East Asia." *Asian Perspective* 21: 153-70.

Kim, Yong-Ho. 1994. "Party Politics and the Process of Democratization in Korea." In *Korea in the Global Wave of Democratization*, eds., Do Chull Shin, Myeong-Han Zoh, and Myung Choy. Seoul: Seoul National University Press.

King, Desmond. 1992. "The Establishment of Work-Welfare Programs in the United States and Britain." In *Structuring Politics: Historical Institutionalism in Comparative Analysis*, eds., Sven Steinmo and Kathleen Thelen, and Frank Longstreth. Cambridge, Massachusetts: Cambridge University Press.

Klare, Michael T. 1993. "The Next Great Arms Race." *Foreign Affairs* 72: 136-52.

Klare, Michael T. and Daniel Volman. 1996. "From Military Aid to Military Markets." In *Foreign Aid toward the Millennium*, ed., Steven W. Hook. Boulder, Colorado: Lynne Rienner.

Koh, Byung-Chul. 1984. *The Foreign Policy Systems of North and South Korea*. Berkeley, California: University of California Press.

Koh, Byung-Chul. 1985. "Policy Toward Reunification." In *The Foreign Policy of the Republic of Korea*, eds., Youngnok Koo and Sung-joo Han. New York: Columbia University Press.

Koh, Byung-Chul. 1994. "Confrontation and Cooperation on the Korean Peninsula: The Politics of Nuclear Non-proliferation." *Korean Journal of Defense Analysis* 6: 53-83.

Koh, Tommy. 1998. *The Quest for World Order: Perspectives of a Pragmatic Idealist*. Singapore: The Institute of Policy Studies.

Kolodziej, Edward A. 1992. "Renaissance in Security Studies? Caveat Lector!" *International Studies Quarterly* 36: 421-38.

Kong, Tat Yan and Dae Hwan Kim. 1997. "Introduction: Aspects of the Transition and Theoretical Considerations." In *The Korean Peninsula in Transition*, eds., Dae Hwan Kim and Tat Yan Kong. New York: St. Martin's Press.

Koo, Hagan and Eun-Mee Kim. 1993. "The Developmental State and Capital Accumulation in South Korea." In *States and Development in the Asia Pacific Rim*, eds., Richard Appelbaum and Jefferey Henderson. Newbury Park, California: Sage.

Koo, Young-Nok. 1975. "The Conduct of Foreign Affairs." In *Korean Politics in Transition*, ed., Edward R. Wright. Seattle, Washington: University of Washington Press.

Koo, Young-Nok and Sungjoo Han. 1985. "Historical Legacy." In *The Foreign Policy of the Republic of Korea*, eds., Young-Nok Koo and Sungjoo Han. New York: Columbia University Press.

Kozak, David C. 1988. "The Bureaucratic Politics Approach: The Evolution of the Paradigm." In *Bureaucratic Politics and National Security: Theory and Practice*, eds., David C. Kozak and James M. Keagle. Boulder, Colorado: Lynne Rienner.

Krasner, Stephen D. 1978. *Defending the National Interest*. Princeton, New Jersey: Princeton University Press.

Krasner, Stephen D. ed. 1983. *International Regimes*. Ithaca, New York: Cornell University Press.

Krasner, Stephen D. 1984. "Approaches to the State: Alternative Conceptions and Historical Dynamics." *Comparative Politics* 16: 223-46.

Kratochwil, Friedrich. 1989. *Rules, Norms, Decisions*. Cambridge, Massachusetts: Cambridge University Press.

Krueger, Anne O. 1979. *The Developmental Role of the Foreign Sector and Aid*. Cambridge, Massachusetts: Harvard University Press.

Krugman, Paul. 1998. "Asia: What Went Wrong." *Fortune* 137: 32-4.

Kuhn, Thomas S. 1970. *The Structure of Scientific Revolution.* Chicago, Illinois: University of Chicago Press.

Kuznetts, Paul W. 1977. *Economic Growth and Structure in the Republic of Korea.* New Haven, Connecticut: Yale University Press.

Kwak, Tae-Hwan and Edward A. Olsen. eds. 1996. *The Major Powers of Northeast Asia: Seeking Peace and Stability.* Boulder, Colorado: Lynne Rienner.

Kwon, Hyunjoo P. 1974. *The Emergency of Military Men in Korean Politics: A Historical Study on the Rise of Military Elites.* Buffalo, New York: State University of New York Press.

Kwon, Jene K. 1990. "The Uncommon Characteristics of Korea's Economic Development." In *Korean Economic Development*, ed., Jene K. Kwon. New York: Greenwood Press.

Lachmann, Richard. 1990. "Class Formation Without Class Struggle: An Elite Conflict Theory of the Transition to Capitalism." *American Sociological Review* 55: 398-414.

Lake, David A. 1997. "Regional Security Complexes: A Systems Approach." In *Regional Orders: Building Security in a New World*, eds., David A. Lake and Patrick M. Morgan. University Park, Pennsylvania: The Pennsylvania State University Press.

Laurence, Edward J. 1992. *The International Arms Trade.* New York: Lexington Books.

Laurence, Henry. 1999. "Financial System Reform and the Currency Crisis in East Asia." *Asian Survey* 39: 349-73.

Layne, Christopher. 1994. "Kant or Cant: The Myth of the Democratic Peace." *International Security* 19: 5-49.

Lebow, Richard N. and Thomas Risse-Kappen. 1995. *International Relations Theory and the End of the Cold War.* New York: Columbia University Press.

Lee, Jong-Gi. 1995. "Study on Possible Establishment of the CSCNA." *Journal of International Affairs* 26: 87-92.

Lee, Jong-Seok. 1995. "Inter-Korean Relations: Kim Jung-Il's Survival Tactic." *Korea Focus* 3: 70-3.

Lee, Kuan Yew. 1992. "What Kinds of New Order in East Asia?" *New Perspective Quarterly* 9: 4-19.

Lee, Min-Young. 1995. "Building Security Regimes in Northeast Asia." *The Journal of East Asian Affairs* 9: 61-85.

Lee, Sam-Sung. 1994. "Peace and Security in Northeast Asia: Reality and Vision." *Asian Perspective* 18: 129-58.

Lee, Sun-Ho and Kwang-Sun Jung. 1996. *Internationalization of Korean Defense (Han-KuK-Bang-Wi-Eui-Sae-Gae-Hwa)*. Seoul: Palbokwon.

Lee, Tae Hwan. 1999. "Korea's Foreign Policy in the Post-Cold War era." *Korea Focus* 7: 1-17.

Lee, Young-ho. 1975. "Politics of Democratic Experiment." In *Korean Politics in Transition*, ed., Edward R. Wright. Seattle, Washington: University of Washington Press.

Leffler, Melvyn P. 1984. The American Conception of National Security and the Beginnings of the Cold War, 1945-48." *American Historical Review* 89: 346-400.

Legro, Jeffrey W. 1997. "Which Norms Matter? Revisiting the 'Failure' of Internationalism." *International Organization* 51: 31-64.

Lehman, Ronald. 1994. "Some Considerations on Resolving the North Korean Nuclear Question." *The Korean Journal of Defense Analysis* 6: 11-33.

Lentner, Howard H. 1974. *Foreign Policy Analysis: A Comparative and Conceptual Approach*. Columbus, Ohio: Bell & Howell.

Levi, Margaret. 1988. *Of Rule and Revenue*. Berkeley, California: University of California Press.

Levin, Norman D. 1993. "US Interests in Korean Security in the Post-Cold War World." In *Asian Flashpoint: Security and the Korean Peninsula*, ed., Andrew Mack. Canberra: Allen & Unwin.

Levin, Norman D. and Richard L. Sneider. 1981. "Korea in Postwar U.S. Security Policy." In *The US-South Korean Alliance: Evolving Patterns in Security Relations*, eds., Gerald L. Curtis and Sung-joo Han. Lexington, Massachusetts: Lexington Books.

Levy, Jack S. 1989. "The Causes of War: A Review of Theories and Evidence." In *Behavior, Society, and Nuclear War*, ed., Philip E. Tetlock. New York: Oxford University Press.

Lim, Dong Won. 1991. "Inter-Korean Relations Oriented toward Reconciliation and Cooperation with an Emphasis on the Basic South-North Agreement." *Korea and World Affairs* 16: 213-23.

Lim, Dong Won. 1993. "Inter-Korean Relations Oriented toward Reconciliation and Cooperation." In *Korea Under Roh Tae-Woo: Democratization, Northern Policy, and Inter-Korean Relations*, ed., James Cotton. Canberra: Allen & Unwin.

Lipschutz, Ronnie D. 1995. "On Security." In *On Security*, ed., Ronnie Lipschutz. New York: Columbia University Press.

Lipset, Martin S. 1959. "Some Social Requisites of Democracy: Economic Development and Political Legitimacy." *American Political Science Review* 53: 69-105.

Lipson, Charles. 1984. "International Cooperation in Economic and Security Affairs." *World Politics* 37: 1-23.

Lohmann, Susanne. 1997. "Linkage Politics." *The Journal of Conflict Resolution* 41: 38-67.

Lowndes, Vivien. 1996. "Varieties of New Institutionalism: A Critical Appraisal." *Public Administration* 74: 181-97.

Lynn-Jones, Sean M. and Steven E. Miller. eds. 1993. *The Cold War and After: Prospects for Peace*. Cambridge, Massachusetts: The MIT Press.

McDougall, Derek. 1997. *The International Relations of the New Asia Pacific*. Boulder, Colorado: Lynne Rienner.

McGinns, Michael D. 1986. "Issue-Linkage and the Evolution of International Cooperation." *Journal of Conflict Resolution* 30: 141-70.

McGinns, Michael D. and John T. Williams. 1993. "Policy Uncertainty in Tow-Level Games: Examples of Correlated Equilibria." *International Studies Quarterly* 37: 29-54.

McKinlay, R. D. and A. Mughan. 1984. *Aid and Arms to the Third World: An Analysis of the Distribution and Impact of US Official Transfers.* New York: St. Martin's Press.

McMichael, Philip. 1990. "Incorporating Comparison within a World-Historical Perspective: An Alternative Comparative Method." *American Sociological Review* 55: 385-97.

Mack, Andrew. 1993. "Security and the Korean Peninsula in the 1990s." In *Asian Flashpoint: Security and the Korean Peninsula*, ed., Andrew Mack. Canberra: Allen & Unwin.

Mack, Andrew. 1994. "A Nuclear North Korea: The Choices Are Narrowing." *World Policy Journal* 11: 27-35.

Mako, William P. 1983. *U.S. Ground Forces and the Defense of Central Europe.* Washington, D.C.: Brookings Institution.

Maniruzzaman, Talukder. 1992. "Arms Transfers, Military Coups, and Military Rule in Developing States." *Journal of Conflict Resolution* 36: 733-55.

Mansfield, Edward D. and Jack Snyder. 1995. "Democratization and the Danger of War." In *Debating the Democratic Peace*, eds., Michael E. Brown, Sean M. Lynn-Jones, and Steven E. Miller. Cambridge, Massachusetts: The MIT Press.

Manzur, Meher. 1993. *Exchange Rates, Prices and World Trade: New Methods, Evidence and Implications.* New York: Routledge.

Maoz, Zeev. 1996. *Domestic Sources of Global Change.* New York: University of Michigan Press.

Maoz, Zeev and N. Abdolali. 1989. "Regime Types and International Conflict, 1816-1976." *Journal of Conflict Resolution* 33: 3-35.

March, James G. 1994. "The Evolution of Evolution." In *Evolutionary Dynamics of Organization*, eds., Joel A. C. Baum and Jitendra V. Singh. New York: Oxford University Press.

March, James G. and Johan P. Olsen. 1989. *Rediscovering Institutions: The Organizational Basis of Politics*. New York: The Free Press.

Mathews, Jessica T. 1989. "Redefining Security." *Foreign Affairs* 18: 162-77.

Matray, James I. 1995. "Hodge Podge: American Occupation Policy in Korea, 1945-1948." *Korean Studies* 19: 17-38.

Mazarr, Michael J. 1995. "The U.S.-DPRK Nuclear Deal." *Korea and World Affairs* 19: 482-509.

Mearsheimer, John. 1990. "Back to the Future: Instability in Europe after the Cold War." *International Security* 15: 5-56.

Mehta, Jagat S. 1985. *Third World Militarization: A Challenge to Third World Diplomacy*. Austin, Texas: University of Texas Press.

Menon, Rajan. 1997. "The Strategic Convergence Between Russia and China." *Survival* 39: 101-25.

Middleton, Lawrence. 1997. "South Korean Foreign Policy." In *The Korean Peninsula in Transition*, eds., Dae Hwan Kim and Tat Yan Kong. New York: St. Martin's Press.

Midlarsky, Manus I. 1983. "The Balance of Power as a Just Historical System." *Polity* 16: 181-200.

Migdal, Joel S. 1988. *Strong Societies and Weak States: State-Society Relations and State Capacities in the Third World*. Princeton, New Jersey: Princeton University Press.

Mill, John S. [1881] 1950. *Philosophy of Scientific Method*. New York: Hafner.

Min, Byung-Chun. 1978. *Thesis on Korean Security* (*Kuk-Ga-Bang-Wi-Ron*). Seoul: Daewangsa.

Mingst, Karen. 1995. "Uncovering the Missing Links: Linkage Actors and Their Strategies in Foreign Policy Analysis." In *Foreign Policy Analysis: Continuity and Change in Its Second Generation*, eds., Laura Neack, Jeanne A.K. Hey, and Patrick J. Haney. Englewood Cliffs, New Jersey: Prentice Hall.

Mo, Jongryn. 1999. "Democratization, Labor Policy, and Economic Performance." In *Democracy and the Korean Economy*, eds., Jongryn Mo and Chung-in Moon. Stanford, California: Hoover Institution.

Moon, Bruce E. 1985. "Consensus or Compliance? Foreign Policy Change and External Dependence." *International Organization* 39: 297-329.

Moon, Bruce E. 1995. "The State in Foreign and Domestic Policy." In *Foreign Policy Analysis: Continuity and Change in Its Second Generation*, eds., Laura Neack, Jeanne A.K. Hey, and Patrick J. Haney. Englewood Cliffs, New Jersey: Prentice Hall.

Moon, Chung-in. 1988. "Complex Interdependence and Transnational Lobbying: South Korea in the U.S." *International Studies Quarterly* 32: 67-89.

Moon, Chung-in. 1999. "Democratization and Globalization as Ideological and Political Foundations of Economic Policy." In *Democracy and the Korean Economy*, eds., Jongryn Mo and Chung-in Moon. Stanford, California: Hoover Institution.

Moon, Chung-in and Seok-soo Lee. 1995. "The Post-Cold War Security Agenda of Korea: Inertia, New Thinking, and Assessments." *The Pacific Review* 8: 99-115.

Moore, Barrington. 1966. *Social Origins of Dictatorship and Democracy*. New York: Beacon.

Moosa, Imad A. and Razzaque H. Bhatti. 1997. *International Parity Conditions: Theory, Economic Testing and Empirical Evidence*. New York: St. Martin's Press.

Moravcsik, Andrew. 1993. "Introduction: Integrating International and Domestic Theories of International Bargaining." In *Double-edged Diplomacy: International Bargaining and Domestic Politics*, eds., Peter B. Evans, Harold K. Jacobson, and Robert D. Putnam. Berkeley, California: University of California Press.

Moravcsik, Andrew. 1997. "Taking Preferences Seriously: A Liberal Theory of International Politics." *International Organization* 51: 513-53.

Morgan, Patrick M. 1997. "Regional Security Complexes and Regional Orders." In *Regional Orders: Building Security in a New World*, eds., David A. Lake and Patrick M. Morgan. University Park, Pennsylvania: The Pennsylvania State University Press.

Morgan, T. Clifton and Sally H. Campbell. 1991. "Domestic Structure, Decisional Constraints, and War: So Why Kant Democracies Fight?" *Journal of Conflict Resolution* 53: 187-211.

Morgenthau, Hans. 1948. *Politics Among Nations: The Struggle for Power and Peace*. New York: Knopf.

Morimoto, Satoshi. 1993. "Japan's Interests in Security on the Korean Peninsula in a Post-Cold War World." In *Asian Flashpoint: Security and the Korean Peninsula*, ed., Andrew Mack. Canberra: Allen & Unwin.

Muller, Herald and Thomas Risse-Kappen. 1993. "From the Outside In and From the Inside Out: International Relations, Domestic Politics, and Foreign Policy." In *The Limits of State Autonomy: Social Groups and Foreign Policy Formulation*, eds., Valerie Hudson and David Skidmore. Boulder, Colorado: Westview.

Muller, Lynn H. 1994. *Global Order: Values and Power in International Politics*. Boulder, Colorado: Westview.

Murphy, Craig and Gareth Evans. 1973. *U.S. Military Personnel Strength by Country of Location since World War II, 1948-1973*. Washington, D.C.: Government Printing Office.

Murray, Douglas J. and Paul R. Viotti. 1989. "Introduction: Defense Policy in Comparative Perspective." In *The Defense Policies of Nations: A Comparative Study*, eds., Douglas J. Murray and Paul R, Viotti. Baltimore, Maryland: The Johns Hopkins University Press.

Mustanduno, Michael, David A. Lake, and G. John Ikenberry. 1989. "Toward a Realist Theory of State Action." *International Studies Quarterly* 33: 457-74.

Nam, Joo-Hong. 1986. *America's Commitment to South Korea: The First Decade of the Nixon Doctrine*. New York: Cambridge University Press.

Neack, Laura. 1995. "Linking State Type with Foreign Policy Behavior." In *Foreign Policy Analysis: Continuity and Change in Its Second Generation*, eds., Laura Neack, Jeanne A.K. Hey, and Patrick J. Haney. Englewood Cliffs, New Jersey: Prentice Hall.

Neack, Laura, Jeanne A. K. Hey, and Patrick J. Haney. 1995. "Generational Change in Foreign Policy Analysis." In *Foreign Policy Analysis: Continuity and Change in Its Second Generation*, eds., Laura Neack, Jeanne A.K. Hey, and Patrick J. Haney. Englewood Cliffs, New Jersey: Prentice Hall.

Nordlinger, Eric. 1981. *On the Autonomy of the Democratic State*. Cambridge, Massachusetts: Harvard University Press.

North, Douglass C. 1990. *Institutions, Institutional Change and Economic Performance*. Cambridge, Massachusetts: Cambridge University Press.

Numazaki, Ichiro. 1998. "The Export-Oriented Industrialization of Pacific Rim Nations and Their Presence in the Global Market." In *The Four Asian Tigers: Economic Development and the Global Political Economy*, ed., Eyn Mee Kim. San Diego, California: Academic Press.

Nye, Joseph. 1971. "Comparing Common Markets: A Revised Neofunctional Model." In *Regional Integration: Theory and Research*, eds., Leon N. Lindberg and Stuart A. Schiengold. Cambridge, Massachusetts: Harvard University Press.

Nye, Joseph and Sean M. Lynn-Jones. 1988. "International Security Studies: A Report of a Conference on the State of the Field." *International Security* 12: 5-27.

Oberdorfer, Don. 1988. "In Bow to Seoul, U.S. Eases Some Restrictions on North Korea." *Washington Post*, November 1, p. A-28.

O'Donnell, Guillermo. 1979. "Tensions in Bureaucratic-Authoritarian State and the Question of Democracy." In *The New Authoritarianism in Latin America*, ed., David Collier. Princeton, New Jersey: Princeton University Press.

O'Donnell, Guillermo, Philippe C. Schmitter, and Laurence Whitehead. 1986. *Transitions from Authoritarianism*. Baltimore, Maryland: The Johns Hopkins University Press.

Officer, Lawrence H. 1982. *Purchasing Power Parity and Exchange Rates: Theory, Evidence and Relevance*. Greenwich, Connecticut: JAI Press.

Oh, Kwan-chi, Young-gu Cha, and Dong-Jun Hwang. 1990. *The Evolution and the Future of Korea-US Military Cooperation Relations (Han-Mi-Gun-Sa-Heup-Reuk-gwan-Gye-Eui-Bal-Jeon-Gwa-Mi-Rae)*. Seoul: Se-Kyung.

Oliver, Robert T. 1978. *Syngman Rhee and American Involvement in Korea, 1941-1960: A Personal Narrative*. Seoul: Panmun Book.

Olsen, Edward A. 1993. "The Diplomatic Dimensions of the Korean Confrontation." In *East Asian Security in the Post-Cold War Era*, ed., Sheldon Simon. New York: M.E. Sharpe.

Olsen, Edward A. 1996. "U.S.-Northeast Asian Security Relations: From Bilateralism to Multilateralism." In *The Major Powers of Northeast Asia: Seeking Peace and Security*, eds., Tae-Hwan Kwak and Edward A. Olsen. Boulder, Colorado: Lynne Rienner.

Organski, A. F. K. 1968. *World Politics*. New York: Knopf.

Organski, A. F. K. and Jacek Kugler. 1980. *The War Ledge*. Chicago, Illinois: University of Chicago Press.

Osgood, Charles E. 1966. *Perspective in Foreign Policy*. Palo Alto, California: Pacific Books.

Owen, John M. 1996. "How Liberalism Produces Democratic Peace." In *Debating the Democratic Peace*, ed., Michael E. Brown. Cambridge, Massachusetts: The MIT Press.

Pae, Sung M. 1986. *Testing Democratic Theories in Korea*. New York: University Press of America.

Papayoanou, Paul A. 1997. "Economic Interdependence and the Balance of Power." *International Studies Quarterly* 41: 113-40.

Park, Jae Kyu. 1985. "Korea and the Third World." In *The Foreign Policy of the Republic of Korea*, eds., Young-Nok Koo and Sung-joo Han. New York: Columbia University Press.

Park, Moon Young. 1995. "Lure North Korea." *Foreign Policy* 97: 97-105.

Park, Myung-Lim. 1996. *The Outbreak and Origins of the Korean War* (*Han-Kuk-Jun-Jang-Eui-Bal-Bal-Gwa-Gi-Won*) Seoul: Nanam.

Park, Sang-seek. 1993. "Northern Diplomacy and Inter-Korean Relations." In *Korea Under Roh Tae-Woo: Democratization, Northern Policy, and Inter-Korean Relations*, ed., James Cotton. Canberra: Allen & Unwin.

Park, Tong-Whan, Dae-Won Ko, and Kyu-Ryoon Kim. 1994. "Democratization and Foreign Policy Change in the East Asian NICs." In *Foreign Policy Restructuring: How Governments Respond to Global Changes*, eds., Jerel A. Rosati, Joe D. Hagan, and Martin W. Sampson. Columbia, South Carolina: University of South Carolina Press.

Perlmutter, Amos. 1981. *Modern Authoritarianism: A Comparative Institutional Analysis*. New Haven, Connecticut: Yale University Press.

Pierre, Andrew J. 1982. *The Global Politics of Arms Sales*. Princeton, New Jersey: Princeton University Press.

Pirages, Dennis. 1987. "Change in the Global System." In *Political Change and Foreign Policies*, eds., Gavin Boyd and Gerald W. Hopple. New York: St. Martin's Press.

Posen, Barry. 1984. *The Sources of Military Doctrine: France, Britain, and Germany between the World Wars*. Ithaca, New York: Cornell University Press.

Posen, Barry. 1989. "Correspondence." *International Security* 13: 144-60.

Posen, Barry and Stephen Van Evera. 1987. "Reagan Administration Defense Policy: Departure from Containment." In *Eagle Resurgent: The Reagan Era in American Foreign Policy*, eds., K. Oye, R. Lieber, and D. Rothchild. Boston, Massachusetts: Little, Brown.

Powell, Robert. 1991. "The Problem of Absolute and Relative Gains in International Relations Theory." *American Political Science Review* 85: 1303-20.

Przeworski, Adam and Henry Teune. 1970. *The Logic of Comparative Social Inquiry*. New York: Wiley-Interscience.

Putnam, Hilary. 1990. "Realism with a Human Face" and "A Defense of Internal Realism." In *Realism with a Human Face*, ed., James Conant. Cambridge, Massachusetts: Harvard University Press.

Putnam, Robert D. 1988. "Diplomacy and Domestic Politics: The Logic of Two Level Games." *International Organization* 42: 427-60.

Ragin, Charles and David Zaret. 1983. "Theory and Method in Comparative Research: Two Strategies." *Social Forces* 61: 731-54.

Reese, David. 1988. *A Short History of Modern Korea.* New York: Hippocrene Books.

Reese, David. 1998. *The Prospects for North Korea's Survival.* Oxford: Oxford University Press.

Riedel, James. 1996. "Intra-regional Trade and Foreign Direct Investment in the Asia-Pacific Region." In *Emerging Growth Pole: The Asia-Pacific Economy*, ed., Dilip K. Das. New York: Prentice Hall.

Riker, William H. 1962. *The Theory of Political Coalitions.* New Haven, Connecticut: Yale University Press.

Risse-Kappen, Thomas. 1995. "Bringing Transnational Relations Back In: Introduction." In *Bringing Transnational Relations Back In: Non-State Actors, Domestic Structures and International Institutions*, ed., Thomas Risse-Kappen. Cambridge, Massachusetts: Cambridge University Press.

Ritzer, George and Pamela Gindoff. 1994. "Agency-Structure, Micro-Macro, Individualism-Holism-Relationism: A Metatheoretical Convergence between the United States and Europe." In *Agency and Structure: Reorienting Social Theory*, ed., Piotr Szetompka. New York: Gordon and Breach.

Robertson, David B. and Dennis R. Judd. 1989. *The Development of American Public Policy: The Structure of Policy Restraint.* Glenview, Illinois: Scott, Foresman and Company.

Rosati, Jerel A. 1987. *The Carter Administration's Quest for Global Community: Beliefs and Their Impact on Behavior.* Columbia, South Carolina: University of South Carolina Press.

Rosati, Jerel A. 1993. *The Politics of United States Foreign Policy.* Dallas, Texas: Harcourt Brace Jovanovitch.

Rosati, Jerel A., Martin W. Sampson, and Joe D. Hagan. 1994. "The Study of Change in Foreign Policy." In *Foreign Policy Restructuring: How Governments Respond to Global Change*, eds., Jerel A. Rosati, Joe D. Hagan, and Martin W. Sampson. Columbia, South Carolina: University of South Carolina Press.

Rose, Gideon. 1998. "Neoclassical Realism and Theories of Foreign Policy." *World Politics* 51: 144-72.

Rosenau, James N. 1969. *Linkage Politics: Essays on the Convergence of National and International Systems.* New York: The Free Press.

Rosenau, James N. 1971. *The Scientific Study of Foreign Policy.* New York: The Free Press.

Rosenau, James N. 1978. "Restlessness, Change, and Foreign Policy Analysis." In *In Search of Global Patterns*, ed., James Rosenau. New York: The Free Press.

Rosenau, James N. 1981. *The Study of Political Adaptation: Essays on the Analysis of World Politics.* New York: Nichols Publishing.

Rosenau, James N. 1990. *Turbulence in World Politics: A Theory of Change and Continuity.* Princeton, New Jersey: Princeton University Press.

Rosenau, James N. 1992. "Governance, Order, and Change in World Politics." In *Governance Without Government: Order and Change in World Politics*, eds., James N. Rosenau and Ernst-Otto Czempiel. Cambridge, Massachusetts: Cambridge University Press.

Ross, Robert E. ed. 1998. *After the Cold War: Domestic Factors and U.S.-China Relations.* New York: M.E. Sharpe.

Rothgeb, John M. Jr. 1995. "The Changing International Context for Foreign Policy." In *Foreign Policy Analysis: Continuity and Change in Its Second Generation*, eds., Laura Neack, Jeanne A. K. Hey, and Patrick J. Haney. Englewood Cliffs, New Jersey: Prentice Hall.

Roy, Denny. 1997. "Introduction: Old and New Agendas." In *The New Security Agenda in the Asia-Pacific Region*, ed., Denny Roy. New York: St. Martin's Press.

Russett, Bruce. 1993. *Grasping the Democratic Peace: Principles for a Post-Cold War World*. Princeton, New Jersey: Princeton University Press.

Russett, Bruce. 1996. "Why Democratic Peace?" In *Debating the Democratic Peace*, eds., Michael E. Brown, Sean M. Lynn-Jones, and Steven E. Miller. Cambridge, Massachusetts: The MIT Press.

Sagan, Scott. 1985. Nuclear Alerts and Crisis Management. *International Security* 11: 151-75.

Sampson, Martin W. 1994. "Exploiting the Seams: External Structure and Libyan Foreign Policy Changes." In *Foreign Policy Restructuring: How Governments Respond to Global Changes*, eds., Jerel A. Rosati, Joe D. Hagan, and Martin W. Sampson. Columbia, South Carolina: University of South Carolina Press.

Sanford, Dan. 1993. "ROK's *nordpolitik* Revisited." *The Journal of East Asian Affairs* 7: 1-31.

Saward, Michael. 1994. "Democratic Theory and Indices of Democratization." In *Defining and Measuring Democracy*, ed., David Beetham. Thousand Oaks, California: Sage.

Scalapino, Robert A. 1976. "The Two Koreas—Dialogue or Conflicts?" In *The Two Koreas in East Asian Affairs*, ed., William J. Barnds. New York: New York University Press.

Scalapino, Robert A. 1986. *Asian Political Institutionalization*. Berkeley, California: Institute of East Asian Studies.

Scalapino, Robert A. 1992. "National Political Institutions and Leadership in Asia." *The Washington Quarterly* 15: 157-72.

Schelling, Thomas C. 1960. *The Strategy of Conflict*. Cambridge, Massachusetts: Harvard University Press.

Schelling, Thomas C. and M. Halperin. 1961. *Strategy and Arms Control*. New York: Twentieth Century Fund.

Schlesinger, Arthur. 1967. "Origins of the Cold War." *Foreign Affairs* 46:22-52.

Schmitter, Philippe and Guillermo O'Donnell. 1986. *Tentative Conclusions about Uncertain Transitions*. Baltimore, Maryland: The Johns Hopkins University Press.

Schmitter, Philippe and Karl Terry. 1991. "What Democracy Is...and Is Not." *Journal of Democracy* 2: 75-88.

Schraeder, Peter J. 1994. "Bureaucratic Incrementalism, Crisis, and Change in U.S. Foreign Policy Toward Africa." In *Foreign Policy Restructuring*, eds., Jerel A. Rosati, Joe D. Hagan, and Martin W. Sampson. Columbia, South Carolina: University of South Carolina Press.

Schroeden, Paul W. 1994. "The New World Order: A Historical Perspective." *The Washington Quarterly* 17: 25-43.

Schweller, Randall L. 1998. *Deadly Imbalances: Tripolarity and Hitler's Strategy of World Conquest*. New York: Columbia University Press.

Scott, W. Richard. 1995. *Institutions and Organizations*. Thousand Oaks, California: Sage.

Segal, Gerald. 1997. "How Insecure is Pacific Asia?" *International Affairs* 73: 235-49.

Seo, Jae-Jin. 1992. *Comparative Analysis on the National Capabilities of North and South Korea (Nam-Buk-Han-Kuk-Neuk-Eui-Bi-Gyo-Yeon-Gu)*. Seoul: The Center of National Unification Studies.

Seo, Ju-Seok. 1999. "Who is Responsible for the Korean War?" *Hankook Daily News*, June 22.

Seung, Ho. 1993. "Tasks for Korean Economic Diplomacy." *Korea Focus* 1: 29-40.

Sheehan, Michael. 1996. *The Balance of Power: History and Theory*. New York: Routledge.

Shin, Hee-Suk. 1993. "Korea's Response to the Changing World Politics: Is a Power Vacuum Developing in Northeast Asia?" *Korea Observer* 26: 603-11.

Shin, Kwang Yeong. 1998. "The Political Economy of Economic Growth in East Asia: South Korea and Taiwan." In *The Four Asian Tigers: Economic Development and the Global Political Economy*, ed., Eun Mee Kim. San Diego, California: Academic Press.

Shin, Myong-sun. 1993. *Discussion of Korean Politics (Han-Kuk-Jung-Chi-Non-Chong)*. Seoul: Pommunsa.

Shirk, Susan L. 1997. "Asia-Pacific Regional Security: Balance of Power or Concert of Powers?" In *Regional Orders: Building Security in a New World*, eds., David A. Lake and Patrick M. Morgan. University Park, Pennsylvania: The Pennsylvania State University Press.

Singer, David. 1961. "The Level-of-Analysis Problem in International Relations." In *The International System: Theoretical Essays*, eds., Klaus Knorr and Sidney Verva. Princeton, New Jersey: Princeton University Press.

Skidmore, David. 1994. "Explaining State Response to International Change: The Structural Sources of Foreign Policy Rigidity and Change." In *Foreign Policy Restructuring*, eds., Jerel A. Rosati, Joe D. Hagan, and Martin W. Sampson. Columbia, South Carolina: University of South Carolina Press.

Skidmore, David and Valerie M. Hudson. 1993. *The Limits of State Autonomy: Societal Groups and Foreign Policy Formulation*. Boulder, Colorado: Westview.

Skocpol, Theda. 1985. "Bringing the State Back In: Strategies of Analysis in Current Research." In *Bringing the State Back In*, eds., Peter B. Evans, Dietrich Rueschemeyer, and Theda Skocpol. Cambridge, Massachusetts: Cambridge University Press.

Skocpol, Theda. 1992. *Protecting Soldiers and Mothers: The Political Origins of Social Policy in the United States*. New York: Cambridge University Press.

Skowronek, Stephen. 1982. *Building a New American State: The Expansion of National Administrative Capacities, 1877-1920*. New York: Cambridge University Press.

Smith, Heather. 1998. "Korea." In *East Asia in Crisis: From Being a Miracle to Needing One?* eds., Ross H. McLeod and Ross Gaunaut. New York: Routledge.

Smith, Steve. 1986. "Theories of Foreign Policy: A Historical Overview." *Review of International Studies* 12: 13-29.

Snidal, Duncan. 1985. "Coordination vs. Prisoner's Dilemma: Implications for International Cooperation and Regimes." *American Political Science Review* 79: 923-42.

Snidal, Duncan. 1993. "Relative Gains and the Pattern of International Cooperation." In *Neorealism and Neoliberalism: The Contemporary Debate*, ed., David Baldwin. New York: Columbia University Press.

Snyder, Glenn. 1961. *Deterrence and Defense: Toward a Theory of National Security*. Princeton, New Jersey: Princeton University Press.

Snyder, Glenn. 1984. *The Ideology of the Offensive: Military Decisionmaking and the Disasters of 1914*. Ithaca, New York: Cornell University Press.

Snyder, Glenn. 1990. "Avoiding Anarchy in the New Europe." *International Security* 14: 5-41.

So, Alvin Y. and Stephen W. K. Chiu. 1995. *East Asia and the World Economy*. Thousand Oaks, California: Sage.

Soh, Byung-Hee. 1997. "*Chaebol* and Politics: Past Ills and Future Tasks." *Korea Focus* 5: 56-65.

Sohn, Hak-Kyu. 1989. *Authoritarianism and Opposition in South Korea*. New York: Routledge.

Son, Chu-Whan. 1999. "North Korean Refugees: Problems and Policy Considerations." *Korea Focus* 7: 1-12.

Song, Hee-hyon. 1990. "Transport System Development Direction in Northeast Asia: With Particular Preference to Korea, USSR and China." Seoul: Korean Maritime Institute.

Sorensen, Georg. 1998. *Democracy and Democratization: Processes and Prospects in a Changing World*. Boulder, Colorado: Westview.

Spanier, John and Steven W. Hook. 1998. *American Foreign Policy Since World War II*. Washington, D.C.: Congressional Quarterly.

Spiro, Daivd E. 1994. "The Significance of the Liberal Peace." *International Security* 19: 50-86.

Stavridis, Stelios and Christopher Hill. 1996. *Domestic Sources of Foreign Policy.* Washington, D.C.: Berg.

Stein, Arthur A. 1982. "Coordination and Collaboration Regimes in an Anarchic World." *International Organization* 36: 229-324.

Steinberg, David I. 1989. *The Republic of Korea: Economic Transformation and Social Change.* Boulder, Colorado: Westview.

Steinberg, S. H. and John Paxton. Various years. *The Statesman's Yearbook: Statistical and Historical Annual of the States of the World.* New York: St. Martin's Press.

Steinbruner, John D. 1974. *The Cybernetic Theory of Decision.* Princeton, New Jersey: Princeton University Press.

Steinbruner, John D. 1976. "Beyond Rational Deterrence: The Struggle for New Conceptions." *World Politics* 28: 223-42.

Stephens, John. 1989. "Democratic Transition and Breakdown in Western Europe, 1870-1939: A Test of the Moore Thesis." *American Journal of Sociology* 94: 1019-77.

Stern, Eric and Bertjan Verbeek, 1998. "Wither the Study of Governmental Politics in Foreign Policymaking?: A Symposium." *Mershon International Studies Review* 42: 205-55.

Stokes, Henry S. 1982. "South Korea Under Chun: New Vigor But Little Shift Toward Democracy." *New York Times*, March 4, p. 6.

Strange, Susan. 1996. *The Retreat of the State: The Diffusion of Power in the World Economy.* Cambridge, Massachusetts: Cambridge University Press.

Stubbs, Richard and Geoffrey Underhill. 1994. "Global Issues and Historical Perspective" and "Global Trends and Regional Patterns." In *Political Economy and the Changing Global Order*, eds., R. Stubbs and G. Underhill. Toronto, Canada: McClelland and Stewart.

Suh, Sang Chul. 1978. "Foreign Capital and Development Strategy in Korea." *Korean Studies* 2: 67-94.

Sundhaussen, Ulf. 1984. "Military Withdrawal from Government Responsibility." *Armed Forces and Society* 10: 543-62.

Taylor, Robert. 1996. *Greater China and Japan: Prospects for an Economic Partnership in East Asia*. New York: Routledge.

Tehranian, Majid. ed. 2000. *Asian Peace: Security and Governance in the Asia-Pacific Region*. New York: I.B. Tauris.

Tellis, Ashley J. 1995. "Reconstructing Political Realism: The Long March to Scientific Theory." *Security Studies* 5: 3-104.

Thelen, Kathleen and Sven Steinmo. 1992. "Historical Institutionalism in Comparative Politics." In *Structuring Politics*, eds., Sven Steinmo, Kathleen Thelen, and Frank Longstreth. Cambridge, Massachusetts: Cambridge University Press.

Thomas, Caroline. 1989. "Southern Instability, Security, and Western Concepts: On an Unhappy Marriage and the Need for a Divorce." In *The State and Instability in the South*, eds., Caroline Thomas and Paikiasothy Saravanamuttu. New York: St. Martin's Press.

Thurow, Lester. 1992. "Communitarian vs. Individualistic Capitalism." *New Perspective Quarterly* 9: 41-5.

Tilly, Charles. 1985. "War Making and State Making as Organized Crime." In *Bringing the State Back In*, eds., Peter Evans, Dietrich Rueschemeyer, and Theda Skocpol. Cambridge, Massachusetts: Cambridge University Press.

Todaro, Michael. 1992. *Economics for a Developing World*. New York: Longman.

Tollison, Robert E. and Thomas D. Willett. 1979. "An Economic Theory of Mutually Advantageous Issue Linkage in International Negotiations." *International Organization* 33: 425-49.

Touraine, Alain. 1998. *What is Democracy?* Trans., David Macey. Boulder, Colorado: Westview.

Tow, William. 1993a. "Northeast Asia and International Security: Transforming Competition to Collaboration." *Australian Journal of International Affairs* 47: 1-28.

Tow, William. 1993b. "The Military Dimensions of the Korean Confrontation." In *East Asian Security in the Post-Cold War Era*, ed., Sheldon W. Simon. New York: M. E. Sharpe.

Tsebelis, George. 1990. *Nested Games*. Berkeley, California: University of California Press.

Tucker, Robert W. 1977. *The Inequality of Nations*. New York: Basic Books.

Tussie, Diana. 1998. "Multilateralism Revisited in a Globalizing World Economy." *Mershon International Studies Review* 42: 183-203.

Ullman, Richard H. 1983. "Redefining Security." *International Security* 8: 129-53.

University Press of America. 1992. "Declaration of Non-Nuclear Korean Peninsula Peace Initiatives." In *Korea in the Pacific Century: Selected Speeches, 1990-1992*. New York: University Press of America.

Van Evera, Stephen W. 1990. "Primed for Peace: Europe After the Cold War." *International Security* 15: 7-57.

Volgy, Thomas J. and John E. Schwarz. 1994. "Foreign Policy Restructuring and the Myriad Webs of Restraint." In *Foreign Policy Restructuring: How Governments Respond to Global Change*, eds., Jerel A. Rosati, Joe D. Hagan, and Martin W. Sampson. Columbia, South Carolina: University of South Carolina Press.

Wade, Robert. 1991. *Governing the Market*. Princeton, New Jersey: Princeton University Press.

Walker, Hugh D. 1975. "Traditional Sino-Korean Relations and Their Contemporary Implications." In *Korea and the New Order in East Asia*, ed., Andrew C. Nahm. Kalamazoo, HI: Center for Korean Studies.

Walt, Stephen M. 1987. *The Origin of Alliances*. Ithaca, New York: Cornell University Press.

Walt, Stephen M. 1991. "The Renaissance of Security Studies." *International Studies Quarterly* 35: 211-39.

Walt, Stephen M. 1997. "Why Alliances Endure or Collapse." *Survival* 39: 156-79.

Waltz, Kenneth N. 1959. *Man, The State, and War: A Theoretical Analysis.* New York: Columbia University Press.

Waltz, Kenneth N. 1979. *Theory of International Politics.* Reading, Massachusetts: Addison-Wesley.

Waltz, Kenneth N. 1986. "Reflections on Theory of International Politics: A Response to My Critics." In *Neorealism and Its Critics*, ed., Robert Keohane. New York: Columbia University Press.

Waltz, Kenneth N. 1993. "The Emerging Structure of International Politics." *International Security* 18: 44-79.

Wanandi, Jusuf. 1996. *Asia Pacific After the Cold War.* Jakarta: Center for Strategic and International Studies.

Warr, Peter G. 1998. "Thailand." In *East Asia in Crisis: From Being a Miracle to Needing One?*" eds., Ross H. McLeod and Ross Garnaut. New York: Routledge.

Weaver, Kent and Bert Rockman. 1993. *Do Institutions Matter? Government Capabilities in the United States and Abroad.* Washington, D.C.: Brookings Institution.

Weber, Max. 1947. *The Theory of Social and Economic Organization.* Trans., A. H. Henderson and Talcott Parsons. New York: The Free Press.

Weir, Margaret. 1992. "Ideas and the Politics of Bounded Innovation." In *Structuring Politics: Historical Institutionalism in Comparative Analysis*, eds., Sven Steinmo, Kathleen Thelen, and Frank Longstreth. Cambridge, Massachusetts: Cambridge University Press.

Welch, David A. 1992. "Organizational Process and Bureaucratic Politics Paradigms: Retrospect and Prospect." *International Security* 17: 112-46.

Wendt, Alexander. 1992. "Level of Analysis vs. Agents and Structures: Part III." *Review of International Studies* 18: 181-85.

White, Gordon. 1982. "North Korea Juche: The Political Economy of Self-Reliance." In *The Struggle for Development: National Strategies in an International Context*, eds., Manfred Bienefeld and Martin Godfrey. New York: John Wiley & Sons.

Wholforth, William C. 1998. "Reality Check: Revising Theories of International Politics in Response to the End of the Cold War." *World Politics* 50: 650-80.

Wilkenfeld, Jonathan. 1973. "Domestic and Foreign Conflict." In *Conflict Behavior and Linkage Politics*, ed., Jonathan Wilkenfeld. New York: McKay.

Wilkinson, David. 1999. "Unipolarity Without Hegemony." *International Studies Review*, Special Issue 1: 141-72.

Winn, Gregory F. T. 1976. *Korean Foreign-Policy Decision Making: Process and Structure*. Honolulu, Hawaii: The Center for Korean Studies.

Wittman, Donald. 1979. "How a War Ends: A Rational Model Approach." *Journal of Conflict Resolution* 23: 743-63.

Wittkopf, Eugene R. and James M. McCormick. eds. 1998. *The Domestic Sources of American Foreign Policy: Insights and Evidence*. New York: Rowman & Littlefield.

Wohlstetter, Albert J. 1959. "The Dedicate Decline of Terror." *Foreign Affairs* 37: 211-34.

Woo-Cumings, Meredith. 1995. "The Korean Bureaucratic States: Historical Legacies and Comparative Perspectives." In *Politics and Policy in the New Korean States*, ed., James Cotton. New York: St. Martin's Press.

Woo-Cumings, Meredith. 1997. "The Political Economy of Growth in East Asia: A Perspective on the State, Market, and Ideology." In *The Role of Government in East Asian Economic Development: Comparative Institutional Analysis*, eds., Masahiro Aoki, Hyung-Ki Kim, and Masahiro Okuno-Fujwara. Oxford: Clarendon Press.

Woo-Cumings, Meredith. 1998. "National Security and the Rise of the Developmental State in South Korea and Taiwan." In *Behind East Asian Growth: The Political and Social Foundations of Prosperity*, ed., Henry S. Rowen. New York: Routledge.

Wood, Robert E. 1986. *From Marshall Plan to Debt Crisis: Foreign Aid and Development Choices in the World Economy*. Berkeley, California: University California Press.

Wover, Ole. 1995. "Securitization and Desecuritization." In *On Security*, ed., Ronnie D. Lipschutz. New York: Columbia University Press.

Wright, Edward R. 1975. "The Constitution and Governmental Structures." In *Korean Politics in Transition*, ed., Edward R. Wright. Seattle, Washington: University of Washington Press.

Wright, Quincy. 1942. *A Study of War*. Chicago, Illinois: University of Chicago Press.

Yang, Jae-In. 1990. *Korean Political Elites* (*Han-Kuk-Jung-Chi-Elite-Ron*). Seoul: Daewangsa.

Yang, Sung-Chul. 1994. *The North and South Korean Political Systems: A Comparative Analysis*. Boulder, Colorado: Westview.

Yang, Yong-shik. 1998. "Kim Dae-Jung Administration's North Korea Policy." *Korea Focus* 6: 48-62.

Yin, Robert. 1993. *Applications of Case Study Research*. Thousand Oaks, California: Sage.

Yin, Robert. 1994. *Case Study Research: Design and Methods*. Thousand Oaks, California: Sage.

Yoo, Jang-Hee. 1999. "Reform with No Caprice: Economic Performance of the Roh Administration." In *Democracy and the Korean Economy*, eds., Jongryn Mo and Chung-in Moon. Stanford, California: Hoover Institution.

Yoon, Dae-kyu. 1990. *Law and Political Authority in South Korea*. Boulder, Colorado: Westview.

Yoon, Dae-kyu. 1994. "Constitutional Change in Korea: Retrospect and Prospects." *Asian Affairs* 25: 178-86.

Yoon, Young-Kwan. 1995. "Globalization: Toward a New Nationalism in Korea." *Korea Focus* 3: 13-28.

Zagoria, Donald S. and Young Kun Kim. 1976. "North Korea and the Major Powers." In *The Two Koreas in East Asian Affairs*, ed., William J. Barnds. New York: New York University Press.

Zakaria, Fareed. 1995. In *The Perils of Anarchy: Contemporary Realism and International Security*, eds., Michael E. Brown, Sean M. Lynn-Jones, and Steven E. Miller. Cambridge, Massachusetts: The MIT Press.

Zucker, Lynne G. 1977. "The Role of Institutionalization in Cultural Persistence." *American Sociological Review* 42: 726-43.


**Official Publications, Documents and Newspapers**

Asian Watch Committee, *Human Rights in Korea*. New York: Asian Watch Committee.

Congressional Quarterly, 1969. *Global Defense: U.S. Military Commitments Abroad*. Washington, D.C.: Congressional Quarterly Service.

Dong-A Daily News, July 4, 1972 and March 29, 1978.

Freedom House, *Annual Survey of Freedom Country Scores*. Washington, D.C.: Freedom House.

Institute of International Affairs, *Korean Defense Yearbook*. Seoul: IIA.

International Monetary Fund, *Direction of Trade Statistics Yearbook*. Washington, D.C.: IMF.

International Monetary Fund, *Financial Statistics Yearbook*. Washington, D.C.: IMF.

Keesing's Contemporary Archives, *Record of World Events*. London: Longman.

Organization of Economic Cooperation and Development, *Geographical Distribution of Financial Flows to Developing Countries*. Paris: OECD.

Republic of Korea (ROK), Bank of Korea, *Economic Statistics Yearbook*. Seoul: BOK.

Republic of Korea (ROK), Economic Planning Board. *Major Statistics of Korean Economy*. Seoul: EPB.

Republic of Korea (ROK), Economic Planning Board. *Economic Trends*. Seoul: EPB.

Republic of Korea (ROK), Election Management Committee, *History of Elections in Korea*. Seoul: EMC.

Republic of Korea (ROK), Korean Trade Promotion Corporation (KOTRA), *Statistical Yearbook*. Seoul: KOTRA.

Republic of Korea (ROK), Ministry of Finance, *Fiscal and Financial Statistics*. Seoul: MOF.

Republic of Korea (ROK), Ministry of Finance, *Trends in Foreign Direct Investment*. Seoul: MOF.

Republic of Korea (ROK), Ministry of Finance and Economy, *Fiscal and Financial Statistics*. Seoul: MOFE.

Republic of Korea (ROK), Ministry of Finance and Economy, *IMF Program for Korea*. Seoul: MOFE.

Republic of Korea (ROK), Ministry of Foreign Affairs, *Diplomacy White Paper*. Seoul: MFA.

Republic of Korea (ROK), Ministry of Foreign Affairs and Trade, *Diplomacy White Paper*. Seoul: MFAT.

Republic of Korea (ROK), Ministry of National Defense, *Defense White Paper*. Seoul: MND.

Republic of Korea (ROK), Ministry of Public Information, *Globalization Blueprint: 1995-2000*. Seoul: MPI.

Republic of Korea (ROK), Ministry of Public Information, *The Governmental Elites of the Republic of Korea.* Seoul: MPI.

Republic of Korea (ROK), Ministry of Unification, *Inter-Korean Trade Volume.* Seoul: MPI.

Republic of Korea (ROK), Ministry of Unification, *Status of South-North Cooperation Fund.* Seoul: MPI.

Republic of Korea (ROK), National Statistical Office, *Korean Statistical Yearbook.* Seoul: NSO.

Republic of Korea (ROK), National Unification Board. *Economic Comparison between North and South Korea.* Seoul: Research Center for Peace and Unification.

Republic of Korea (ROK), National Unification Board. *Humanitarian Aid to North Korea.* Seoul: Research Center for Peace and Unification.

Stockholm International Peace Research Institute, *World Armaments and Disarmament Yearbook.* London: Taylor & Francis.

United Nations, *Direction of Trade Statistics.* New York: The UN Printing Office.

United Nations, *General Assembly Resolution 195 (III),* December 12, 1948.

United Nations, *International Trade Statistics Yearbook.* New York: The UN Printing Office.

United Nations, *Official Records of the General Assembly,* Third Session, Part I, 1948.

United Nations, *Yearbook of National Accounts Statistics.* New York: The UN Printing Office.

United Nations Development Program, *Human Development Report.* Oxford: Oxford University Press.

United States Arms Control and Disarmament Agency, *World Military Expenditures and Arms Transfers.* Washington, D.C.: Government Printing Office.

United States Central Intelligence Agency, *The World FactBook*. Washington, D.C.: Government Printing Office.

U.S. Department of Commerce, *The Statistical Abstract of the United States*. Washington, D.C.: Government Printing Office.

U.S. Department of Defense, *Report of the Secretary of Defense to the President and the Congress*. Washington, D.C.: Government Printing Office.

U.S. Department of State, *Country Reports on Human Rights Practice*. Washington, D.C.: Government Printing Office.

U.S. Senate, Committee on Foreign Relations, *Hearings on the Mutual Defense Treaty with Korea*, 83rd Congress, 2nd Session, 1954.

World Bank, *Private Capital Flows to Developing Countries: The Road to Financial Integration*. London: Oxford University Press.

World Bank, *World Bank Atlas*. Washington, D.C.: World Bank.

World Bank, *World Bank Indicators*. Washington, D.C.: World Bank.

World Bank, *World Development Report*. Washington, D.C.: World Bank.

Yonhap News Agency, *Korea Annual*. Seoul: YNA.

T - #0114 - 270225 - C0 - 216/148/14 - PB - 9780415792905 - Gloss Lamination